THE PREACHER'S HEBREW / GREEK COMPANION SERIES

General Editor / Old Testament Editor

JONATHAN G. KLINE, PHD
Senior Editor
Hendrickson Publishers

New Testament Editor

SEAN M. MCDONOUGH, PHD
Professor of New Testament
Gordon-Conwell Theological Seminary

The Preacher's Hebrew Companion Series

Ecclesiastes

THE PREACHER'S HEBREW COMPANION TO

Ecclesiastes

A Selective Commentary for
Meditation and Sermon Preparation

Russell L. Meek

HENDRICKSON
ACADEMIC

The Preacher's Hebrew Companion to Ecclesiastes:
A Selective Commentary for Meditation and Sermon Preparation

Published by Hendrickson Academic
3 Centennial Drive
Peabody, Massachusetts 01960
www.hendricksonpublishers.com

ISBN 979-8-4005-0984-1

First Printing — September 2025

Library of Congress Control Number: 2025935882

CONTENTS

ECCLESIASTES 3:16–22

Telling the Truth about the World Turned Upside Down

ECCLESIASTES 4:4–12

Relationships Matter

ECCLESIASTES 5:12–19 [13–20]

What Makes Us "Rich"?

ECCLESIASTES 6:1–9

God Is Sovereign over His Gifts and the Ability to Enjoy Them

ECCLESIASTES 7:1–14

Proverbial Reflections

ECCLESIASTES 8:10–15

Coping with Injustice

ECCLESIASTES 9:1–10

Death Is Coming, So Enjoy Life

ECCLESIASTES 11:1–10

The Limits of Human Knowledge (and What to Do about It)

SERIES EDITORS' PREFACE

Overview

Like many preachers, you may wish you could use the biblical languages in your sermon preparation, but the task seems daunting. Perhaps you lack confidence in your language skills—especially if it's been a long time since you studied Greek or Hebrew—and when you turn to technical commentaries, you feel overwhelmed. Or perhaps you simply don't have the time to do the laborious work of digging into the original-language texts. To help you overcome these challenges, we designed this series, the Preacher's Hebrew Companion (as well as its New Testament counterpart series, the Preacher's Greek Companion). In collaboration with the series authors, our goal as series editors is to gently guide you, the busy preacher, through the Hebrew text of select biblical passages in a way that will empower you to integrate original-language exegesis and homiletics. Our prayer is that you will find this book and the other volumes in this series spiritually and intellectually encouraging as well as pleasant to use. We hope your use of the series will make your sermon preparation a more profound and satisfying process and will invigorate your preaching.

Structure

Each volume in this series includes the following three features for a given biblical book (or portion of a book):

- **a curated selection of passages** we believe many preachers would likely choose to preach on from the biblical book (or portion of the book) in question; **or, for shorter biblical books, the entire book**, broken up into manageable passages
- all the basic **lexical and grammatical tools** you need (whatever your Hebrew skill level may be) **to work through and meditate on the Hebrew text** of these passages in a way that strengthens your sermon preparation and empowers you to preach more effectively
- **succinct, select comments** intended to help you responsibly and effectively bridge the gap between reading the Hebrew text and delivering a sermon on it

The Preacher's Hebrew Companion is not a traditional commentary series, as is reflected in its title and subtitle: "*Companion*" (not "Commentary") and "*Selected* Passages for *Meditation* and *Sermon Preparation*." That is, we conceived this series as a *supplement* to the wealth of fine commentaries that already exist, not as a replacement for any of them. We recommend using this series alongside traditional commentaries, which by design include helpful information that is not covered in ours.

The Selection of Passages

Each volume in the Preacher's Hebrew Companion series provides the Hebrew text of **approximately ten to twelve passages** from a particular biblical book (or portion thereof):

- In addition to having expertise in Hebrew and exegesis, our series authors typically have extensive preaching experience or are full-time preachers by vocation. Unless the biblical book in question is short enough to be included in full, they chose **passages** they think **preachers would most likely desire to preach**. In order to encourage preaching through the biblical book in an "expository" rather than a thematic manner, these passages are presented in canonical order. That said, for longer books (such as Isaiah or Matthew), we encouraged authors to choose passages that highlight or represent important themes found in the book; for such books, however, the chosen passages are still presented in canonical order. The curated, limited number of passages in each series volume allows you, if you wish, to use the passages as the basis for a "ready-made" sermon series of whatever length suits your schedule (e.g., for a series consisting of, say, four, seven, ten, or twelve sermons). Alternatively, you might choose to preach a series using some of the passages in a volume and then supplement these with passages from the biblical book in question that are not found in the volume.

- The aims of the series guided our decisions about passage length. On the one hand, we encouraged authors to choose **passages that are not too long**, so that the portions of text won't be daunting to you if your Hebrew skills are rudimentary; nor do we want you to be overwhelmed by wading through dozens of verses in Hebrew. For this reason, our ideal length for most passages has been approximately ten verses. On the other hand, in order to do justice to the natural boundaries of longer passages, we have taken care not to artificially truncate such texts. Consider, for example, the account of the crossing of the Red Sea (Exod 14–15) or the story of the raising of Lazarus (John 11). Although these texts are far too long to be included in full in a volume in this series, each constituent part of these texts is vital to understanding their narrative development and message. For such passages, we asked authors to focus—as a preacher might typically do when delivering a sermon on a lengthy passage—on what they consider to be the most salient verses from the passage. Accordingly, we have provided the Hebrew text for only these verses, with the author summarizing the other verses (in English).

- Finally, when authors deemed it helpful (especially for longer biblical books), they have indicated, on the first page devoted to each passage, the **larger literary unit to which the passage belongs**,[1] thus helping you see the passage in question as part of a larger whole rather than as an isolated pericope. In cases where this larger literary context is indicated, we encourage you to pick up a Bible and read and dwell on this context while using this volume to work through the passage.

The Presentation of Each Passage

This volume helps you work through each passage it contains by presenting the Hebrew text of the passage along with the lexical and grammatical information you need in order to dig into this original-language text. Designed to be highly accessible, this format is intended (1) to enable you to work through the text in manageable chunks and according to your abilities, regardless of your skill level in Hebrew; (2) to simultaneously facilitate both study and devotion; and (3) in conjunction with the author's commentary, to help you bridge the gap, as easily and seamlessly as possible, between the original-language text and preaching.

More specifically, this volume contains the following five sections for each passage:

- A **brief introduction** to the passage—typically comprising only a few sentences—is included in order to set the stage for the passage and highlight its important themes.
- For ease of reading and to encourage you to slow down and contemplate the text, the passage is typically divided into subunits. For each of these subunits, we provide the **Hebrew text** of each clause or phrase, along

1. Occasionally, such a literary unit is coterminous with the passage itself.

with **transliteration** (as a pronunciation help for those whose Hebrew is at a rudimentary level) and the author's **translation.**[2]

- Next, each clause or phrase from the subunit is presented in an interlinear fashion, notably with **a contextual gloss (or multiple contextual glosses) and parsing for each word.**[3] For example:

1a	בְּרֵאשִׁית בָּרָא אֱלֹהִים		
	In the beginning, God created		
בְּרֵאשִׁית	in beginning of/ when . . . began	CST W/ PREP בְּ	noun
רֵאשִׁית	*bə · rē᾽ · **šîṯ***		
בָּרָא	(he) created	QAL PF 3MS	verb
ברא	*bā · **rā᾽***		
אֱלֹהִים	God	ABS	noun
אֱלֹהִים	*ʾĕ · lō · **hîm***		

This formatting allows you to easily analyze each word in the clause or phrase (by helping you on the level of semantics and morphology) and to perceive how the words work together as a whole (by helping you on the level of syntax).

- A key feature of each volume in this series is the inclusion of **concise comments** to accompany some clauses and phrases. These have two primary goals: (1) to enable you to understand and exegete the text more deeply than might be possible from reading it in English, and (2) to equip

2. The Hebrew text used in this series has been taken from the Michigan-Claremont-Westminster Electronic Hebrew Bible, a popular electronic version based on the BHS that has been revised by its creators on the basis of comparison with the Leningrad Codex. This electronic text is in the public domain and has been made available courtesy of the J. Alan Groves Center for Advanced Biblical Research. For simplicity's sake, whenever there is a *ketiv-qere*, only the *qere* has been presented (without being marked as such). Interested readers should feel free to consult critical editions, such as the BHS, to see where instances of *ketiv-qere* or other text-critical issues occur.

3. The glosses are the author's own and intentionally err on the "literal" end of the spectrum, in order to help you apprehend the basic meaning(s) of each word in context. The parsings have been supplied by the team at Hendrickson. Naturally, some words can plausibly be parsed more than one way in context; in such cases, the parsing provided is the one we deemed to make the most sense, but other parsings could have been listed instead.

you with insights into the original-language text that will be of direct value for your preaching. To help you focus and not become overwhelmed with too much information, we encouraged our authors to comment only on those clauses and phrases for which they thought doing so would accomplish these two goals. In addition, because the volumes in this series are not only language aids but—ultimately and more importantly—preaching aids, we asked authors to highlight those features in the Hebrew text that bring out key themes, rhetorical and theological emphasis, narrative development, character development, connections with other biblical texts, and the like. Although noting various other features in the Hebrew text may have been intrinsically interesting from a grammatical perspective or helpful for strengthening your language skills, authors have generally refrained from commenting on such features when doing so would not be likely to aid you in moving from text to sermon in any substantial way.[4] In short, an author's brief, select comments are intended—in conjunction with the volume's language aids—to provide you both with *focus* and with *space* to slow down, meditate, wonder, and mature in your understanding and experience of the text, as you form your own judgments on it and prepare to proclaim the divine word to your hearers. The author's comments are not intended to circumscribe the possible interpretive options with one single answer (especially for texts whose interpretation is the particular subject of debate among Christian believers). Rather, they are meant to stimulate your thinking, to help you see features of the text (and connections with other texts) that you may not have perceived before, and to prompt you to ask questions that may not have previously occurred to you.

Each passage ends with a brief section titled **"From Text to Sermon,"** in which our authors, building on their comments, suggest ways you can move from working through the Hebrew text to the task of homiletics, highlighting potential points of emphasis or particular insights you may wish to share with your audience. In this way, the authors provide you with possible ways to bring the text to life for your audience (e.g., types

4. Another way we have kept the presentation streamlined and uncluttered, so that you can achieve maximum focus, is by intentionally keeping source citations to a minimum. Authors' comments on a given passage are the fruit of their scholarly research on the passage, their personal reflection on it, and their experience preaching and teaching it. They cite secondary sources only when they draw a specific insight from one particular source or wish to point you to a particularly helpful resource for further reading. As stated above, we naturally encourage you to also use traditional commentaries (which typically provide more documentation) in your study and sermon preparation.

of illustrations you might use). Because individual preachers (and each of our series authors) bring their own particular skills, perspectives, backgrounds, and oratorial approaches to bear on the homiletical task, and because every biblical text has its own unique features, we encouraged our authors to structure the "From Text to Sermon" section as a free-form series of short paragraphs whose content and emphases are guided by their own personal judgment about what is most helpful for a variety of preachers in different places, cultures, and times. The remarks in this section are always grouped according to rubrics (in the form of inline headers); but rather than restrict authors with a "one-size-fits-all" set of rubrics, we allowed them to create their own rubrics and even, if helpful, to vary these rubrics across passages within their volume in light of the unique features and emphases of each passage.[5] We view the resulting diversity of approaches and emphases across this series (and even within a given volume) as a strength, and we hope this aspect of the series will encourage you to use your own judgment about how to preach each passage in a way that best suits you and your listeners, being sensitive to the promptings and guidance of the Spirit of God.

Audience and Theological Perspective

Since our hope is that many different kinds of people will find the volumes in this series useful, we have designed the Preacher's Hebrew Companion to be helpful to a broad spectrum of Christian preachers:

- Our intention is that the series will be **useful and accessible to a large and diverse group of preachers serving a variety of communities throughout the world**. For this reason, we encouraged authors to exercise sensitivity and broad-mindedness in their comments and particularly when writing the "From Text to Sermon" section, in which they could run the risk of being too culturally specific. In particular, we asked authors that any sermon illustrations they included in this section generally be as universal as possible or that, instead of providing specific illustrations, they point to themes from the passage you may wish to illustrate in one way or another. That said, because specificity is essential for good communication, we also allowed authors to suggest—when they deemed

5. That said, we suggested the following possible rubrics to authors as starting points to consider: theological themes, themes for application and illustration, integrating the broader historical and literary context, learning from the language, and (as deemed helpful and not reductionistic) "the big idea" of the passage.

it particularly helpful—concrete, culturally specific examples as springboards to help you think about examples that will be relevant for your own context.

- We asked our authors to express any **theological perspectives** in a way that is **consistent with the beliefs stated in the Apostles' Creed**. Because this series aims to meet the needs of Christian preachers of various theological viewpoints, we encouraged a diversity of theological perspectives within these bounds across the volumes in the series. In addition, because the series has a joint focus on exegesis (close attention to what a specific text says) and homiletics (how to preach said text), we advised authors when making any theological comments to let these flow naturally from the text at hand, rather than using the text as a springboard to discuss issues that would more properly fall under the rubric of systematic theology. Although we asked authors to avoid reading any given passage through the lens of a theological system grounded in other biblical texts, we also strongly encouraged them to discuss allusions to other biblical passages or other innerbiblical literary connections if they felt that doing so would help you understand the message of the text at hand and know how to preach it more effectively.

Acknowledgments

We would like to offer our heartfelt gratitude to the following individuals, who have played a central role in the creation of this series:

- Arley Kangas, Marco Resendes, and Tyler Comer, for their excellent work on various aspects of the making of these volumes, especially transliterating, proofreading, and generating the indexes.
- Phil Frank, for his expert typesetting and for patiently working with us, in our capacity as series editors, to achieve the desired formatting and aesthetic for these volumes.
- The series authors, for joining us in this unique project and for sharing our vision and lending their considerable skills to the task. These volumes are the result of a fruitful collaboration between the Hendrickson team and the series authors (with both parties contributing to the content). We are truly grateful for the opportunity to have worked on this project together.

All of us—the series editors, the series authors, and the team at Hendrickson—pray that the volume you now hold in your hands will empower and encourage you to work through the Hebrew text of the Bible in order to deepen your sermon preparation and strengthen your proclamation of the word of God. We nurture a deep respect and appreciation for the challenging work that you as a preacher do on the "front lines," and we recognize the many challenges (logistical, mental, emotional, spiritual, and more) that you encounter on a weekly, indeed a daily, basis. We are honored to come alongside you and support you in your important labors, and we pray that your use of this book will bear much fruit for the kingdom of God.

Jonathan G. Kline
Sean M. McDonough

AUTHOR'S INTRODUCTION

Qoheleth found me as a young man stumbling through life and looking for a way to embrace the faith that my grandmother had passed down to me. Looking back, it is clear that I had been "deconstructing" for several years; as a last grasp, I turned to the book of Ecclesiastes. There I met a person who had also struggled with life's tragedies and injustices, and by the grace of God he had both made it through and chronicled his journey for the sojourners who would come after him.

Qoheleth gave his readers the gift of a vision of life with God that includes honest wrestling with the reality of this world. This life so often doesn't turn out how we think it should—how the Bible seems to indicate it should. In this upside-down world, the righteous suffer, the wicked prosper, the fastest runner doesn't always win the race, and sometimes religious leaders bring tremendous harm to the people they're supposed to shepherd. Qoheleth teaches us that Christians can say such things out loud—we can, like he did, voice our frustration with injustice and the brevity of life.

But Qoheleth doesn't leave us there, lost in the hopelessness of the world turned upside down. Rather, he presents a compelling apologetic for faith in the Lord, the Creator of heaven and earth. He tells his readers that *because* life so often goes so wrong, seems so hopeless, and just doesn't make sense—*because* this is reality, our only hope is to enjoy the gifts God gives us—food, work, a spouse, and wine—and to live in right relationship with God. Qoheleth shows us that the only way to live, to *really live*, is to abandon ourselves to the God of the universe and to eagerly and gratefully embrace every gift he gives us. Qoheleth's vision of life, his apologetic for walking with Yahweh, includes deep community with God and others, joyful feasting, and genuine joy in the work of our hands. He takes the very things we often use to cope when life is hard—food, alcohol, sex, and work—and he puts them in their proper place. God didn't intend his gifts to numb us or to fulfill our deepest longings—or even our shallowest longings. Rather, he intended his gifts to be embraced and enjoyed within a relationship with him and in community with others.

All of this is why I often tell my students that Ecclesiastes is the most Christian book in the Old Testament, and it's most definitely the book that we need today. It presents a compelling vision of life that beckons its readers into relationship with God and relationship with others, relationships marked by feasting, joy, and fulfillment but also loss, death, and struggle. So, friend, let's open this little book together, and let's "taste and see that Yahweh is good" (Ps 34:9).

For my wife and sons: Knowing you is a gift.

Ari, may the Lord make you strong and brave like a lion.

Abel, may the Lord give you the courage and faithfulness to always bring your best to God, no matter what.

Elijah, may the Lord give you the boldness and fortitude to speak truth to power.

And Brittany, "the wife whom [I] love" (Eccl 9:9), you prove daily that

> "He who finds a wife finds a good thing,
> and has obtained favor from Yahweh" (Prov 18:22).

LIST OF ABBREVIATIONS

1	first person	IMPV	imperative
2	second person	indef	indefinite
3	third person	INF	infinitive
ABS	absolute	INTERR/interr	interrogative
adj	adjective	JUSS	jussive
adv	adverb	M	masculine
ATTR	attributive	NIPH	Niphal
C	common	P	plural
COHORT	cohortative	PASS	passive
CONJ/conj	conjunction	PF	perfect
CST	construct	PRED	predicative
DEF. ART.	definite article	PREP/prep	preposition
demonstr	demonstrative	PRON/pron	pronoun
DSS	Dead Sea Scrolls	PTCP	participle
F	feminine	S	singular
HIPH	Hiphil	SUBST	substantive
HITH	Hithpael	SX	suffix
HOPH	Hophal	w/	with
IMPF	imperfect	WAYY	wayyiqtol

NOTE: All verse numbers in this volume refer to the Hebrew text; when the English verse numbering differs, it is listed in brackets following the Hebrew numbering.

INTRODUCTORY EXCURSUS: THE MEANING OF הֶבֶל (*HEVEL*) IN ECCLESIASTES

The key word of Ecclesiastes is indisputably הֶבֶל, typically translated in English versions as "vanity" or "meaningless" or another similarly negative term.[1] The meaning of this word is disputed, with suggestions ranging from "enigmatic" to "absurd" to "nothing" to more colorful options that need not be repeated here.[2] Throughout the commentary below, we will examine different places where it is clear that the theology of Ecclesiastes is Genesis-shaped. Qoheleth, the author of Ecclesiastes, regularly alludes to Genesis through repeated vocabulary and overlapping themes, which in turn informs how we understand his use of the key word הֶבֶל, the very name of Abel in Gen 4. Though a full treatment of the question is not in order here, in this section I aim to show that Ecclesiastes is best understood when we read הֶבֶל as a reference to Abel. We begin by examining the word's usage outside of Ecclesiastes.

What Does הֶבֶל Mean?

The word הֶבֶל appears in the Old Testament eighty-six times.[3] It is used almost entirely in a metaphorical sense, with translations such as "vanity," "meaningless," and "absurd," though some passages use its concrete meaning: "vapor" or "breath" (e.g., Ps 62:10). In some contexts, the metaphorical use refers to idolatry, while in others it refers to the brevity of human life, the emptiness of words, or the fleetingness of ill-gotten wealth.

Regardless of the specific context in which הֶבֶל appears, it almost exclusively refers to some aspect of either idols or humans, often in contrast to God. Most

1. This chapter is a slightly modified version of Russell L. Meek, "Abel and the Meaning of 'Vanity,'" in *Ecclesiastes and the Search for Meaning in an Upside-Down World* (Peabody, MA: Hendrickson, 2022), 29–50. Used with permission from the publisher.

2. For a thorough overview of the word's recent history of interpretation, see Russell L. Meek, "Twentieth- and Twenty-First Century Readings of Hebel (הֶבֶל) in Ecclesiastes," *Currents in Biblical Research* 14.3 (2016): 279–97.

3. Gen 4:2 (2x), 4 (2x), 8 (2x), 9, 25; Deut 32:21; 1 Kgs 16:13, 26; 2 Kgs 17:15 (2x); Job 7:16; 9:29; 21:34; 27:12 (2x); 35:16; Pss 31:7; 39:6, 7, 12; 62:10 (2x), 11; 78:33; 94:11; 144:4; Prov 13:11; 21:6; 31:30; Eccl 1:2 (5x), 14; 2:1, 11, 15, 17, 19, 21, 23, 26; 3:19; 4:4, 7, 8, 16; 5:6, 9; 6:2, 4, 9, 11, 12; 7:6, 15; 8:10, 14 (2x); 9:9 (2x); 11:8; 11:10; 12:8 (3x); Isa 30:7; 49:4; 57:13; Jer 2:5 (2x); 8:19; 10:3, 8, 15; 14:22; 16:19; 23:16; 51:18; Lam 4:17; Jon 2:9; Zech 10:2.

importantly, הֶבֶל often describes things that do not produce their intended results. For example: neither idols nor Egypt can save Israel; "vain" talk cannot comfort; inappropriately gained wealth doesn't provide security; death levels all; and righteousness does not always prove innocence, as Job's heartrending story shows us. The following survey organizes הֶבֶל around its referents.

Idolatry

Outside of Ecclesiastes, הֶבֶל most often refers to idolatry, either to idols themselves or to the result of worshiping idols. In the second instance, it is used to say that idolaters become like their idols: nothing, inconsequential, vaporous. In such cases, the reference to הֶבֶל is set in contrast with Yahweh and is often accompanied by language that describes the provocation of the Lord's anger against idolatry (e.g., Deut 32:21; 1 Kgs 16:13, 26; 2 Kgs 17:15 [2x]; Jer 2:5; 8:19).

This use of הֶבֶל is most common in the prophetic books, particularly Jeremiah (2:5; 8:19; 10:3, 8, 15; 16:19; 51:18). Jonah (2:8) and Zechariah (10:2) also use הֶבֶל to talk about idolatry. Isaiah 57:13 uses הֶבֶל to refer to the fleetingness of idols, stating that they can be blown away by a "breath" and that a "vapor" (הֶבֶל) will carry them off (Blenkinsop 2003:153). Outside of the prophetic books, הֶבֶל refers to idols in Ps 31:6: "I hate those who are devoted to *worthless* idols, but as for me, I trust in Yahweh."

Isaiah 30:7 also uses הֶבֶל in the broad context of idolatry; that is, looking to something other than God for what only God can do (see also Lam 4:7). In this passage, Israel is looking to Egypt, rather than to the Lord, for help. Though the context is slightly different from out-and-out idolatry, the takeaway remains the same: no one but Yahweh is capable to act on Israel's behalf.

In Prov 31, the poem of the valiant woman, הֶבֶל appears again, this time in reference to beauty. In this passage, most English translations render הֶבֶל as "fleeting" to communicate the transient nature of beauty. For example, the CSB says, "Charm is deceptive and beauty is *fleeting*" (Prov 31:30; see also NLT, CEB, NIV, NET, NKJV).

However, הֶבֶל is parallel to another Hebrew word that means "falsehood" or "deceptive" (שֶׁקֶר). Further, the next line highlights what really matters for this "valiant woman": "a woman who fears the Lord will be praised." In context, then, הֶבֶל refers *not* to the fleetingness of beauty but rather to its inherent deceitfulness, as the author likewise describes "charm." Like idols, beauty and charm are untrustworthy because they do not make good on their promises. This untrustworthiness of outward appearance contrasts with the person who fears Yahweh—an inward disposition that by its nature is not as obvious as charm and beauty or the external features of a person.

Human Life

הֶבֶל is also used to describe human life in its denotative sense of "breath" or "vapor," which is sometimes expanded to the concept of "brevity" or "transience." This usage can be seen in Ps 39, where the psalmist speaks of the fleeting nature of his life (see Pss 39:6–7, 12; 78:33; 94:11; 144:4).[4] הֶבֶל is used this way once in Job (7:16), where Job states that he "will not live forever" because his "days are a *breath*" (CSB).

Words

הֶבֶל sometimes refers to the "emptiness" or "nothingness" of words, such as in Job 21:34 and 35:16, and possibly in Isa 49:4. Job (21:34) accuses his friends of comforting him with הֶבֶל; that is, their words are "empty" or "nothing" because they do not actually do what they are meant to do, which is comfort (or even convince!) Job. Similarly, in 35:16, Elihu accuses Job of speaking words that amount to "nothing," words that fail in their purpose of exonerating Job.

In Isa 49:4, the prophet complains that "for emptiness and הֶבֶל I spent my strength." Here, Isaiah appears to be complaining that his strength has been spent for "nothing." His words have come to naught, or הֶבֶל, in that they have not produced the intended result of repentance. Words, then, are הֶבֶל when they do not accomplish their intended purpose.

Wealth

Proverbs employs הֶבֶל twice in the context of wealth. Proverbs 13:11 contrasts הֶבֶל with hard work, stating that wealth gained from הֶבֶל will diminish, but wealth gained from working hard will increase. While some see this passage as referring to the transience of ill-gotten wealth, the verse's parallelism indicates that הֶבֶל here is actually contrasted with hard work. Thus the word appears to mean something along the lines of "deception," similar to how it is used in contexts that address idolatry—ill-gotten wealth does not do what it is supposed to do. Rather than providing peace and security, it passes through one's fingers and is therefore הֶבֶל (Waltke 2004:561). Psalm 62:10 and Prov 21:6 similarly use הֶבֶל to describe ill-gained wealth.

Unexpected Results

Finally, in Job 9:29, Job uses הֶבֶל to refer to a broken relationship between actions and their expected consequences. He states, "I am condemned. Why then

4. When הֶבֶל is used in this sense, its surrounding context often includes terms such as יוֹם ("day"; e.g., Pss 39:6, 7, 12; 78:33; 144:4) to indicate that the author is referring to a span of time.

do I toil with הֶבֶל?" Throughout the book, Job protests his suffering because he is *innocent*. He's done nothing to deserve the suffering he is experiencing. His protests of innocence, though, do nothing to stop the deluge of suffering. He is condemned, and so he wonders why he labors with הֶבֶל, or "in a way that does not produce the expected results." His righteous life and protestations of innocence should have relieved his suffering, but neither is effective, neither produces the intended results.

So, Again, What Does הֶבֶל Mean?

Now we return to the initial question: What does הֶבֶל mean? Context determines meaning, and words are used in different ways in different contexts. For example, consider the English word *bread*, which can refer to all sorts of things made of the basic ingredients of flour, sugar, water, and sometimes yeast. A donut is not a dinner roll, but both are "bread." Thus "Pass me the bread" said at dinner would refer to an altogether different thing than it would at breakfast; and the word's meaning is even more different when someone says, "Painting houses is my bread and butter." Or, "This horse is a real breadwinner!" Context determines meaning.

Broadly speaking, based on the discussion above, we can categorize הֶבֶל as a word with both metaphorical and concrete meanings. Its concrete meaning is "breath" or "vapor," which is then expanded metaphorically to refer to basically two different sorts of things:

(1) things that do not last, and

(2) things that do not produce their intended results; that is, a disconnect between actions and their rewards, or the breakdown of the retribution principle.

The story of Abel (הֶבֶל in Hebrew) beautifully illustrates both aspects of this word, and I think that tragic story is what Qoheleth wants us to consider when we read the word הֶבֶל in his book.

Retribution Theology in the Life of Abel

In Gen 4, the wicked Cain refuses to conquer the sin that is "crouching at the door" (Gen 4:7). Instead, he vents his anger and embarrassment over God's rebuke by murdering his brother. The Bible is clear that Abel did nothing to deserve Cain's wrath, in which Cain persisted despite God's pleading with him to do right and turn back to God. Abel was righteous. Cain was not. Abel the righteous, however, was murdered by Cain the unrighteous.

In order to fully grasp what's going on in this story—particularly, to understand the role it plays in Ecclesiastes—we need to fast-forward just a bit in the narrative of the Bible. The Cain and Abel story is not just about jealousy and murder and improper worship. It's also about the failure of actions to produce their expected outcomes; that is, the failure of "retribution theology." We can see this theology most clearly in places like Deuteronomy and Job, where we now turn before revisiting the two brothers.

The covenant God made with Israel when he brought them out of Egypt is alternately called the Deuteronomic covenant, the Mosaic covenant, the Sinaitic covenant, and the old covenant. This covenant is grounded in Yahweh's choice of Israel, which Deuteronomy traces back to the covenant relationship between Yahweh and Abraham, Isaac, and Jacob (Deut 1:8). Throughout Deuteronomy, the Lord reminds Israel that the basis of their relationship is Yahweh's grace—not their own merit. However, as with the rest of the Bible (even the New Testament), human actions matter. In the Deuteronomic covenant, Israel's obedience or disobedience to Yahweh mattered both in the people's relationship with Yahweh and their way of life. Because God loves his people and wants to live in a good relationship with them, Deuteronomy outlines the stipulations of this covenant and the results of either keeping or failing to keep these stipulations. This is similar to how good parents set boundaries, establish consequences both good and bad, and explain all of this to their children.

Although these boundaries and subsequent consequences are laced throughout Deuteronomy, we'll focus on just a few passages here. Deuteronomy 7:11–15 delineates the blessings contingent on Israel's obedience to God. If the people obey Yahweh's commands and statutes, then he will give them descendants, abundant crops and herds, and good health. The passage goes on to assure the Israelites that they will possess the land of their enemies, which represents the fulfillment of Yahweh's promise to Abraham in Gen 22. The path to these blessings is straightforward: obedience to the covenant requirements. The context also shows that blessing comes from Yahweh because of his love and faithfulness to Israel's ancestors. Thus the Bible holds in tension human obedience and God's grace: obedience to the covenant is paramount, but Yahweh's grace is ultimately responsible for blessing.

Deuteronomy 24:17–22 provides another example of the relationship between God's grace and Israel's responsibility to keep the covenant requirements. In this passage, Israel is commanded to relate to the underprivileged in society with justice and fairness. The rationale given for their treatment of the underprivileged is twofold: (1) because Yahweh redeemed Israel from slavery in Egypt, and (2) so that Yahweh might bless them. Again, blessing comes from obedience, but God's grace is fully responsible for blessings.

In Deut 30:11–20, Moses assures the Israelites that these commandments can be obeyed, for they are near to them in their hearts (vv. 11–14). The people cannot charge God with making the conditions of blessing too difficult. This passage also explains what blessing consists of: descendants, reputation, physical provision—both sustenance and victory over enemies—land, and long life. In sum, Deuteronomy shows that blessing is contingent on obedience to the covenant *and* streams from Yahweh's grace.

Other biblical books confirm this basic understanding of the relationship between actions and consequence: obedience results in blessing, and disobedience results in curses. For example, Proverbs argues that righteous living leads to being blessed and unrighteous living leads to being cursed. Though Proverbs does not present a rigid retribution theology, it certainly presents a worldview governed by the principles of retribution theology. The book of Job also contains the basic formulation that actions and their results should have a predictable relationship, but Job introduces another piece to this puzzle. As a righteous person, he should not suffer the curses brought upon him, and that's why his friends are so adamant that he must have sinned: their theological system doesn't allow for a righteous sufferer.

Let's press pause briefly on this conversation and keep it in the back of our minds as we look again at the first few chapters of Genesis—and why Qoheleth picks up on this story as a way to wrestle with retribution theology in particular. The basic formulation of retribution theology—obedience results in blessing while disobedience results in curses—was operative in the first few chapters of Genesis. For example, in Gen 3 disobedience resulted in being cursed. Adam and Eve suffered the consequences of their sin—death, separation from God, pain, and strenuous work (Gen 3:14–19). This pattern of sin and punishment, however, does not hold true for the Cain and Abel narrative.

As we know, Abel offered an acceptable sacrifice to Yahweh and Cain did not. After Yahweh rejected Cain's sacrifice, he warned an angry Cain that sin was ready to devour him, and he admonished Cain to "overtake" sin before it consumed him. Cain failed to heed this warning and instead murdered his brother. Although Yahweh cursed him (Gen 4:11–12), Cain protested that the punishment was too severe. In response, Yahweh mitigated the curse by placing on Cain a sign of protection (4:13–15). His life was prolonged, he had many descendants, and he built a city (4:17). *Cain, "who belonged to the evil one"* (1 John 3:12 NIV), *received the blessings for obedience* (outlined later in Deuteronomy; see esp. 7:11–15; 28:1–14; 30:11–20).

On the other hand, *"righteous Abel"* (as Jesus referred to him in Matt 23:35) *suffered the consequences of disobedience* (also outlined in Deuteronomy; see esp. 28:15–68). His life was cut short, ostensibly leaving him with no children, no heritage, and no material wealth. The one-to-one relationship between disobedience and curses or obedience and blessing had been reversed. At this point, the world has clearly been turned upside down. The righteous suffer and the unrighteous prosper.

This brief, early narrative of the first time when the expected relationship between actions and consequences breaks down is one of the key ways in which הֶבֶל is used in the Old Testament. Centuries later, Qoheleth presented Abel as the embodiment of human tragedy, which everyone since—including us today—has experienced in one way or another.

Abel in Ecclesiastes

Ecclesiastes 1:2 loudly proclaims that everything is הֶבֶל—a word that Qoheleth's readers might remember from the Cain and Abel (הֶבֶל) narrative. In the Old Testament, names often reveal some aspect of a person's character, or as scholar Tremper Longman (1998:177) says, "Naming captures the essential nature of a person or thing." For example, Cain was "gotten" by Eve (Gen 4:1), and Abraham is the "father of a multitude" (Gen 17:5).

The same holds true for Abel. The nonmetaphorical meaning of his name is "breath" or "vapor," which by its nature is ephemeral and transient. Jacques Ellul (1990:50) states that Abel was so named for this very reason. Even though he is the righteous character in the narrative, Cain cuts short Abel's life. Abel is thus the embodiment of transience. Joseph Blenkinsopp (2011:84–85) also argues that Abel's name presupposes his murder at the hands of his brother, indicating that Abel is "breath"—a theme Qoheleth develops by commenting on the transience of all humans (e.g., Eccl 3:19–20). This allusion continues throughout the book. By using הֶבֶל as a leitmotif—a recurring thematic word—Qoheleth expands this theme of transience and injustice introduced in Gen 4 (see Fredericks 1993:11–32): Everyone and everything in life is subject to the reversal that Abel experienced.

However, it seems more is at work in Qoheleth's writing than simply the matter of transience. He also uses הֶבֶל to invoke Abel as a symbol in his discussion of the various ways that human life has mirrored the tragedy of Abel since the day Cain murdered him. Instead of explicitly stating his assessment of something gone wrong, Qoheleth leaves it to us to decide which aspect of Abel's story he's talking about: transience, the broken relationship between actions and rewards, the injustice suffered, the inability to attain lasting value—all of which are summed up in the failure of the retribution principle in Abel's case.

In Eccl 1:14, Qoheleth states that he has seen all the works done under the sun and that they are all הֶבֶל and a pursuit of wind. By making הֶבֶל parallel with pursuing wind, Qoheleth points to the inability of all people, like Abel, to grasp anything with lasting value. The obedient *should* experience tangible blessings that add value to their lives. For Qoheleth, however, the one-to-one correspondence between actions and rewards has been blown away, so now trying to attain anything of lasting value is like trying to grasp the wind.

In 2:15, Qoheleth laments that the wise and foolish are alike in their end: they all die. No one escapes Abel's fate—the culmination of the curses that God pronounced after the fall (Anderson 1998). The anticipated relationship between actions and rewards makes no sense. Fool or wise—both are subject to the same fate.

In 3:19, Qoheleth says that "humans have no advantage over the beasts, for all are הֶבֶל." We all share the same breath of life and the same fate of death. Just as Abel's life was fleeting, so is everything else—human and animal alike. Similarly, the "Royal Experiment" (Krüger 2001:45) of Eccl 2 finds that everything in life is ephemeral, lacking any lasting value, and that our only recourse is to enjoy the gifts of God: eating, drinking, a spouse, and pleasurable toil, which are themselves also transient (2:24–25).

Another aspect of Abel's life that Qoheleth discusses is the disconnect between hard work and the fruit of our labor. For example, he states in 4:4,

> And I myself saw all the toil and all the skill of work, that this is from the envy of a man of his fellow. This also is הֶבֶל, and a pursuit of wind.

Qoheleth indicates that labor and work—the effort to acquire—result from envying others. Instead of working as a way to fulfill God's design for humanity (Gen 2:15) and reap the blessings it brings to us and those around us, Qoheleth tells us that hard work comes from envy. The desire to keep up with the Joneses, not the desire to contribute meaningfully to society or enjoy one's work, drives achievement in the post-fall, upside-down world we inhabit. The right order of the world is reversed.

In 4:8, we can see how the person who has no children resembles Abel:

> And for whom am I laboring and depriving myself from the good?
> This also is הֶבֶל and an evil task.

This person works tirelessly to establish wealth and honor, yet he does not receive the blessing of descendants to inherit his wealth. This is a grievous wrong since wealth represents blessing from Yahweh, a "normal reward for righteous living" (Ellis 2010). Yahweh, however, has withheld the blessing of progeny. Since he obtained the blessing of wealth, shouldn't he also experience the blessing of children? The former without the latter is an "evil" thing.

Finally, Qoheleth states in 8:14, "There is הֶבֶל that is done upon the earth: that there are righteous to whom it happens according to the deeds of the wicked, and there are wicked to whom it happens according to the deeds of the righteous. I said that this also is הֶבֶל." This passage is Ecclesiastes's most explicit reference to the reversal of the expected order of life. As in the Cain and Abel narrative, so in the rest of life, sometimes the disobedient receive blessing while the obedient receive curses. As we all are painfully aware, the world is often turned upside down, which is what Qoheleth asks us to remember when he says,

"Abel of Abels, everything is Abel."

Conclusion

If we read הֶבֶל in Ecclesiastes as a reference to Abel's life, then the implications for how we understand "the Bible's strangest book" (Crenshaw 1987:23) are enormous. First, reading the book as an examination of the "Abelness" of life (when the relationship between actions and expected results is turned upside down) helps us see that Ecclesiastes is not the rumblings of a discontented sage. Rather, it's a book written from the wrestling of a faithful follower of God.

Second, if Qoheleth is indeed using הֶבֶל to refer to Abel's life—and all that went wrong in it—then Ecclesiastes is not at all about the "meaninglessness" or "vanity" of life. Rather, it's a book that guides us through the vagaries of life in this fallen world, offering the solution for how to navigate such a dark and twisted place.

The solution is to be faithfully obedient to God and enjoy his gifts.

Taken together, these two implications—wrestling with life and offering the solution—mean that this ancient book is not only relevant for Qoheleth's ancient audience but for us as well. It is for *every* human struggling to figure out what it means to live and to follow God in a world turned upside down.

EVERYTHING CHANGES; EVERYTHING STAYS THE SAME

As much as everything changes, it all seems to stay the same. Even though humans clearly experience change and growth in our individual lives, when we think beyond our personal experiences and consider life across time and culture, the universal sameness and cyclical nature of the human experience remains. Qoheleth opens his treatise on life with a poem that invites his readers to consider that life is basically the same for all of us. And that consideration forms the foundation for the book's primary theological message, which we can summarize in three parts. (1) All humans experience a life characterized by injustice and suffering because of the fall, as exemplified in the story of Abel (הֶבֶל). (2) Given #1, humans must take every opportunity to enjoy the gifts of God that Adam and Eve experienced in the garden of Eden, and (3) to live in a trusting, obedient relationship with God.

1:1

1a דִּבְרֵי֙ קֹהֶ֣לֶת

divrê qōhelet

The words of Qoheleth,

1b בֶּן־דָּוִ֖ד מֶ֥לֶךְ בִּירוּשָׁלָֽםִ׃

ben-dāwid melek bîrûšālāim.

the son of David, king in Jerusalem.

1a דִּבְרֵי֙ קֹהֶ֣לֶת

The words of Qoheleth,

דִּבְרֵי֙ / דָּבָר	words of / *div·rê*	CST	noun
קֹהֶ֣לֶת / קֹהֶ֫לֶת	Qoheleth/gatherer/assembler / *qō·he·let*	ABS	noun

Ecclesiastes 1:1 and 12:9–14 form what has been called a "narrative frame" around the book of Ecclesiastes (Fox 1977). Verse 1 introduces readers to the primary speaker in the book, "Qoheleth," translated variously as "the Teacher" (CSB, NIV, CEB, NET) and "the Preacher" (KJV, ESV, NASB). It is the feminine participle form of קהל, "to assemble" or "to gather." The Septuagint renders this Ἐκκλησιαστής, or "assembler," from which the English title "Ecclesiastes" derives. Qoheleth is thus "one who assembles [people]" (as in the Septuagint; cf. 1 Kgs 8:1 in reference to Solomon) or "one who gathers [proverbs]." The latter understanding is consistent with the book's association with Solomon and the closing epilogue, which describes Qoheleth as one who "taught the people knowledge and . . . weighed, searched out, and made clear many proverbs" (Eccl 12:10).

1b בֶּן־דָּוִד מֶלֶךְ בִּירוּשָׁלִָם׃

the son of David, king in Jerusalem.

בֶּן־	son of	CST	noun
בֵּן	*ben-*		
דָּוִד	David	ABS	noun
דָּוִד	*dā·**wid***		
מֶלֶךְ	king	ABS	noun
מֶלֶךְ	***me**·lek̠*		
בִּירוּשָׁלִָם׃	in Jerusalem	ABS W/ PREP בְּ	noun
יְרוּשָׁלַ͏ִם	*bî·rû·šā·**lā**·im*		

The noun בֵּן, "son," in the phrase בֶּן־דָּוִד is definite because it is in construct with the proper noun "David." "Son of" most often describes an immediate direct descendant, just as people used to call me "Len's boy" (I'm from Arkansas). In the plural, it can refer to an entire people group (e.g., "the sons of Israel") or to members of a particular profession (e.g., "the sons of Asaph" in 2 Chr 35:15 are singers, and the "sons of the prophets" [2 Kgs 2:3] are prophets). Less often, "son of" can refer to a more distant descendant, as in the New Testament usage of "Son of David" to refer to Jesus as a royal descendant of David. בֶּן־דָּוִד occurs ten times in the Old Testament and refers to a specific, direct son of David in nine of its usages; in six occurrences, Solomon is named (Prov 1:1; 1 Chr 29:22; 2 Chr 1:1; 13:6; 30:26; 35:3); once Absalom (2 Sam 13:1); once Amnon (2 Sam 13:1); and once Jerimoth (2 Chr 11:18). The only other occurrence is here, where no name is given. (For arguments for and against Solomonic authorship, and why we cannot know for certain who authored the book, see Meek 2015.)

2a הֲבֵל הֲבָלִים

*hă**vēl** hăvā**lîm***

“Abel of Abels,”

2b אָמַר קֹהֶלֶת

*ʾā**mar** qō**he**let*

says Qoheleth,

2c הֲבֵל הֲבָלִים

*hă**vēl** hăvā**lîm***

“Abel of Abels.

2d הַכֹּל הָבֶל׃

*hak**kōl** **hā**vel.*

Everything is Abelish.”

3a מַה־יִּתְרוֹן לָאָדָם

*mah-yit**rôn** lāʾā**dām***

What profit is there for the human

3b בְּכָל־עֲמָלוֹ שֶׁיַּעֲמֹל תַּחַת הַשָּׁמֶשׁ׃

*bəḵol-ʿămā**lô** šeyyaʿă**mōl** **ta**ḥat haš**šā**meš.*

in all of his toil at which he toils under the sun?

2a הֲבֵל הֲבָלִים

“Abel of Abels,”

הֲבֵל הֶבֶל	Abel/mist/vapor/breath of *hă·**vēl***	CST	noun

הֲבָלִים הֶבֶל	Abels/mists/vapors/breaths *hă·vā·**lîm***	ABS	noun

The meaning of הֶבֶל is widely debated, with most English translations opting for a negative rendering of the word, such as "vanity" (e.g., NIV, ESV) or "meaningless" (e.g., NLT). In the opening excursus on the meaning of הֶבֶל (*hevel*), I argue that this term is a reference to Abel (see Gen 4) and will translate it as such throughout. This rendering is quite unusual, but the present volume allows this to work because the Hebrew is constantly before us alongside the translation, and keeping "Abel" at the forefront of our minds helps us to understand more fully how the original readers would have heard Qoheleth's use of הֶבֶל. Please see above for further discussion.

This Hebrew construction, a singular noun in construct with the same noun in the plural, is one way of communicating the superlative in Hebrew. We see the same construction in "holy of holies" (e.g., Exod 29:33; 1 Kgs 6:16), which refers to the most holy place in the tabernacle and temple.

2b אָמַר קֹהֶלֶת

says Qoheleth,

אָמַר אמר	(he) said/says *ʾā·**mar***	QAL PF 3MS	verb
קֹהֶלֶת קֹהֶלֶת	Qoheleth/gatherer/assembler *qō·**he**·let*	ABS	noun

2c הֲבֵל הֲבָלִים

"Abel of Abels.

הֲבֵל הֶבֶל	Abel/mist/vapor/breath of *hă·**vēl***	CST	noun
הֲבָלִים הֶבֶל	the Abels/mists/vapors/breaths *hă·vā·**lîm***	ABS	noun

2d	הַכֹּ֥ל הָֽבֶל׃			
	Everything is Abelish."			
הַכֹּ֥ל כֹּל	everything/the whole/ all (of it) *hak·kōl*	ABS W/ DEF. ART.	noun
הָֽבֶל׃ הֶ֫בֶל	Abel/mist/vapor/breath *hā·vel*	ABS	noun

The author is using repetition and hyperbole here to communicate that the human experience (life "under the sun," see 1:3b) after the fall is in some way like Abel.

3a	מַה־יִּתְר֖וֹן לָֽאָדָ֑ם			
	What profit is there for the human			
מַה־ מָה	what? *mah-*	---	interr pron
יִּתְר֖וֹן יִתְרוֹן	profit/gain/surplus/ advantage *yit·rôn*	ABS	noun
לָֽאָדָ֑ם אָדָם	for/to the man/human *lā·'ā·dām*	ABS W/ PREP לְ + DEF. ART.	noun

The term יִתְרוֹן ("advantage") is derived from the root יתר, which means "to remain" or "be left over." In its nominal form it refers to "profit" or that which is "left over." Some translations, such as NIV and ESV, render the term with "gain." Throughout Ecclesiastes the author argues (or implies, as here) that there is no "profit"—that is, nothing "left over"—for humans despite all of their toil on the earth. There is no "gain" from anything done on the earth; with Job, we can affirm that "naked I came from my mother's womb, and naked I will leave this life" (Job 1:21 CSB). However, Ecclesiastes presents an alternative to despair; for while there is no "profit" or "left-over portion," there is a חֵלֶק, "portion" or "reward," in this life, which Qoheleth will later identify as food, work, wine, and a spouse (see e.g., Eccl 3:22; 9:7–10). Thus, Ecclesiastes argues that while we should recognize the folly of working for some ultimate gain to be taken with us (there is none), we can and must enjoy gifts from God as he gives them. We will return to the concept of "reward" periodically, as it features prominently in Qoheleth's thought.

3b בְּכָל־עֲמָלוֹ שֶׁיַּעֲמֹל תַּחַת הַשָּׁמֶשׁ׃

in all of his toil at which he toils under the sun?

בְּכָל־ / כֹּל	in all of / *bə·kol-*	CST W/ PREP בְּ	noun
עֲמָלוֹ / עָמָל	his toil/labor / *ʿă·mā·**lô***	CST W/ 3MS SX	noun
שֶׁיַּעֲמֹל / עמל	(at) which he toils/labors / *šey·ya·ʿă·**mōl***	QAL IMPF 3MS W/ RELATIVE PRON שֶׁ	verb
תַּחַת / תַּחַת	under / ***ta**·ḥat*	---	prep
הַשָּׁמֶשׁ׃ / שֶׁמֶשׁ	the sun / *haš·**šā**·meš*	ABS W/ DEF. ART.	noun

Qoheleth uses the phrase תַּחַת הַשָּׁמֶשׁ ("under the sun") twenty-nine times and its approximate synonym תַּחַת הַשָּׁמַיִם ("under the heavens") three times to refer to that which occurs on earth. This does not mean that Qoheleth has an "earthly perspective" rather than a "heavenly perspective," as some have argued. Such a reading over-spiritualizes the metaphor, thus reading into it a meaning that the author did not intend. Rather, it means that Qoheleth is discussing how to navigate human life faithfully.

"Toil" seems to be one of Qoheleth's favorite words—it appears in its verbal or nominal form thirty-five times in Ecclesiastes (the noun and verb, as in English, share the same root: עמל). Qoheleth prefers "toil," which has negative connotations of hard labor, over the more neutral עבד, "work," which Genesis uses to describe humanity's purpose in the garden (Gen 2:15: "to work it and to preserve it"). However, as we will see below, Qoheleth still sees work as a gift from God—as long as it is enjoyed as God's gift rather than used a means for "profit."

Verse 3 as a whole functions as a rhetorical question that invites the reader to consider what is to be gained—that is, *ultimately* gained, or taken with us—during life on earth. We know the answer is "nothing," as does Qoheleth. However, we often live as if we do *not* believe that we'll be leaving this earth just as we entered it (Job 1:21). Qoheleth therefore wants readers to examine our hearts and lives and to point us toward a better way of living—namely, of embracing God's gifts as they come rather than attempting to "gain" what we cannot keep.

1:4–11

4a דּוֹר הֹלֵךְ וְדוֹר בָּא

dôr hōlēḵ wədôr bā’

A generation goes and a generation comes,

4b וְהָאָרֶץ לְעוֹלָם עֹמָדֶת׃

wəhā’āreṣ lə‘ôlām ‘ōmādet.

but the earth stands forever.

5a וְזָרַח הַשֶּׁמֶשׁ וּבָא הַשָּׁמֶשׁ

wəzāraḥ haššemeš ûvā’ haššāmeš

The sun rises and the sun sets,

5b וְאֶל־מְקוֹמוֹ שׁוֹאֵף זוֹרֵחַ הוּא שָׁם׃

wə’el-məqômô šō’ēf zôrēaḥ hû’ šām.

and to its home gasping [for air], there it rises.

6a הוֹלֵךְ אֶל־דָּרוֹם

hôlēḵ ’el-dārôm

Blowing to the south

6b וְסוֹבֵב אֶל־צָפוֹן

wəsôvēv ’el-ṣāfôn

and circling around to the north,

6c סוֹבֵב ׀ סֹבֵב הוֹלֵךְ הָרוּחַ

sôvēv sōvēv hôlēḵ hārûaḥ

circling, circling goes the wind,

6d וְעַל־סְבִיבֹתָיו שָׁב הָרוּחַ׃

wə‘al-səvîvōtāyw šāv hārûaḥ.

and upon its circuit, the wind returns.

7a כָּל־הַנְּחָלִים֙ הֹלְכִ֣ים אֶל־הַיָּ֔ם

*kol-hannəḥā**lîm** hōlə**ḵîm** ʾel-hay**yām***

All the rivers run into the sea,

7b וְהַיָּ֖ם אֵינֶ֣נּוּ מָלֵ֑א

*wəhay**yām** ʾê**nen**nû mā**lēʾ***

but the sea is never full.

7c אֶל־מְק֗וֹם שֶׁ֤הַנְּחָלִים֙ הֹֽלְכִ֔ים

*ʾel-mə**qôm** šehannəḥā**lîm** hōlə**ḵîm***

To the place where the rivers run,

7d שָׁ֛ם הֵ֥ם שָׁבִ֖ים לָלָֽכֶת׃

***šām hēm** šā**vîm** lā**lā**ḵet.*

there they return to run.

8a כָּל־הַדְּבָרִ֣ים יְגֵעִ֔ים

*kol-haddəvā**rîm** yəgē**ʿîm***

Everything is overwhelming;

8b לֹא־יוּכַ֥ל אִ֖ישׁ לְדַבֵּ֑ר

*lōʾ-yû**ḵal** **ʾîš** lədab**bēr***

people can’t even talk about it!

8c לֹא־תִשְׂבַּ֥ע עַ֙יִן֙ לִרְא֔וֹת

*lōʾ-tiś**baʿ** **ʿa**yin lir**ʾôt***

The eye is never sated with seeing,

8d וְלֹא־תִמָּלֵ֥א אֹ֖זֶן מִשְּׁמֹֽעַ׃

*wəlōʾ-timmā**lēʾ** **ʾō**zen miššə**mō**aʿ*

and the ear is never full of hearing.

9a מַה־שֶּֽׁהָיָה֙ ה֣וּא שֶׁיִּהְיֶ֔ה

*mah-šehā**yâ** **hûʾ** šeyyih**ye***

Whatever has been is that which will be,

9b וּמַה־שֶּֽׁנַּעֲשָׂ֔ה ה֖וּא שֶׁיֵּעָשֶׂ֑ה

ûmah-šenna'ăśâ hû' šeyyē'āśe

and whatever has been done is that which will be done,

9c וְאֵ֥ין כָּל־חָדָ֖שׁ תַּ֥חַת הַשָּֽׁמֶשׁ׃

wə'ên kol-ḥādāš taḥat haššāmeš.

and there is nothing new under the sun.

10a יֵ֥שׁ דָּבָ֛ר שֶׁיֹּאמַ֥ר

yēš dāvār šeyyō'mar

Someone has said,

10b רְאֵה־זֶ֖ה חָדָ֣שׁ ה֑וּא

rə'ē-ze ḥādāš hû'

"Look! This—it is new!"

10c כְּבָר֙ הָיָ֣ה לְעֹֽלָמִ֔ים אֲשֶׁ֥ר הָיָ֖ה מִלְּפָנֵֽנוּ׃

kəvār hāyâ lə'ōlāmîm 'ăšer hāyâ milləfānēnû.

It has long ago existed in the ages that came before us.

11a אֵ֥ין זִכְר֖וֹן לָרִאשֹׁנִ֑ים

'ên zikrôn lāri'šōnîm

There is no remembering former people,

11b וְגַ֨ם לָאַחֲרֹנִ֜ים שֶׁיִּהְי֗וּ

wəgam lā'aḥărōnîm šeyyihyû

and also the people to come

11c לֹא־יִהְיֶ֤ה לָהֶם֙ זִכָּר֔וֹן

lō'-yihye lāhem zikkārôn

will not be remembered

11d עִ֥ם שֶׁיִּהְי֖וּ לָאַחֲרֹנָֽה׃

'im šeyyihyû lā'aḥărōnâ.

by those who come later.

4a	דּ֣וֹר הֹלֵ֗ךְ וְד֣וֹר בָּ֔א

A generation goes and a generation comes,

דּ֣וֹר דּוֹר	generation/age *dôr*	ABS	noun
הֹלֵ֗ךְ הלך	walks/goes *hō·lēḵ*	QAL PTCP MS	verb
וְד֣וֹר דּוֹר	and a generation *wə·dôr*	ABS W/ CONJ וְ	noun
בָּ֔א בוא	comes/enters *bā'*	QAL PTCP MS	verb

4b	וְהָאָ֖רֶץ לְעוֹלָ֥ם עֹמָֽדֶת׃

but the earth stands forever.

וְהָאָ֖רֶץ אֶרֶץ	but the earth/land *wə·hā·'ā·reṣ*	ABS W/ CONJ וְ + DEF. ART.	noun
לְעוֹלָ֥ם עוֹלָם	for/to a long time/ forever/eternity *lə·'ô·lām*	ABS W/ PREP לְ	noun
עֹמָֽדֶת׃ עמד	stands/remains/endures *'ō·mā·ḏet*	QAL PTCP FS	verb

Verse 4 opens Qoheleth's poem on life's cyclical nature. His primary point in the poem is that everything changes, and yet everything stays the same. You and I will each have varied experiences in life, but the human race as a whole has the same basic experience. One generation comes, another goes, and the earth keeps spinning on its axis. We should not take his statement that "the earth stands forever" to contradict Genesis's teaching that God created the earth. He is not arguing that the earth has literally always existed, nor is he presenting an eschatological view as John the Revelator does in Rev 21. Rather, he is speaking poetically to communicate the general principle that people die and the earth remains. As will become clear throughout the book, the impermanence of individual humans deeply troubles Qoheleth—as it likely does the rest of us.

5a **וְזָרַח הַשֶּׁמֶשׁ וּבָא הַשָּׁמֶשׁ**

The sun rises and the sun sets,

וְזָרַח זרח	rise/appear/shine *wə·zā·**raḥ***	QAL PF 3MS W/ CONJ וְ	verb
הַשֶּׁמֶשׁ שֶׁמֶשׁ	the sun *haš·**še**·meš*	ABS W/ DEF. ART.	noun
וּבָא בוא	and comes/enters *û·**vā**ʾ*	QAL PF 3MS W/ CONJ וְ	verb
הַשָּׁמֶשׁ שֶׁמֶשׁ	the sun *haš·**šā**·meš*	ABS W/ DEF. ART.	noun

5b **וְאֶל־מְקוֹמוֹ שׁוֹאֵף זוֹרֵחַ הוּא שָׁם׃**

and to its home gasping [for air], there it rises.

וְאֶל־ אֶל	and to/toward *wə·ʾel-*	--- W/ CONJ וְ	prep
מְקוֹמוֹ מָקוֹם	its place/home/site *mə·qô·**mô***	CST W/ 3MS SX	noun
שׁוֹאֵף שׁאף	panting/heaving/gasping *šô·**ʾēf***	QAL PTCP MS	verb
זוֹרֵחַ זרח	rises/appears/shines *zô·**rē**·aḥ*	QAL PTCP MS	verb
הוּא הוּא	she/it ***hûʾ***	---	personal pron
שָׁם׃ שָׁם	there ***šām***	---	adv

In addition to the cyclic nature of humanity (i.e., "generation") described in v. 4, in vv. 5–7 Qoheleth illustrates how other features of creation (cf. Gen 1) likewise cycle endlessly. Here he mentions the sun, which he follows up with wind and water in the next two verses. In each case, the movement continues endlessly, with no real sense of fulfillment; in other words, even the sun, rivers, and earth lack any "profit" for their labors. שׁוֹאֵף describes heaving or "gasping" for air, as a woman in throes of labor (Isa 42:14). The sun's toil is difficult—and it never ceases.

6a הוֹלֵךְ אֶל־דָּרוֹם

Blowing to the south

הוֹלֵךְ הלך	walking/going *hô·lēḵ*	QAL PTCP MS	verb
אֶל־ אֶל	to/toward *ʾel-*	---	prep
דָּרוֹם דָּרוֹם	south *dā·rôm*	ABS	noun

6b וְסוֹבֵב אֶל־צָפוֹן

and circling around to the north,

וְסוֹבֵב סבב	and turning/surrounding/circling *wə·sô·vēv*	QAL PTCP MS W/ CONJ וְ	verb
אֶל־ אֶל	to/toward *ʾel-*	---	prep
צָפוֹן צָפוֹן	north *ṣā·fôn*	ABS	noun

6c סוֹבֵב ׀ סֹבֵב הוֹלֵךְ הָרוּחַ

circling, circling goes the wind,

סוֹבֵב ׀ סבב	turning/surrounding/circling *sô·vēv*	QAL PTCP MS	verb
סֹבֵב סבב	turning/surrounding/circling *sō·vēv*	QAL PTCP MS	verb

הוֹלֵךְ הלך	walks/goes *hô·lēḵ*	QAL PTCP MS	verb
הָרֽוּחַ רוּחַ	the wind *hā·rû·aḥ*	ABS W/ DEF. ART.	noun

6d **וְעַל־סְבִיבֹתָיו שָׁב הָרֽוּחַ׃**

and upon its circuit, the wind returns.

וְעַל־ עַל	and upon/on/over *wə·ʿal-*	--- W/ CONJ וְ	prep
סְבִיבֹתָיו סָבִיב	its circuit/vicinity *sə·vî·vō·ṯāyw*	CST W/ 3MS SX.	noun
שָׁב שׁוּב	returns/goes back *šāv*	QAL PTCP MS	verb
הָרֽוּחַ׃ רוּחַ	the wind *hā·rû·aḥ*	ABS W/ DEF. ART.	noun

This verse includes a striking amount of alliteration, with its repetition of "s" sounds, making it both memorable and pleasing to the ears of the original audience. As with the previous verses, Qoheleth here describes the cyclical nature of the wind, whose continuous activity does not actually "gain" anything. It simply continues on its never-ending circuit.

7a **כָּל־הַנְּחָלִים֙ הֹלְכִ֣ים אֶל־הַיָּ֔ם**

All the rivers run into the sea,

כָּל־ כֹּל	all/each of *kol-*	CST	noun
הַנְּחָלִים֙ נַ֫חַל	the rivers/streams *han·nə·ḥā·lîm*	ABS W/ DEF. ART.	noun
הֹלְכִים הלך	walking/going/running *hō·lə·ḵîm*	QAL PTCP MP	verb
אֶל־ אֶל	to/toward *ʾel-*	---	prep

הַיָּם יָם	the sea *hay·**yām***	ABS W/ DEF. ART.	noun

7b **וְהַיָּם אֵינֶנּוּ מָלֵא**

but the sea is never full.

וְהַיָּם יָם	and/but the sea *wə·hay·**yām***	ABS W/ CONJ וְ + DEF. ART.	noun
אֵינֶנּוּ אַיִן	it is not/there is not to it *ʾê·**nen**·nû*	--- W/ 3MS SX.	particle
מָלֵא מָלֵא	full/fullness *mā·**lēʾ***	MS PRED	adj

7c **אֶל־מְקוֹם שֶׁהַנְּחָלִים הֹלְכִים**

To the place where the rivers run,

אֶל־ אֶל	to/toward *ʾel-*	---	prep
מְקוֹם מָקוֹם	place/home/site of *mə·**qôm***	CST	noun
שֶׁהַנְּחָלִים נַחַל	where the rivers/streams *še·han·nə·ḥā·**lîm***	ABS W/ RELATIVE PRON שֶׁ + DEF. ART.	noun
הֹלְכִים הלך	walking/going/running *hō·lə·**ḵîm***	QAL PTCP MP	verb

7d **שָׁם הֵם שָׁבִים לָלָכֶת׃**

there they return to run.

שָׁם שָׁם	there ***šām***	---	adv
הֵם הֵם	they/those ***hēm***	---	personal pron

שָׁבִים שׁוב	returns/goes back *šā·**vîm***	QAL PTCP MP	verb
לָלָכֶת׃ הלך	to walk/go/run *lā·**lā**·ḵet*	QAL INF CST W/ PREP לְ	verb

In v. 4, Qoheleth introduced the contrast between the earth's permanence and the impermanence of human life. Verses 5–7 highlight similarities between human life and other natural features—namely, the sun, wind, and rivers. Qoheleth makes this comparison clear through his use of personification. Just as the generations הלך ("go"—i.e., pass on), so also the wind הלך ("goes"—i.e., blows) and the rivers הלך ("go"—i.e., run). Though we use different English words to describe the movements of humans, wind, and streams, Qoheleth uses the same Hebrew term to highlight their cyclical nature over against the "standing" of the earth. The sun likewise exhibits human characteristics as it "gasps" around the earth each day. By comparing generations of humans with the never-ending work of earth's natural features, Qoheleth gives us the answer to his question, "What profit is there for the human in all of his toil at which he toils under the sun?" (1:2). There is no profit, nothing left over, because human generations—like the sun, streams, and wind—are stuck on repeat, with the added tragedy that though humanity continues, individual humans die.

8a כָּל־הַדְּבָרִים יְגֵעִים

Everything is overwhelming;

כָּל־ כֹּל	all/each of *kol-*	CST	noun
הַדְּבָרִים דָּבָר	the words/matters/things *had·də·vā·**rîm***	ABS W/ DEF. ART.	noun
יְגֵעִים יָגֵעַ	wearisome/troubling *yə·gē·**ʿîm***	MP PRED	adj

8b לֹא־יוּכַל אִישׁ לְדַבֵּר

people can't even talk about it!

לֹא־ לֹא	not *lō'-*	---	particle

יוּכַל יכל	(he) is able/can *yû·kal*	QAL IMPF 3MS	verb
אִישׁ אִישׁ	man/person *ʾîš*	ABS	noun
לְדַבֵּר דבר	to speak/state *lə·dab·bēr*	PIEL INF CST W/ PREP לְ	verb

Qoheleth regularly uses two Hebrew terms to refer to people: אִישׁ (10x) and אָדָם (49x). Both can be translated as "man," and both are used in the Hebrew Bible to refer generically to a "person" or "people." אָדָם often refers to humanity in general and almost always occurs with the definite article in Ecclesiastes (39x out of 49x), as is the case in Gen 1–11 (37x with the definite article out of 44x used); we will examine below the significance of this for the relationship between Genesis and Ecclesiastes. For now, we simply recognize that while אִישׁ and אָדָם can refer to a "man," in contexts like this one they refer generically to "people" or "humanity."

Interpreters of Ecclesiastes—scholars and laypeople like—often view Qoheleth as a pessimist, a glass-half-full kind of person who struggles to see the good in life. It is understandable when we read sentences like this (v. 8a–b), but let's hold off on letting that cast set just yet. This sentence represents just one part of the picture he paints, though it is a part of the picture we must acknowledge. As the father of three children, one adopted out of foster care, I have often uttered prayers like, "This is too much, God," and "If you don't help, there's no way through this." I am certain you can easily think of similarly despair-inducing times during your own life and the lives of your congregants. Life *can* be overwhelming (יְגֵעִים), and it *can* be too much to talk about it (לֹא־יוּכַל אִישׁ לְדַבֵּר). Qoheleth's frank acknowledgment of life's difficulties is a key reason for its ongoing relevance. He puts to words what many of us are afraid to say, and in so doing, he frees us to acknowledge our own struggles to navigate the post-fall world we inhabit.

8c **לֹא־תִשְׂבַּע עַיִן לִרְאוֹת**

The eye is never sated with seeing,

לֹא־ לֹא	not *lōʾ-*	---	particle
תִשְׂבַּע שׂבע	(it) is sated/filled/satisfied *tiś·baʿ*	QAL IMPF 3FS	verb

עַ֫יִן עַ֫יִן	eye *ʿa·yin*	ABS	noun
לִרְא֔וֹת ראה	to see/look at *lir·ʾôt*	QAL INF CST W/ PREP לְ	verb

8d **וְלֹא־תִמָּלֵ֥א אֹ֖זֶן מִשְּׁמֹֽעַ׃**

and the ear is never full of hearing.

וְלֹא־ לֹא	and not *wə·lōʾ-*	--- W/ CONJ וְ	particle
תִמָּלֵ֥א מלא	(it) is full/filled/satisfied *tim·mā·lēʾ*	NIPH IMPF 3FS	verb
אֹ֖זֶן אֹ֫זֶן	ear *ʾō·zen*	ABS	noun
מִשְּׁמֹֽעַ׃ שׁמע	to hear/listen *miš·šə·mō·aʿ*	QAL INF CST W/ PREP מִן	verb

Qoheleth cleverly personifies ears and eyes with the use of two Hebrew words with overlapping meaning: שׂבע ("to be sated") and מלא ("to be full, satisfied"). No matter how much ears hear, there is always room for more, and no matter how much eyes see, they always have space to see more. Unlike the belly, eyes and ears never get enough. They are like a black hole that consumes all that comes its way. But we shouldn't view this negatively; they are functioning as God intended as they consume everything within earshot or eyesight. The point is that—like the sun, wind, streams, and humanity itself—their work is never quite finished.

9a **מַה־שֶּֽׁהָיָה֙ ה֣וּא שֶׁיִּֽהְיֶ֔ה**

Whatever has been is that which will be,

מַה־ מָה	what *mah-*	---	interr pron
שֶּֽׁהָיָה֙ היה	which/that was/has been *še·hā·yâ*	QAL PF 3MS W/ RELATIVE PRON שֶׁ	verb
ה֣וּא הוּא	it/that *hûʾ*	---	personal pron

שֶׁיִּהְיֶה היה	which/that is/will be *šey·yih·ye*	QAL IMPF 3MS W/ RELATIVE PRON שֶׁ	verb

9b **וּמַה־שֶּׁנַּעֲשָׂה הוּא שֶׁיֵּעָשֶׂה**

and whatever has been done is that which will be done,

וּמַה־ מָה	and what *û·mah-*	--- W/ CONJ וְ	interr pron
שֶּׁנַּעֲשָׂה עשׂה	which is done/ has been done *šen·na·ʿă·śâ*	NIPH PF 3MS W/ RELATIVE PRON שֶׁ	verb
הוּא הוּא	it/that *hûʾ*	---	personal pron
שֶׁיֵּעָשֶׂה עשׂה	will be done *šey·yē·ʿā·śe*	NIPH IMPF 3MS W/ RELATIVE PRON שֶׁ	verb

9c **וְאֵין כָּל־חָדָשׁ תַּחַת הַשָּׁמֶשׁ׃**

and there is nothing new under the sun.

וְאֵין אַיִן	and there is not *wə·ʾên*	--- W/ CONJ וְ	particle
כָּל־ כֹּל	all/anything *kol-*	ABS	noun
חָדָשׁ חָדָשׁ	new *ḥā·dāš*	MS ATTR	adj
תַּחַת תַּחַת	under *ta·ḥat*	---	prep
הַשָּׁמֶשׁ׃ שֶׁמֶשׁ	the sun *haš·šā·meš*	ABS W/ DEF. ART.	noun

This verse is full of pronouns that perform multiple functions in Hebrew, making an exact translation difficult if not impossible. The relative pronoun שֶׁ ("that") is repeated four times, the interrogative pronoun מָה appears twice, and the third-person masculine pronoun הוּא ("he, it") appears twice. These can all be translated various ways; however, we benefit greatly from the author's use of parallelism in this verse. Each of these three lines is in synonymous parallelism—they state essentially the same thing—so we can understand the meaning of the first two, more difficult, lines by the clearly stated third line: "There is nothing new under the sun." As with previous poetic statements, we should not take this to mean that Qoheleth used an electric light bulb to illuminate the desk on which he wrote Ecclesiastes. He is not stating that technological advances are a fantasy; rather, he is pointing to the overall cyclical nature of human life, more akin to something I heard regularly in my more ornery moments as a child: "I hope you have a kid just like you when you grow up." (Indeed, that hope has been fulfilled.)

Qoheleth again uses the phrase תַּ֣חַת הַשָּֽׁמֶשׁ ("under the sun"), which we saw a few verses above. As mentioned at 1:3b, this phrase appears twenty-nine times in the book of Ecclesiastes and is not used anywhere else in the Hebrew Bible. The importance of this phrase for understanding Ecclesiastes is significant. It is often taken to refer to a "worldly" perspective on life as opposed to "heavenly" one; however, that reading derives from reading the book as a whole negatively, which in turn results from reading the book's key word, הֶבֶל ("Abel/breath/vapor"), negatively. In addition, the "worldly" reading of "under the sun" does not account for the immediate context, which utilizes imagery from the natural world to communicate realities of the shared human experience. It likewise ignores the larger context of Ecclesiastes, which regularly elevates the enjoyment of earthly realities such as food, work, a spouse, and wine. Thus, rather than seeing Qoheleth's discussion as framed by a "worldly" view of life, we should see it as a frank discussion of what life on earth, or life "under the sun," is like. Understood this way, Qoheleth is not so much a sage urging us to turn aside from immorality (though he does that) as he is a sage helping his readers to navigate the dark yet delightful world we inhabit.

10a	יֵ֥שׁ דָּבָ֛ר שֶׁיֹּאמַ֥ר			
	Someone has said,			
יֵ֥שׁ יֵשׁ	there is *yēš*	---	particle
דָּבָ֛ר דָּבָר	a word/matter/thing *dā·vār*	ABS	noun
שֶׁיֹּאמַ֥ר אמר	which (he) said *šey·yō'·mar*	QAL IMPF 3MS W/ RELATIVE PRON שֶׁ	verb

The Hebrew of this text more woodenly reads, "There is a word that he speaks." The idiomatic rendering provided here captures the same meaning. Some translations (such as the ESV, CSB, and KJV) translate this as a question, "Is there a thing of which it is said?" (ESV). Whether rendered as a question or a statement, the intent is to introduce and then refute an argument Qoheleth's hearers/readers might make.

10b רְאֵה־זֶ֖ה חָדָ֣שׁ ה֑וּא

"Look! This—it is new!"

רְאֵה־ ראה	look/see/investigate *rə·ʾē-*	QAL IMPV MS	verb
זֶ֖ה זֶה	this ***ze***	---	demonstr pron
חָדָ֣שׁ חָדָשׁ	new *ḥā·**dāš***	MS PRED	adj
ה֑וּא הוּא	it ***hûʾ***	---	personal pron

This is the content of the statement Qoheleth anticipates from his hearers/readers. Just as a good professor will anticipate and then answer her students' questions, Qoheleth does the same. He imagines that, after listening to his opening words, someone might object that some things indeed *are* new.

10c כְּבָר֙ הָיָ֣ה לְעֹֽלָמִ֔ים אֲשֶׁ֥ר הָיָ֖ה מִלְּפָנֵֽנוּ׃

It has long ago existed in the ages that came before us.

כְּבָר֙ כְּבָר	already, long ago *kə·**vār***	---	adv
הָיָ֣ה היה	it was/existed *hā·**yâ***	QAL PF 3MS	verb
לְעֹֽלָמִ֔ים עוֹלָם	for/to a long time/ forever/eternity *lə·ʿō·lā·**mîm***	ABS W/ PREP לְ	noun
אֲשֶׁ֥ר אֲשֶׁר	that/which *ʾă·**šer***	---	relative pron

הָיָה היה	(it) was/existed *hā·yâ*	QAL PF 3MS	verb
מִלְּפָנֵנוּ׃ לִפְנֵי	from before us *mil·lə·fā·nē·nû*	--- W/ PREP מִן + 1CP SX	prep

As in the previous statements where Qoheleth uses hyperbole to great effect, so also here he is not saying that batteries and remote-controlled cars already existed in the ancient Near East. Rather, he is pointing to the cyclical nature of human life. Today we might say, "History repeats itself," with the same intent.

11a אֵין זִכְרוֹן לָרִאשֹׁנִים

There is no remembering former people,

אֵין אַיִן	there is not *'ên*	---	particle
זִכְרוֹן זִכָּרוֹן	remembering/memorial/ remembrance of *zik·rôn*	CST	noun
לָרִאשֹׁנִים רִאשׁוֹן	the former people/things *lā·ri'·šō·nîm*	MP SUBST W/ PREP לְ + DEF. ART.	adj

Translations vary on how they understand the term רִאשֹׁנִים ("former people"). The ESV sees it as a reference to "things," as does the KJV and the NASB. Other versions, such as the NIV and CSB, read רִאשֹׁנִים as referring to "those" (i.e., people; CSB) or "generations" (NIV). The NLT renders the word with "events." The Hebrew allows for any of these translations. Given the ambiguity in Hebrew, I have opted for "people" in v. 11 because v. 9 refers to events ("whatever has been") and actions ("whatever has been done") and v. 10 refers to things ("This—it is new!"). Taken together, then, vv. 9–11 cover the gamut of what humans experience, including humans themselves.

זִכָּרוֹן ("remembering"; used twice in this verse) is a noun derived from the root זכר ("to remember"). It can refer to "memorials" to events, such as the stones set up to memorialize Yahweh damming up the Jordan River as the Israelites crossed into Canaan (Josh 4:7). But it is also used in reference to memorials to people. For example, in Mal 3:16–18 the term refers to a "book of remembrance" or "memorial book" used to record the names of those who "feared Yahweh." In Exod 28:12 "memorial stones" or "stones of remembrance" are affixed to the high priest's ephod to represent the people of Israel, and in Num 31:54 the spoil from war is brought into the tent of meeting as a "memorial" or "remembrance" for the people of Israel before Yahweh. Whether it is translated "memorial," "remembrance," or "remembering" in Eccl 1:11, the significance is that the vast majority of people are lost to history (can you name, much less describe, your great-great-grandmother?).

11b **וְגַם לָאַחֲרֹנִים שֶׁיִּהְיוּ**

and also the people to come

וְגַם גַּם	and also/even/too/likewise *wə·**gam***	--- W/ CONJ וְ	adv
לָאַחֲרֹנִים אַחֲרוֹן	to/for the latter people/things *lā·ʾa·ḥă·rō·**nîm***	MP SUBST W/ PREP לְ + DEF. ART.	adj
שֶׁיִּהְיוּ היה	which will be *šey·yih·**yû***	QAL IMPF 3MP W/ RELATIVE PRON שֶׁ	verb

Following the same rationale given for translating רִאשֹׁנִים as "former people" above, אַחֲרֹנִים here and אַחֲרֹנָה in v. 11d are taken to refer to people.

11c **לֹא־יִהְיֶה לָהֶם זִכָּרוֹן**

will not be remembered

לֹא־ לֹא	not *lō*ʾ-	---	particle
יִהְיֶה היה	(he) will be *yih·**ye***	QAL IMPF 3MS	verb
לָהֶם לְ	to/for them *lā·**hem***	--- W/ 3MP SX	prep
זִכָּרוֹן זִכָּרוֹן	remembering/memorial/ remembrance *zik·kā·**rôn***	ABS	noun

11d	עִם שֶׁיִּהְי֖וּ לָאַחֲרֹנָֽה׃
	by those who come later.

עִ֫ם עִם	among/with *'im*	---	prep
שֶׁיִּהְי֖וּ היה	which will be *šey·yih·**yû***	QAL IMPF 3MP W/ RELATIVE PRON שֶׁ	verb
לָאַחֲרֹנָֽה׃ אַחֲרוֹן	to/for the latter person/thing *lā·'a·ḥă·rō·**nâ***	FS SUBST W/ PREP לְ + DEF. ART.	adj

Verse 11 closes the opening poem that introduces the book of Ecclesiastes and hints at key themes that Qoheleth will develop in the coming chapters. Verse 11, in particular, subtly introduces a prominent motif: the injustice of death. While Qoheleth does not explicitly discuss death as he will later in the book (e.g., 3:20; 8:8; 9:2–3), he points to ultimate death—the loss of one's memory among the living (see, e.g., Deut 25:5–10; 29:16–21; Josh 7:9; 1 Sam 24:20–22; Zeph 1:4; Zech 13:2). This great tragedy—death—hints at another theme in Qoheleth that we have already seen above—in-the-moment (and momentary) enjoyment of God's gifts. There is no "profit" (Eccl 1:3), and there is no "remembering," so humans can and must take hold of that which God gives them *today*, for that is our "portion" or "reward." It certainly troubles Qoheleth that legacy (i.e., a זִכָּרוֹן, "memorial/remembrance") remains out of (nearly) everyone's grasp, but his solution is neither hopelessness nor nihilism, as is so often the solution today; instead he advocates trust in, or fear of, God (Eccl 12:13) and enjoyment of his gifts.

From Text to Sermon

Reading Ecclesiastes with Fresh Eyes. Ecclesiastes is a difficult book for many Christians to understand. I, for one, first studied the book because I thought its author was as disillusioned with life as I was. If a person who thought everything was "meaningless" could write a book of the *Bible*, I thought, then perhaps there was hope for me. As I studied the book and examined its Hebrew more closely, though, I realized that I had it all wrong, and at the root of my misunderstanding was its Christian history of interpretation. Since Jerome's Vulgate translation, which rendered הֶבֶל as *vanitas*, "vanity," the negative reading of the book has dominated Christian interpretation. Thus, it is likely your congregation will have many misunderstandings and misconceptions about the book of Ecclesiastes, and this sermon on the first chapter gives you the opportunity to begin the work of helping your people read the book with fresh eyes. There are many ways to accomplish this task, but in the spirit of the book of Ecclesiastes, perhaps this first sermon is a good place to introduce the topics to which you will return throughout the series, such as death, work, joy, and living in relationship with God.

A primary obstacle to overcome in preaching Ecclesiastes is the book's cyclical and meandering structure, which can be frustrating for many Western Christians. (Why can't he just state things plainly like Paul?!?) One way to help your people relate to this structure is to share insights from studies on trauma, which indicates that trauma survivors do not process their experiences in a linear, logical fashion.

Take my experience, for example. I had a very difficult childhood that included an alcoholic father, an abusive stepfather who was a deacon at my church, and the much too early death of my grandmother. I began using drugs in elementary school, was expelled from junior high, and eventually Jesus saved me just before college—but it took many years to really understand and address all that I had experienced, both at the hands of others and because of my own decisions. All of my experiences of loss, abuse, and destructive coping mechanisms became jumbled in my heart and mind, and just as I thought I was "over" a certain part of it, a seemingly innocuous interaction would suddenly transform me into a young boy cowering in my room, weeping at the dining room table, or stuffing pills down my throat to feel better. What's worse, every time I thought I had recovered from something I experienced, two weeks later—and then a week after that and two months after that—I would have to process it all over again. In other words, like Qoheleth, I kept returning to the same issues over and over and over again. My healing was not linear; it was cyclical. And my experience with trauma is not unique, as studies of trauma survivors have shown. While Ecclesiastes is not a modern text on trauma, it is definitely an ancient text on the traumas we all face—death, injustice, and the seeming inability of our lives to *matter*. So, while Qoheleth's cyclical approach to these topics can be irritating, it is also quite comforting to know that he—just like me, and perhaps you, and definitely many in your congregation—kept circling around to the same problems again and again.

Besides discussing the book's cyclical nature, you could also touch on issues such as the meaning of "under the sun" and how it introduces us to Qoheleth's concern for navigating human life. In addition, he broaches the topic of work, hinting at both the problem of work—that it doesn't fulfill us in any lasting way as we think it should—and the solution to that problem—not asking or expecting work to fulfill us. Finally, Qoheleth introduces the greatest injustice in life: death. Qoheleth will, like the wind and sun in his poem, return to these topics in the coming chapters. And in this opening, he primes the pump with his poem about cycles that introduces topics he will cycle through in a way that mimics how we humans process and heal from trauma—in cycles. Ecclesiastes is a masterful book with the ability to radically change your congregation's experience of life "under the sun." Welcome them to its wonders!

THE ROYAL EXPERIMENT

These several verses form the backbone of the argument for Solomonic authorship of Ecclesiastes, for it is here where the author embarks upon a grand building project that mirrors Solomon's accomplishments (though Deuteronomy would be loathe to call them "accomplishments"; see Deut 17:14–17) listed in 1 Kgs 3 11 (see Meek 2015:77 79; Seow 1997:150–52). In particular, the statement in 2:9, "I became greater than—and I surpassed—all who were before me in Jerusalem," echoes 1 Kgs 10:23: "Solomon the king became greater than all the kings of the earth with regard to wisdom and riches." In addition to echoing the narrative of Solomon's reign in 1 Kings, this passage also fits squarely within the ancient Near Eastern tradition of royal garden building (Galling 1932). Most importantly, though, this passage echoes the narrative of God's creation of his own garden in Gen 1–2, thus inviting readers to view Qoheleth's garden project in light of God's garden project. This relationship between Genesis and Ecclesiastes will be further developed below, as will its implications for interpreting and preaching Ecclesiastes.

LARGER LITERARY CONTEXT › 2:1–17

2:4–9

4a הִגְדַּ֖לְתִּי מַעֲשָׂ֑י

*hig**dal**tî ma'ă**śāy***

I increased my achievements.

4b בָּנִ֥יתִי לִי֙ בָּתִּ֔ים

*bā**nî**tî **lî** bāt**tîm***

I built for myself palaces.

4c נָטַ֥עְתִּי לִ֖י כְּרָמִֽים׃

*nā**ṭa**'tî **lî** kərā**mîm**.*

I planted for myself vineyards.

5a עָשִׂ֣יתִי לִ֔י גַּנּ֖וֹת וּפַרְדֵּסִ֑ים

*'ă**śî**tî **lî** gan**nôt** ûfardē**sîm***

I made for myself gardens and parks,

5b וְנָטַ֥עְתִּי בָהֶ֖ם עֵ֥ץ כָּל־פֶּֽרִי׃

*wənā**ṭa**'tî vā**hem** 'ēṣ kol-**pe**rî.*

and I planted in them trees of every (kind of) fruit.

6a עָשִׂ֥יתִי לִ֖י בְּרֵכ֣וֹת מָ֑יִם

*'ă**śî**tî **lî** bərē**ḵôt** **mā**yim*

I made for myself pools of water

6b לְהַשְׁק֣וֹת מֵהֶ֔ם יַ֖עַר צוֹמֵ֥חַ עֵצִֽים׃

*ləhaš**qôt** mē**hem** **ya**'ar ṣô**mē**aḥ 'ē**ṣîm**.*

from which to irrigate a forest of sprouting trees.

7a קָנִ֙יתִי֙ עֲבָדִ֣ים וּשְׁפָח֔וֹת

*qā**nî**tî 'ăvā**dîm** ûšəfā**ḥôt***

I bought male and female slaves,

7b וּבְנֵי־בַיִת הָיָה לִי

*ûvənê-**vayit** **hāyâ** **lî***

and slaves were born in my house.

7c גַּם מִקְנֶה בָקָר וָצֹאן הַרְבֵּה הָיָה לִּי

gam** miq**ne** vā**qār** wā**ṣō'n** har**bē** **hāyâ** **lî

I also owned enormous herds of large livestock and small livestock,

7d מִכֹּל שֶׁהָיוּ לְפָנַי בִּירוּשָׁלָֽםִ׃

*mik**kōl** šehā**yû** ləfā**nay** bîrûšā**lā**im.*

more than all who came before me in Jerusalem.

8a כָּנַסְתִּי לִי גַּם־כֶּסֶף וְזָהָב

*kā**nas**tî **lî** gam-**ke**sef wəzā**hāv***

I also gathered for myself silver and gold,

8b וּסְגֻלַּת מְלָכִים וְהַמְּדִינוֹת

*ûsəgul**lat** məlā**ḵîm** wəhamməd**înôt***

and the treasure of kings and provinces.

8c עָשִׂיתִי לִי שָׁרִים וְשָׁרוֹת וְתַעֲנוּגֹת בְּנֵי הָאָדָם שִׁדָּה וְשִׁדּוֹת׃

*'ā**sî**tî **lî** šā**rîm** wəšā**rôt** wəta'ănû**gōt** bənê hā'ā**dām** šid**dâ** wəšid**dôt**.*

I amassed for myself male and female singers
and the luxuries of humanity—servant upon servant.

9a וְגָדַלְתִּי וְהוֹסַפְתִּי

*wəgā**dal**tî wəhô**saf**tî*

I became greater—and I surpassed—

9b מִכֹּל שֶׁהָיָה לְפָנַי בִּירוּשָׁלָםִ

*mik**kōl** šehā**yâ** ləfā**nay** bîrûšā**lā**im*

all who were before me in Jerusalem.

9c אַף חָכְמָתִי עָמְדָה לִּי׃

*'**af** ḥoḵ**mā**tî '**ā**mədâ **lî**.*

What's more, my wisdom remained with me.

4a	הִגְדַּ֫לְתִּי מַעֲשָׂ֑י		
	I increased my achievements.		
הִגְדַּ֫לְתִּי גדל	I increased/magnified/ made great *hig·**dal**·tî*	HIPH PF 1CS	verb
מַעֲשָׂ֑י מַעֲשֶׂה	my works/products/ achievements *ma·ʿă·**śāy***	CST W/ 1CS SX	noun

Twice in this chapter (2:4, 9) and once in ch. 1 (1:16) Qoheleth uses the root גדל ("to be/become great / make great / increase / magnify") to describe himself or his accomplishments. As mentioned in the introduction to this section, גדל is also used to describe Solomon in 1 Kgs 10:23: "Solomon the king became greater than all the kings of the earth with regard to wisdom and riches." The choice of verb here, along with the boasts in the rest of this section, indicates the author wants readers to associate Qoheleth with King Solomon. Such self-boasting in a book associated with Solomon is ironic, given the hard line against it in Proverbs, another Solomonic work: "Let another praise you, and not your own mouth; a stranger, and not your own lips" (Prov 27:2). Perhaps the self-boasting is intended to cause us to look askance at Qoheleth, or perhaps he is simply establishing his credibility to make the argument that unfolds in the following verses.

4b	בָּנִ֥יתִי לִי֙ בָּתִּ֔ים		
	I built for myself palaces.		
בָּנִ֥יתִי בנה	I built *bā·**nî**·tî*	QAL PF 1CS	verb
לִי֙ לְ	for myself ***lî***	--- W/ 1CS SX	prep
בָּתִּ֔ים בַּ֫יִת	palaces/houses *bāt·**tîm***	ABS	noun

בָּתִּים ("houses") is the same term used for the "house" David wanted to build for Yahweh and for the "house" (2 Sam 7:5) Solomon built for himself (1 Kgs 7:1) and for at least one of his wives (1 Kgs 7:8). In keeping with the royal language of this passage and the term's usage for Yahweh's temple and Solomon's palaces, I have opted for the translation "palace" here. This communicates more clearly the grandeur of the building project—having more than one house is opulent, particularly in the ancient Near East; having more than one palace is even more so, especially when those palaces were built by a conscripted labor force (see 1 Kgs 5:13; 9:21–22).

4c **נָטַעְתִּי לִי כְּרָמִים׃**

I planted for myself vineyards.

נָטַעְתִּי נטע	I planted *nā·ṭaʿ·tî*	QAL PF 1CS	verb
לִי לְ	to/for me/myself *lî*	--- W/ 1CS SX	prep
כְּרָמִים׃ כֶּרֶם	vineyards *kə·rā·**mîm***	ABS	noun

The use of the term נטע ("planted") is significant, for it is the first of many overlapping terms between this passage and Yahweh's creation of the garden of Eden in Gen 1–2 (see the chart below at "From Text to Sermon"). Here and in 2:5, Qoheleth "plants" a garden, and in Gen 2:8 Yahweh likewise "plants" a garden. As we continue in this passage, we will see further overlapping vocabulary between the two passages, and the passages also exhibit clear overlap in their subject matter: the creation of a garden by a ruler.

Note also the repetition of first-person verbs and the לִי ("for myself") construction. Whereas Yahweh planted a garden in Eden for the human (Adam), Qoheleth planted a garden only for himself.

5a **עָשִׂיתִי לִי גַּנּוֹת וּפַרְדֵּסִים**

I made for myself gardens and parks,

עָשִׂיתִי עשׂה	I made/did *ʿā·**śî**·tî*	QAL PF 1CS	verb

לִּי לְ	for myself *lî*	--- W/ 1CS SX	prep
גַּנּוֹת גַּן	gardens *gan·nôt*	ABS	noun
וּפַרְדֵּסִים פַּרְדֵּס	and parks/orchards/forests *û·far·dē·sîm*	ABS W/ CONJ וְ	noun

Qoheleth here continues describing his building project, adding "gardens and parks" to his "palaces" and "vineyards." The "gardens" (גַּנּוֹת) that Qoheleth planted are another repetition from the Genesis story, when God likewise planted a "garden" (גַּן; Gen 2:8). Qoheleth also echoes Genesis when he says that he "made" (עשׂה) his garden and parks. Genesis 2:2 reports that God completed "the work that he made" (עשׂה) and Gen 2:8 tells us that God rested from all the work that he "made" (עשׂה). Notice again, though, that Qoheleth has built gardens and parks *for himself* (לִי), whereas the work of God in Genesis is for the benefit of his image bearers. The term פַּרְדֵּס is likely a Persian loanword and refers to "an enclosed park or garden" (Schoors 2013:155). This is one of its three usages in the Hebrew Bible. In Song 4:13 it refers to an "orchard of pomegranates" and in Neh 2:8 it refers to King Artaxerxes's "forest" from which Nehemiah would harvest timber for his rebuilding project.

5b וְנָטַעְתִּי בָהֶם עֵץ כָּל־פֶּרִי׃

and I planted in them trees of every (kind of) fruit.

וְנָטַעְתִּי נטע	and I planted *wə·nā·ṭa‘·tî*	QAL PF 1CS W/ CONJ וְ	verb
בָהֶם בְּ	in them *vā·hem*	--- W/ 3MP SX	prep
עֵץ עֵץ	tree of *‘ēṣ*	CST	noun
כָּל־ כֹּל	all/every *kol-*	CST	noun
פֶּרִי׃ פְּרִי	fruit *pe·rî*	ABS	noun

Qoheleth's "planting" (נטע) of "trees of every (kind of) fruit" also strongly echoes the Genesis creation narrative. In Gen 2:8 God "planted (נטע) a garden in Eden" (see also 2:9, 10, 15, 16), which he filled with "fruit trees" (עֵץ פְּרִי; Gen 1:11, 12, 29; see also 2:9).

6a	עָשִׂיתִי לִי בְּרֵכוֹת מָיִם		
	I made for myself pools of water		
עָשִׂיתִי עשׂה	I made/did *ʿā·śî·tî*	QAL PF 1CS	verb
לִי לְ	for myself *lî*	--- W/ 1CS SX	prep
בְּרֵכוֹת בְּרֵכָה	pools of *bə·rē·ḵôt*	CST	noun
מָיִם מַיִם	water *mā·yim*	ABS	noun

6b	לְהַשְׁקוֹת מֵהֶם יַעַר צוֹמֵחַ עֵצִים׃		
	from which to irrigate a forest of sprouting trees.		
לְהַשְׁקוֹת שׁקה	to irrigate/cause to drink *lə·haš·qôt*	HIPH INF CST W/ PREP לְ	verb
מֵהֶם מִן	from them *mē·hem*	--- W/ 3MP SX	prep
יַעַר יַעַר	forest/woods *ya·ʿar*	ABS	noun
צוֹמֵחַ צמח	sprouting/growing *ṣô·mē·aḥ*	QAL PTCP MS	verb
עֵצִים׃ עֵץ	trees *ʿē·ṣîm*	ABS	noun

The allusions to the creation narrative continue in this verse as Qoheleth describes the forest of trees he has planted as "sprouting" (צמח), just as the trees in God's garden are caused to "sprout" (צמח; Gen 2:9). And just as Qoheleth "irrigates" (שׁקה) his garden with a system of pools, so God "irrigates" (שׁקה) the garden of Eden with a system of rivers (Gen 2:10). Overall, Eccl 2:4–6 repeats an astonishing amount of vocabulary from the Genesis creation account, and both narratives address the same basic idea: creation of a garden by a ruler. This is but one of the many sections in which Qoheleth points readers backward to Genesis as he develops his own thoughts on what it means to live in a world turned upside down by sin. We will discuss the theological implications of the garden of Eden echoes more fully in "From Text to Sermon" below.

7a	קָנִ֫יתִי עֲבָדִ֣ים וּשְׁפָח֔וֹת

I bought male and female slaves,

קָנִ֫יתִי קנה	I bought/acquired *qā·nî·tî*	QAL PF 1CS	verb
עֲבָדִ֣ים עֶ֫בֶד	slaves/servants *ʿă·vā·dîm*	ABS	noun
וּשְׁפָח֔וֹת שִׁפְחָה	and female slaves/ maidservants *û·šə·fā·ḥôt*	ABS W/ CONJ וְ	noun

7b	וּבְנֵי־בַ֖יִת הָ֣יָה לִ֑י

and slaves were born in my house.

וּבְנֵי־ בֵּן	and sons/children of *û·və·nê-*	CST W/ CONJ וְ	noun
בַ֖יִת בַּ֫יִת	house *va·yit*	ABS	noun
הָ֣יָה היה	(it) was *hā·yâ*	QAL PF 3MS	verb
לִ֑י לְ	to/for me *lî*	--- W/ 1CS SX	prep

A wooden translation of this phrase is, "and children of (the) house were to me." הָיָה לִי ("were to me") indicates possession. Idiomatically, Qoheleth is stating that in addition to purchasing slaves (2:7a), those purchased slaves had children, who were therefore born his slaves. Abraham uses a similar phrase in Gen 15:3 when he tells Yahweh that "a son of my house [i.e., a slave] will be my heir" (בֶן־בֵּיתִי יוֹרֵשׁ אֹתִי). In this passage and in

Genesis, the context makes clear that a "son of the house" refers to a person born into slavery in a particular home.

7c גַּם מִקְנֶה בָקָר וָצֹאן הַרְבֵּה הָיָה לִי

I also owned enormous herds of large livestock and small livestock,

גַּם גַּם	also/even *gam*	---	adv
מִקְנֶה מִקְנֶה	cattle/thing purchased *miq·ne*	ABS	noun
בָקָר בָּקָר	cattle/livestock *vā·qār*	ABS	noun
וָצֹאן צֹאן	and sheep/goats/ small livestock *wā·ṣōʼn*	ABS W/ CONJ וְ	noun
הַרְבֵּה רבה	to be many/much *har·bē*	HIPH INF ABS	verb
הָיָה היה	(it) was *hā·yâ*	QAL PF 3MS	verb
לִי לְ	to/for me *lî*	--- W/ 1CS SX	prep

7d מִכֹּל שֶׁהָיוּ לְפָנַי בִּירוּשָׁלָם׃

more than all who came before me in Jerusalem.

מִכֹּל כֹּל	from all *mik·kōl*	CST W/ PREP מִן	noun
שֶׁהָיוּ היה	who were *še·hā·yû*	QAL PF 3CP W/ RELATIVE PRON שֶׁ	verb
לְפָנַי לִפְנֵי	before me *lə·fā·nay*	--- W/ 1CS SX	prep
בִּירוּשָׁלָם׃ יְרוּשָׁלַםִ	in Jerusalem *bî·rû·šā·lā·im*	ABS W/ PREP בְּ	noun

If one does not live in a rural or farming community, the significance of enormous herds of livestock may not be readily apparent. However, livestock in the ancient Near East, as in many parts of the world today, both indicates and generates wealth, much like a large stock portfolio in the modern world.

8a	כָּנַ֣סְתִּי לִ֗י גַּם־כֶּ֙סֶף֙ וְזָהָ֔ב

I also gathered for myself silver and gold,

כָּנַ֣סְתִּי כנס	I gathered/collected *kā·**nas**·tî*	QAL PF 1CS	verb
לִ֗י לְ	for myself ***lî***	--- W/ 1CS SX	prep
גַּם־ גַּם	also/even *gam-*	---	adv
כֶּ֙סֶף֙ כֶּ֫סֶף	silver ***ke**·sef*	ABS	noun
וְזָהָ֔ב זָהָב	and gold *wə·zā·**hāv***	ABS W/ CONJ וְ	noun

Qoheleth continues to recount the enormous amount of wealth he has accumulated for himself. "Silver and gold" (כֶּ֙סֶף֙ וְזָהָ֔ב) is a common, idiomatic way of saying, "a lot of money." We expect monarchs and heads of state to be wealthy, but Yahweh commanded Israelite kings *not* to accumulate wealth, using a very similar expression to what Qoheleth uses here: "silver and gold he must not multiply much to himself" (Deut 17:17). Thus, while modern readers may be impressed, Torah readers will know that an Israelite king who boasts of "silver and gold" indicts himself.

8b	וּסְגֻלַּ֥ת מְלָכִ֖ים וְהַמְּדִינ֑וֹת

and the treasure of kings and provinces.

וּסְגֻלַּ֥ת סְגֻלָּה	and treasure/possession of *û·sə·gul·**lat***	CST W/ CONJ וְ	noun
מְלָכִ֖ים מֶ֫לֶךְ	kings *mə·lā·**kîm***	ABS	noun

וְהַמְּדִינוֹת מְדִינָה	and provinces/districts *wə·ham·mə·dî·**nôt***	ABS W/ CONJ וְ + DEF. ART.	noun

סְגֻלָּה ("treasure") is a somewhat rare word in the Hebrew Bible, occurring only eight times. In six occurrences it refers to Israel as Yahweh's possession (Exod 19:5; Deut 7:6; 14:2; 26:18; Mal 3:7; Ps 135:4). Here and in 1 Chr 29:3 it appears in parallel with "silver and gold" and refers to the personal possessions of a king (Schoors 2013:160–61). Whereas here Qoheleth glories in the "treasure" he gathered to himself, in 1 Chronicles, David states that his "devotion for the house of God" is so great that he has given his own "treasure" or "private collection" for its construction.

8c עָשִׂ֨יתִי לִ֜י שָׁרִ֣ים וְשָׁר֗וֹת וְתַעֲנוּגֹ֛ת בְּנֵ֥י הָאָדָ֖ם שִׁדָּ֥ה וְשִׁדּֽוֹת׃

I amassed for myself male and female singers
and the luxuries of humanity—servant upon servant.

עָשִׂ֨יתִי עשׂה	I acquired/amassed *ʿā·**śî**·tî*	QAL PF 1CS	verb
לִ֜י לְ	for myself ***lî***	--- W/ 1CS SX	prep
שָׁרִ֣ים שׁיר	male singers *šā·**rîm***	QAL PTCP MP	verb
וְשָׁר֗וֹת שׁיר	female singers *wə·šā·**rôt***	QAL PTCP FP W/ CONJ וְ	verb
וְתַעֲנוּגֹ֛ת תַּעֲנוּג	and pleasures/delights/ luxuries of *wə·ta·ʿă·nû·**gōt***	CST W/ CONJ וְ	noun
בְּנֵ֥י בֵּן	the sons/children of *bə·**nê***	CST	noun
הָאָדָ֖ם אָדָם	the man/human/humanity *hā·ʾā·**dām***	ABS W/ DEF. ART.	noun
שִׁדָּ֥ה שִׁדָּה	servant/concubine (?) *šid·**dâ***	ABS	noun
וְשִׁדּֽוֹת׃ שִׁדָּה	and servants/concubines (?) *wə·šid·**dôt***	ABS W/ CONJ וְ	noun

The term (עשׂה) is typically translated "do/make," but its range of meaning is broad. In many contexts, as here, it indicates acquisition (e.g., people, Gen 12:5; wealth, Deut 8:18; a new heart and a new spirit, Ezek 18:31). תַּעֲנוּגֹת ("pleasures") may refer to sexual pleasure, as in Song 7:7, but it usually refers generally to luxury or delight—the "finer things" of life that wealthy people enjoy. This is especially true because בְּנֵי הָאָדָם ("humanity," lit., "the sons of men") refers to humanity in general, rather than men in particular, in each of its other occurrences in Ecclesiastes (Eccl 1:13; 2:3; 3:10, 18, 21; 8:11; 9:3, 12). On the other hand, the next phrase, שִׁדָּה וְשִׁדּוֹת, is most often translated "concubines," but this is the word's only occurrence in the Hebrew Bible and its meaning is unclear (see fuller discussion in Schoors 2013:162–66). Here I have translated the word as "servant" because of the inclusive use of בְּנֵי הָאָדָם ("humanity") throughout Ecclesiastes, the nonsexualized use of תַּעֲנוּגֹת ("luxuries") in the Hebrew Bible, and the broader context of royal boasting in this passage.

9a **וְגָדַלְתִּי וְהוֹסַפְתִּי**

I became greater—and I surpassed—

וְגָדַלְתִּי גדל	and I became greater *wə·gā·**dal**·tî*	QAL PF 1CS W/ CONJ וְ	verb
וְהוֹסַפְתִּי יסף	and I surpassed *wə·hô·**saf**·tî*	HIPH PF 1CS W/ CONJ וְ	verb

9b **מִכֹּל שֶׁהָיָה לְפָנַי בִּירוּשָׁלִָם**

all who were before me in Jerusalem.

מִכֹּל כֹּל	than/from all *mik·**kōl***	ABS W/ PREP מִן	noun
שֶׁהָיָה היה	who were/existed *še·hā·**yâ***	QAL PF 3MS W/ RELATIVE PRON שֶׁ	verb
לְפָנַי לִפְנֵי	before me *lə·fā·**nay***	--- W/ 1CS SX	prep
בִּירוּשָׁלִָם יְרוּשָׁלַםִ	in Jerusalem *bî·rû·šā·**lā**·im*	ABS W/ PREP בְּ	noun

9c	אַ֣ף חָכְמָתִ֔י עָ֥מְדָה לִּֽי׃		
	What's more, my wisdom remained with me.		
אַ֣ף אַף	even/also/moreover/indeed *'af*	---	conj
חָכְמָתִ֔י חָכְמָה	my wisdom *ḥoḵ·mā·tî*	CST W/ 1CS SX	noun
עָ֥מְדָה עמד	(it) remained/stood *'ā·mə·dâ*	QAL PF 3FS	verb
לִּֽי׃ לְ	to me *lî*	--- W/ 1CS SX	prep

Verse 9 closes out this section of boasting, with vv. 10–11 providing a summary of the results of Qoheleth's royal experiment. Here, he reminds readers again that he excelled to the greatest degree—"before all who were before me in Jerusalem"—and emphasizes that he remained wise during the entire pursuit. This claim bears significance in light of the excesses Qoheleth luxuriated in—excesses that the book of Proverbs would caution against. In addition to the various echoes of the Solomon narrative we have already seen in this passage, v. 9 calls to mind 1 Kgs 10:7, in which the queen of Sheba states that Solomon's wisdom "surpassed" (the same *hiphil* form of יסף found here) what she had heard about him.

10a וְכֹל֙ אֲשֶׁ֣ר שָׁאֲל֣וּ עֵינַ֔י

wəḵōl ʾăšer šāʾălû ʿênay

And everything that my eyes asked for,

10b לֹ֥א אָצַ֖לְתִּי מֵהֶ֑ם

*lōʾ ʾāṣaltî mē**hem***

I did not withhold from them.

10c לֹא־מָנַ֨עְתִּי אֶת־לִבִּ֜י מִכָּל־שִׂמְחָ֗ה

*lōʾ-mā**na**ʿtî ʾet-lib**bî** mikkol-śim**ḥâ***

I did not refuse my heart any joy,

10d כִּֽי־לִבִּ֤י שָׂמֵ֙חַ֙ מִכָּל־עֲמָלִ֔י וְזֶֽה־הָיָ֥ה חֶלְקִ֖י מִכָּל־עֲמָלִֽי׃

*kî-lib**bî** śā**mē**aḥ mikkol-ʿămā**lî** wəze hā**yâ** ḥel**qî** mikkol-ʿămā**lî**.*

for my heart rejoiced in all of my toil,
and this was my reward from all of my toil.

11a וּפָנִ֣יתִֽי אֲנִ֗י

*ûfā**nî**tî ʾă**nî***

So I myself looked

11b בְּכָל־מַעֲשַׂי֙ שֶׁעָשׂ֣וּ יָדַ֔י

*bəḵol-maʿă**śay** šeʿā**śû** yā**day***

at all my works that my hands accomplished

11c וּבֶֽעָמָ֖ל שֶׁעָמַ֣לְתִּי לַעֲשׂ֑וֹת

*ûveʿā**māl** šeʿā**mal**tî laʿă**śôt***

and at my toil at which I toiled to do.

11d וְהִנֵּ֨ה הַכֹּ֥ל הֶ֙בֶל֙ וּרְע֣וּת ר֔וּחַ

*wəhin**nē** hak**kōl** **he**vel ûrə**ʿût** **rû**aḥ*

And look! All of it is Abelish and striving after wind,

11e **וְאֵ֥ין יִתְר֖וֹן תַּ֥חַת הַשָּֽׁמֶשׁ׃**

*wəʾ**ên** yit**rôn** **ta**ḥat haš**šā**meš.*

and there is no profit under the sun.

10a **וְכֹל֙ אֲשֶׁ֣ר שָׁאֲל֣וּ עֵינַ֔י**

And everything that my eyes asked for,

וְכֹל֙ כֹּל	and all/everything *wə·**kōl***	ABS W/ CONJ וְ	noun
אֲשֶׁ֣ר אֲשֶׁר	which/that *ʾă·**šer***	---	relative pron
שָׁאֲל֣וּ שׁאל	(they) asked for/demanded *šā·ʾă·**lû***	QAL PF 3CP	verb
עֵינַ֔י עַיִן	my eyes *ʿê·**nay***	CST W/ 1CS SX	noun

10b **לֹ֥א אָצַ֖לְתִּי מֵהֶ֑ם**

I did not withhold from them.

לֹ֥א לֹא	not *lōʾ*	---	particle
אָצַ֖לְתִּי אצל	I withheld *ʾā·**ṣal**·tî*	QAL PF 1CS	verb
מֵהֶ֑ם מִן	from them *mē·**hem***	--- W/ 3MP SX	prep

The word שׁאל in v. 10a, typically translated as "desired," more commonly means "to ask, ask for, demand," and the like. Here, Qoheleth is personifying his eyes by attributing to them the agency to ask for things. The sentiment is similar to how we might describe a spoiled child today: "His parents give him everything he wants." Despite his insistence that his wisdom remained with him (2:9), every parent knows that it is altogether *unwise* to give a person (or one's eyes) everything they ask for.

10c **לֹֽא־מָנַ֫עְתִּי אֶת־לִבִּי מִכָּל־שִׂמְחָה**

I did not refuse my heart any joy,

לֹֽא־ לֹא	not *lōʾ-*	---	particle
מָנַ֫עְתִּי מנע	I refused/denied/withheld *mā·**na**ʿ·tî*	QAL PF 1CS	verb
אֶת־ אֵת	*(direct object marker)* *ʾet-*	---	particle
לִבִּ֫י לֵב	my heart/mind *lib·**bî***	CST W/ 1CS SX	noun
מִכָּל־ כֹּל	from all/each *mik·kol-*	CST W/ PREP מִן	noun
שִׂמְחָה שִׂמְחָה	joy/mirth/happiness *śim·**ḥâ***	ABS	noun

10d **כִּֽי־לִבִּי שָׂמֵ֫חַ מִכָּל־עֲמָלִי וְזֶה־הָיָה חֶלְקִי מִכָּל־עֲמָלִי׃**

for my heart rejoiced in all of my toil,
and this was my reward from all of my toil.

כִּֽי־ כִּי	for/because *kî-*	---	conj
לִבִּי לֵב	my heart/mind *lib·**bî***	CST W/ 1CS SX	noun
שָׂמֵ֫חַ שָׂמֵחַ	rejoiced/took joy/was happy *śā·**mē**·aḥ*	QAL PTCP MS	verb
מִכָּל־ כֹּל	from all/each of *mik·kol-*	CST W/ PREP מִן	noun
עֲמָלִ֫י עָמָל	my toil/labor *ʿă·mā·**lî***	CST W/ 1CS SX	noun
וְזֶה־ זֶה	and this *wə·**ze***	--- W/ CONJ וְ	demonstr pron

הָיָה היה	(it) was *hā·yâ*	QAL PF 3MS	verb
חֶלְקִי חֵלֶק	my portion/reward *ḥel·**qî***	CST W/ 1CS SX	noun
מִכָּל־ כֹּל	from all of *mik·kol-*	CST W/ PREP מִן	noun
עֲמָלִי׃ עָמָל	my toil/labor *ʿă·mā·**lî***	CST W/ 1CS SX	noun

In the comments on 1:3a–b we looked at Qoheleth's lament that there is no "gain" or "profit" for a person's toil during this life, and there we mentioned that later in Ecclesiastes, Qoheleth points out that though there is no *ultimate* gain or "leftover" portion for one's work, there *is* a "reward" for our work. After toiling hard to create a garden and avail himself of every luxury that his immense wealth could afford him, Qoheleth concludes that "rejoic[ing] in all of my toil . . . was the reward from all of my toil." Thus, very early on in the book, readers learn that the antidote to the despair caused by our inability to produce anything lasting in our work is neither hopelessness nor ceasing from toil. Rather, it is to embrace the fleeting joy that our toil affords us. Rather than seeking from vocation some fulfillment that it cannot give ("profit" or "gain"), we instead should embrace what it does give: joy in the work itself.

11a **וּפָנִיתִי אֲנִי**

So I myself looked

וּפָנִיתִי פנה	and/so I turned/looked *û·fā·**nî**·tî*	QAL PF 1CS W/ CONJ וְ	verb
אֲנִי אֲנִי	I *ʾă·**nî***	---	personal pron

The personal pronoun אֲנִי is translated as "myself" to communicate the emphasis added by Qoheleth's including it in addition to the embedded subject in the verb וּפָנִיתִי ("and I turned"). פנה means "to turn" in its most basic sense, but it carries the connotation here and elsewhere of "turning toward," "regarding," or "looking at" something, in this case the "work" that Qoheleth has done.

11b	בְּכָל־מַעֲשַׂ֫י שֶׁעָשׂ֣וּ יָדַ֔י

at all my works that my hands accomplished

בְּכָל־ / כֹּל	at/in all of *bə·ḵol-*	CST W/ PREP בְּ	noun
מַעֲשַׂ֫י / מַעֲשֶׂה	my works/products/ achievements *ma·ʿă·**śay***	CST W/ 1CS SX	noun
שֶׁעָשׂ֣וּ / עשׂה	that (they) accomplished/ did/made *še·ʿā·**śû***	QAL PF 3CP W/ RELATIVE PRON שֶׁ	verb
יָדַ֔י / יָד	my hands *yā·**day***	CST W/ 1CS SX	noun

In addition to the presence of the personal pronoun אֲנִי ("I") in the first clause of this verse, here Qoheleth refers to "my works" and "my deeds," thus beckoning the reader to experience Qoheleth's royal experiment from his perspective as he reflects on what he "accomplished" (עשׂה).

11c	וּבֶֽעָמָ֖ל שֶׁעָמַ֣לְתִּי לַעֲשׂ֑וֹת

and at my toil at which I toiled to do.

וּבֶֽעָמָ֖ל / עָמָל	and at/in toil//labor *û·ve·ʿā·**māl***	ABS W/ CONJ וְ + PREP בְּ + DEF. ART.	noun
שֶׁעָמַ֣לְתִּי / עמל	that I toiled *še·ʿā·**mal**·tî*	QAL PF 1CS W/ RELATIVE PRON שֶׁ	verb
לַעֲשׂ֑וֹת / עשׂה	to do/make *la·ʿă·**śôt***	QAL INF CST W/ PREP לְ	verb

11d	וְהִנֵּ֨ה הַכֹּ֥ל הֶ֛בֶל וּרְע֥וּת ר֖וּחַ

And look! All of it is Abelish and striving after wind,

וְהִנֵּ֨ה / הִנֵּה	and look/behold *wə·hin·**nē***	--- W/ CONJ וְ	particle
הַכֹּ֥ל / כֹּל	the whole/all *hak·**kōl***	ABS W/ DEF. ART.	noun

הֶ֫בֶל֮	Abel/mist/vapor/breath	ABS	noun
הֶ֫בֶל	*he · vel*		
וּרְע֣וּת	and chasing/striving after	CST W/ CONJ וְ	noun
רְעוּת	*û · rə · 'ût*		
ר֑וּחַ	wind/breath	ABS	noun
רוּחַ	*rû · aḥ*		

The basic idea of רְעוּת רוּחַ ("striving after wind") is clear: wind does what it wills and resists all human effort to control or manipulate it.

11e **וְאֵ֥ין יִתְר֖וֹן תַּ֥חַת הַשָּֽׁמֶשׁ׃**

and there is no profit under the sun.

וְאֵ֥ין	and there is not	--- W/ CONJ וְ	particle
אַיִן	*wə · 'ên*		
יִתְר֖וֹן	profit/gain/surplus/ advantage	ABS	noun
יִתְרוֹן	*yit · rôn*		
תַּ֥חַת	under	---	prep
תַּחַת	*ta · ḥat*		
הַשָּֽׁמֶשׁ׃	the sun	ABS W/ DEF. ART.	noun
שֶׁמֶשׁ	*haš · šā · meš*		

In 1:3 Qoheleth asked the question, "What profit is there for the human in all of his toil at which he toils under the sun?" Here in 2:11 he concludes—after accomplishing more than most of us will ever attempt—that there is "no profit under the sun." However, all is not lost, for while there is no "profit" or "gain" from all the work that we do in this life ("under the sun"), there *is* a "reward" or "portion" for our "toil/labor" (עמל): taking joy in the work itself. Learning to take joy in our tasks, rather than looking to them for "gain" or some sort of ultimate satisfaction, is a crucial aspect of effectively navigating life "under the sun."

From Text to Sermon

Echoes of Genesis. Above we examined the multiple points of overlap between Eccl 2:4–6 and Gen 2. As scholar Arian Verheij (1991:114) has pointed out, "Taken separately, these words are not remarkable: for the most part they are indeed very common in Biblical Hebrew. It is their combined occurrence here and in Genesis that establishes a firm link between the texts." In addition to the sheer number of repeated terms, the context is very similar in that both passages describe the construction of a garden by a ruler, complete with sprouting trees and an irrigation method (see chart below). Though Qoheleth cast himself in the image of the Creator by recreating God's efforts in the creation of the cosmos, Qoheleth's efforts failed because "there is no profit [יִתְרוֹן] under the sun" (Eccl 2:11). God's creation, on the other hand, was good (e.g., Gen 1:4, 10, 12, 18, 21, 25, 31), producing the sort of lasting value for which Qoheleth longed. By juxtaposing these efforts, Qoheleth intends his hearers/readers to think on God's good creation in contrast to the efforts of humanity. Humans are not, it turns out, God. Understanding—and living within—this contrast between humanity and God is a key aspect of navigating life well.

	Ecclesiastes 2:4–6	Genesis 2:2, 8–10
Repeated Terms	נָטַעְתִּי (2x)	וַיִּטַּע
	עָשִׂיתִי (2x)	עָשָׂה (2x)
	גַּנּוֹת	גַּן (3x)
	עֵץ כָּל־פֶּרִי	כָּל־עֵץ
	לְהַשְׁקוֹת	לְהַשְׁקוֹת
	צוֹמֵחַ	וַיַּצְמַח
Repeated Themes	Creation of a garden by a ruler	Creation of a garden by a ruler

Profit vs. Reward. In 1:16 Qoheleth boasted that his wisdom surpassed "all who came before me in Jerusalem," in 2:7 he repeated the boast as it relates to his herds of sheep and cattle, and in 2:9 crowed again that "I became greater than—and I surpassed—all who were before me in Jerusalem." As mentioned above, these boasts echo 1 Kgs 10:23—"Solomon the king became greater than all the kings of the earth with regard to wisdom and riches"—and thus associate Qoheleth with Solomon. The overall point Qoheleth makes with these boasts is that he is uniquely qualified to embark on a journey such as this one—a journey to determine the "profit" to be had by working, being wise, and acquiring all that one could desire. Ultimately, he finds out that there is no "profit" or "ultimate gain" in working. However, there is a "reward" or "portion" in work, and that is to take joy in the work itself. This perspective of taking joy in work while refusing to find ultimate value in our vocation is a key to righteous living and navigating the difficulties of life. We cannot escape the curse of difficult labor in this life, but we can push back against the curse—looking behind us to Eden and ahead of us to the new heavens and new earth—by taking genuine, momentary joy in the tasks God gives us.

ECCLESIASTES 3:16–22

TELLING THE TRUTH ABOUT THE WORLD TURNED UPSIDE DOWN

Some readers see this passage as a depressing, maybe even nihilistic, statement about the sad state of the world. Viewed through the lens of trauma studies, though, this passage illustrates disclosure, the process of naming the trauma a person has experienced and telling one's story. Many people who have experienced trauma find disclosure quite difficult, yet "when the truth is finally recognized," writes scholar Judith Herman, "survivors can begin their recovery" (Herman 1997:1). As a young Christian—and now as an older Christian—I wavered most in my faith when I saw the praise and admiration that the church heaped upon my stepfather, who was an entirely different person at home than he was at church. Seeing this disconnect, I thought that God either does not care about injustice or else is unjust himself. However, reading this passage in Ecclesiastes, where Qoheleth acknowledges injustice, breathed new life into my relationship with God by modeling for me what disclosure, or truth telling, looks like. The honesty of Qoheleth's statements about the injustice of death and the reward of the wicked gave me hope that God really does see and really does care, and that hope gave me the boldness to talk to God about—to disclose—my anger and frustration. Those conversations with God, and eventually others, made healing possible for me. So rather than viewing this passage negatively, let us see in it a faithful model of being honest with ourselves, God, and others, and having the courage to tell the truth.

LARGER LITERARY CONTEXT › 3:16–22

3:16–17

16a וְע֥וֹד רָאִ֖יתִי תַּ֣חַת הַשָּׁ֑מֶשׁ

*wəʿ**ôd** rāʾ**î**tî **ta**ḥat haš**šā**meš*

And further, I observed this under the sun:

16b מְק֤וֹם הַמִּשְׁפָּט֙ שָׁ֣מָּה הָרֶ֔שַׁע

*mə**qôm** hammiš**pāṭ** **šā**mmâ hā**re**šaʿ*

The place of justice—there was injustice!

16c וּמְק֥וֹם הַצֶּ֖דֶק שָׁ֥מָּה הָרָֽשַׁע׃

*ûmə**qôm** haṣ**ṣe**deq **šā**mmâ hā**rā**šaʿ.*

And the place of righteousness—there was injustice!

17a אָמַ֤רְתִּֽי אֲנִי֙ בְּלִבִּ֔י

*ʾā**mar**tî ʾă**nî** bəlib**bî***

I myself said in my heart,

17b אֶת־הַצַּדִּיק֙ וְאֶת־הָ֣רָשָׁ֔ע יִשְׁפֹּ֖ט הָאֱלֹהִ֑ים

*ʾet-haṣṣad**dîq** wəʾet-hārā**šā**ʿ yiš**pōṭ** hāʾĕlō**hîm***

"The righteous person and the wicked person, God will judge,

17c כִּי־עֵ֣ת לְכָל־חֵ֔פֶץ וְעַ֥ל כָּל־הַֽמַּעֲשֶׂ֖ה שָֽׁם׃

*kî-ʿ**ēt** ləkol-**ḥē**feṣ wəʿ**al** kol-hammaʿă**śe** **šām**.*

for there is a time for every matter,
and concerning every deed there is a destiny."

16a	וְעוֹד רָאִיתִי תַּחַת הַשָּׁמֶשׁ

And further, I observed this under the sun:

וְעוֹד עוֹד	and also/further/moreover *wə·ʿôd*	--- W/ CONJ וְ	adv
רָאִיתִי ראה	I saw/observed *rā·ʾî·tî*	QAL PF 1CS	verb
תַּחַת תַּחַת	under *ta·ḥat*	---	prep
הַשָּׁמֶשׁ שֶׁמֶשׁ	the sun *haš·šā·meš*	ABS W/ DEF. ART.	noun

Following his poem of "times" in 3:1–8 and discussion of work, joy in God's gifts, and God's purposes for humans in 3:9–15, Qoheleth turns to discuss another feature of life "under the sun" (תַּחַת הַשָּׁמֶשׁ), or in the lived human experience, that remains particularly problematic today: injustice. Qoheleth speaks about this injustice from experience; it is something that he personally "observed" or "saw" (ראה). Speaking from experience performs a few rhetorical functions that engage ancient and modern readers alike. First, his "seeing" invites us likewise to "see" from his perspective, thus drawing us into his life and experience. And once in his shoes, many of us will realize that our experiences are not so different. Like Qoheleth, we also "see" injustice around us. Second, speaking from his own experience emboldens us to, like Qoheleth, acknowledge the injustice we see and experience. Thus, the personal nature of his reflections ("*I* saw") gives readers the tools we need to tell the truth, just as Qoheleth does in this passage.

16b	מְקוֹם הַמִּשְׁפָּט שָׁמָּה הָרֶשַׁע

The place of justice—there was injustice!

מְקוֹם מָקוֹם	the place of *mə·qôm*	CST	noun
הַמִּשְׁפָּט מִשְׁפָּט	of justice *ham·miš·pāṭ*	ABS W/ DEF. ART.	noun
שָׁמָּה שָׁם	there *šām·mâ*	--- W/ LOCATIVE ה	adv

הָרֶ֫שַׁע רֶ֫שַׁע	wickedness/injustice *hā·re·šaʿ*	ABS W/ DEF. ART.	noun

"The place of justice" refers to the legal or court system. Though the courts function differently in modern culture than in the ancient Near East, in both cases there exists a fundamental expectation of justice. In the Old Testament, justice is portrayed as flowing out of God's nature. He "show[s] no partiality and tak[es] no bribe. He executes justice for the fatherless and the widow, and loves the resident alien, giving him food and clothing" (Deut 10:17–18 CSB). It is the last place one would expect to find "injustice," and yet there Qoheleth has observed it.

16c **וּמְקוֹם הַצֶּדֶק שָׁמָּה הָרָשַׁע׃**

And the place of righteousness—there was injustice!

וּמְקוֹם מָקוֹם	and in the place of *û·mə·qôm*	CST W/ CONJ וְ	noun
הַצֶּדֶק צֶ֫דֶק	righteousness *haṣ·ṣe·deq*	ABS W/ DEF. ART.	noun
שָׁמָּה שָׁם	there *šām·mâ*	--- W/ LOCATIVE ה	adv
הָרָשַׁע׃ רֶ֫שַׁע	wickedness/injustice *hā·rā·šaʿ*	ABS W/ DEF. ART.	noun

These two lines (16b and 16c) lack both verbs and prepositions, though most English translations supply "in" or "at" in order to smooth out the statements. The effect in Hebrew is to communicate emotion. That is, Qoheleth is not making a calm, detached observation about injustice; he is rather exclaiming that in the very place he (and everyone else) expected justice, there was injustice.

The Hebrew Bible often pairs justice (מִשְׁפָּט) and righteousness (צֶדֶק) as the ideal that God himself exhibits (e.g., Ps 9:7–8), that the Messiah will establish (Isa 42:1–4; Mal 3:1–5), and to which God calls his people (Jer 22:3; Amos 5:24). These two features are indeed the hallmark of true Israelite faith, and their lack in the very place where they are most expected disturbs Qoheleth as much as it disturbs us today.

17a	אָמַ֤רְתִּֽי אֲנִי֙ בְּלִבִּ֔י

I myself said in my heart,

אָמַרְתִּי אמר	(I) said *ʾā·**mar**·tî*	QAL PF 1CS	verb
אֲנִי אֲנִי	I *ʾă·**nî***	---	personal pron
בְּלִבִּי לֵב	in my heart/mind *bə·lib·**bî***	CST W/ PREP בְּ + 1CS SX	noun

Qoheleth's use of the personal pronoun אֲנִי ("I"), which is unnecessary because the subject is embedded in the verb אָמַרְתִּי ("I said"), indicates emphasis. Further, each of the three Hebrew words in this phrase includes some form of the first-person pronoun. As noted above, Qoheleth's rhetorical style invites readers into his personal experience.

17b	אֶת־הַצַּדִּיק֙ וְאֶת־הָ֣רָשָׁ֔ע יִשְׁפֹּ֖ט הָאֱלֹהִ֑ים

"The righteous person and the wicked person, God will judge,

אֶת־ אֵת	*(direct object marker)* *ʾet-*	---	particle
הַצַּדִּיק צַדִּיק	the righteous person/one *haṣ·ṣad·**dîq***	MS SUBST W/ DEF. ART.	adj
וְאֶת־ אֵת	and *(direct object marker)* *wə·ʾet-*	--- W/ CONJ וְ	particle
הָרָשָׁע רָשָׁע	the wicked person/one *hā·rā·**šāʿ***	MS SUBST W/ DEF. ART.	adj
יִשְׁפֹּט שׁפט	(he) will judge *yiš·**pōṭ***	QAL IMPF 3MS	verb
הָאֱלֹהִים אֱלֹהִים	the God *hā·ʾĕ·lō·**hîm***	ABS W/ DEF. ART.	noun

Qoheleth sees plainly the injustice in life ("under the sun"; v. 16), as in the Cain and Abel narrative. Nevertheless, he also demonstrates faith in God by expressing his conviction that despite what his eyes tell him, God will be just. Like the psalmist in Ps 58:11 and Abraham in Gen 18:25, Qoheleth is certain that God judges justly. Rather than seeing this statement as an insertion by a later editor, we should recognize in it the struggle that faithful people have experienced for millennia, captured memorably in Mark's Gospel: "I believe; help my unbelief!" (Mark 9:24). Despite what our experience tells us, God calls us to live by faith in him and his promise to judge the world rightly.

17c	כִּי־עֵת לְכָל־חֵפֶץ וְעַל כָּל־הַמַּעֲשֶׂה שָׁם׃		
	for there is a time for every matter, and concerning every deed there is a destiny."		
כִּי־ כִּי	for/because *kî-*	---	conj
עֵת עֵת	a time *ʿēt*	ABS	noun
לְכָל־ כֹּל	for all/every of *lə·kol-*	CST W/ PREP לְ	noun
חֵפֶץ חֵפֶץ	matter/delight *ḥē·feṣ*	ABS	noun
וְעַל עַל	and concerning/about *wə·ʿal*	--- W/ CONJ וְ	prep
כָּל־ כֹּל	all/every of *kol-*	CST	noun
הַמַּעֲשֶׂה מַעֲשֶׂה	deed/action/behavior *ham·ma·ʿa·śe*	ABS W/ DEF. ART.	noun
שָׁם׃ שָׁם	destiny/designation *šām*	ABS	noun

The meaning of the term שָׁם ("there") in this context is unclear. Bartholomew (2009:175) and Longman (1998:125) translate it as "too" or "as well." Most English translations leave the word untranslated (e.g., CSB, ESV), though NASB reads it as "there." The translation here follows Seow (1997:166–67) in understanding it as a nominal form from the root שׂים ("put, place, designate") that is in parallel with עֵת ("time"). In this verse Qoheleth confirms what Scripture teaches elsewhere: God sees human deeds and will not leave the guilty unpunished. God's just judgment provides great hope for those who have experienced wrongdoing, and while we long for justice in this life, hope for it in the next offers a significant strategy for developing resilience when we experience suffering and injustice "under the sun."

3:18–21

18a אָמַ֤רְתִּֽי אֲנִי֙ בְּלִבִּ֔י

ʾāmartî ʾănî bəlibbî

I myself said in my heart

18b עַל־דִּבְרַת֙ בְּנֵ֣י הָאָדָ֔ם לְבָרָ֖ם הָאֱלֹהִ֑ים

ʿal-divrat bənê hāʾādām ləvārām hāʾĕlōhîm

concerning the manner of humans, "God makes clear to them

18c וְלִרְא֕וֹת שְׁהֶם־בְּהֵמָ֥ה הֵ֖מָּה לָהֶֽם׃

wəlirʾôt šəhem-bəhēmâ hēmmâ lāhem.

so that they see that they are beasts—they are like them.

19a כִּי֩ מִקְרֶ֨ה בְנֵֽי־הָאָדָ֜ם

kî miqre vənê-hāʾādām

For the fate of humans

19b וּמִקְרֶ֣ה הַבְּהֵמָ֗ה

ûmiqre habbəhēmâ

and the fate of beasts—

19c וּמִקְרֶ֤ה אֶחָד֙ לָהֶ֔ם

ûmiqre ʾeḥād lāhem

one fate for them!

19d כְּמ֥וֹת זֶה֙ כֵּ֣ן מ֣וֹת זֶ֔ה

kəmôt ze kēn môt ze

As dies this one, so dies that one,

19e וְר֥וּחַ אֶחָ֖ד לַכֹּ֑ל

wərûaḥ ʾeḥād lakkōl

and all have the same breath.

19f וּמוֹתַ֨ר הָאָדָ֤ם מִן־הַבְּהֵמָה֙ אָ֔יִן

*ûmô**tar** hāʾā**dām** min-habbəhē**mâ** ʾāyin*

Humans have no advantage over beasts!

19g כִּ֥י הַכֹּ֖ל הָֽבֶל׃

kî** hak**kōl** hā**vel.

Indeed, everything is Abel.

20a הַכֹּ֥ל הוֹלֵ֖ךְ אֶל־מָק֣וֹם אֶחָ֑ד

*hak**kōl** hô**lēḵ** ʾel-mā**qôm** ʾe**ḥād***

All go to one place.

20b הַכֹּל֙ הָיָ֣ה מִן־הֶֽעָפָ֔ר

*hak**kōl** hā**yâ** min-heʿā**fār***

All are from the dust,

20c וְהַכֹּ֖ל שָׁ֥ב אֶל־הֶעָפָֽר׃

*wəhak**kōl** **šāv** ʾel-heʿā**fār.***

and all return to the dust.

21a מִ֣י יוֹדֵ֗עַ ר֚וּחַ בְּנֵ֣י הָֽאָדָ֔ם הָעֹלָ֥ה הִ֖יא לְמָ֑עְלָה

mî** yô**dēa**ʿ **rû**aḥ bə**nê** hāʾā**dām** hāʿō**lâ** **hîʾ** ləmāʿ**lâ

Who knows? Does the spirit of humans ascend upwards?

21b וְר֙וּחַ֙ הַבְּהֵמָ֔ה הַיֹּרֶ֥דֶת הִ֖יא לְמַ֥טָּה לָאָֽרֶץ׃

*wə**rû**aḥ habbəhē**mâ** hayyō**re**det **hîʾ** lə**maṭ**ṭâ lāʾā**reṣ**.*

And does the spirit of beasts descend to the earth beneath?"

18a	אָמַ֤רְתִּֽי אֲנִי֙ בְּלִבִּ֔י

I myself said in my heart

אָמַ֤רְתִּֽי אמר	(I) said *ʾā·**mar**·tî*	QAL PF 1CS	verb
אֲנִי֙ אֲנִי	I *ʾă·**nî***	---	personal pron
בְּלִבִּ֔י לֵב	in my heart/mind *bə·lib·**bî***	CST W/ PREP בְּ + 1CS SX	noun

As in 3:17, the use of "myself" in this translation is to draw out Qoheleth's emphatic use of the first-person pronoun אֲנִי ("I").

18b	עַל־דִּבְרַת֙ בְּנֵ֣י הָאָדָ֔ם לְבָרָ֖ם הָאֱלֹהִ֑ים

concerning the manner of humans, "God makes clear to them

עַל־ עַל	concerning/with regard to *ʿal-*	---	prep
דִּבְרַת֙ דִּבְרָה	manner/cause of *div·**rat***	CST	noun
בְּנֵ֣י בֵּן	the sons of *bə·**nê***	CST	noun
הָאָדָ֔ם אָדָם	the man/human/humanity *hā·ʾā·**dām***	ABS W/ DEF. ART.	noun
לְבָרָ֖ם ברר	to make clear/test/ purify them *lə·vā·**rām***	QAL INF CST W/ PREP לְ + 3MP SX	verb
הָאֱלֹהִ֑ים אֱלֹהִים	the God *hā·ʾĕ·lō·**hîm***	ABS W/ DEF. ART.	noun

The majority of English translations render this statement (לְבָרָם הָאֱלֹהִים) along the lines of "God tests them." However, the meaning "to test" for ברר is not clearly attested anywhere else in the Old Testament (Longman 1998:128); rather, in the Old Testament the term means to "purify" or "cleanse" Longman (1998:128) lists as examples Neh 5:18; Ezek 20:38; Dan 11:35, stating, "From these meanings I derive the translation 'test' based on the present context" and support "by some of the ancient versions." In

Mishnaic Hebrew, ברר is clearly attested with the meaning "to make clear" or "prove," as in b. Kettubot 46a: "The court clarifies [ברר] the matter like a new garment." If we follow this later-attested meaning of ברר (though it is unclear whether this is relevant for the biblical attestation here), "the point would be that God allows human injustice to exist in the world in order to make it clear to mankind that they are essentially no better than the beasts" (NET translation note c on Eccl 3:18). Despite the difficulties of the Hebrew, the context is clear that God is making known something about humans to humans.

18c **וְלִרְא֕וֹת שְׁהֶם־בְּהֵמָ֥ה הֵ֖מָּה לָהֶֽם׃**

so that they see that they are beasts—they are like them.

וְלִרְא֕וֹת ראה	and to see *wə·lir·'ôt*	QAL INF CST W/ CONJ וְ + PREP לְ	verb
שְׁהֶם־ שְׁ	that they *šə·hem-*	--- W/ 3MP SX	prep
בְּהֵמָה בְּהֵמָה	beasts/animals *bə·hē·mâ*	ABS	noun
הֵמָּה הֵמָּה	they *hēm·mâ*	---	personal pron
לָהֶֽם׃ לְ	to/for them *lā·hem*	--- W/ 3MP SX	prep

What God is making clear to humans is that they are like beasts. Taken in isolation, we may be tempted to take this as a blanket statement that humans and animals are the same in every regard. However, in the following verses Qoheleth will clarify exactly how humans are like animals—and it gives him no comfort.

19a **כִּ֩י מִקְרֶ֨ה בְֽנֵי־הָאָדָ֜ם**

For the fate of humans

כִּ֩י כִּי	for/because *kî*	---	conj
מִקְרֶ֨ה מִקְרֶה	fate/fortune/chance of *miq·re*	CST	noun

בְּנֵי־ בֵּן	sons of *və·nê-*	CST	noun
הָאָדָם אָדָם	the man/human/humanity *hā·ʾā·**dām***	ABS W/ DEF. ART.	noun

As noted in 2:8c, בְּנֵי־הָאָדָם refers to "humans" or "people" in general throughout Eccliesiastes, not to an individual man.

19b וּמִקְרֵה הַבְּהֵמָה

and the fate of beasts—

וּמִקְרֵה מִקְרֶה	and fate/fortune/chance of *û·miq·**re***	CST W/ CONJ וְ	noun
הַבְּהֵמָה בְּהֵמָה	the animal/beast *hab·bə·hē·**mâ***	ABS W/ DEF. ART.	noun

In the creation account of Gen 1, בְּהֵמָה ("beasts") refers to land animals as opposed to fish, birds, and "creeping things" (Gen 1:26). We should not take this comparison of humans to "beasts" in either the negative sense of "That person is an animal!" or the positive sense of "That athlete is a beast!" He is comparing humans and animals to each other without the connotations typically carried in modern American English usage.

19c וּמִקְרֶה אֶחָד לָהֶם

one fate for them!

וּמִקְרֶה מִקְרֶה	and fate/fortune/chance *û·miq·**re***	ABS W/ CONJ וְ	noun
אֶחָד אֶחָד	one *ʾe·**ḥād***	ABS	cardinal number
לָהֶם לְ	to/for them *lā·**hem***	--- W/ 3MP SX	prep

19d כְּמוֹת זֶה כֵּן מוֹת זֶה

As dies this one, so dies that one,

כְּמוֹת מָוֶת	like/as death of *kə·**môt***	CST W/ PREP כְּ	noun
זֶה זֶה	this/this one ***ze***	---	demonstr pron
כֵּן כֵּן	thus/so ***kēn***	---	adv
מוֹת מָוֶת	like/as death of ***môt***	CST	noun
זֶה זֶה	this/this one ***ze***	---	demonstr pron

19e וְרוּחַ אֶחָד לַכֹּל

and all have the same breath.

וְרוּחַ רוּחַ	and spirit/breath *wə·**rû**·aḥ*	ABS W/ CONJ וְ	noun
אֶחָד אֶחָד	one *ʾe·**ḥād***	ABS	cardinal number
לַכֹּל כֹּל	to/for all *lak·**kōl***	ABS W/ PREP לְ + DEF. ART.	noun

Humans and animals are alike in this most important matter: both die. They share the same breath, and the same fate awaits every living thing. Death as the great equalizer—and great injustice—troubles Qoheleth, just as it troubles us today.

19f וּמוֹתַר הָאָדָם מִן־הַבְּהֵמָה אָיִן

Humans have no advantage over beasts!

וּמוֹתַר מוֹתָר	and advantage/profit of *û·mô·**tar***	CST W/ CONJ וְ	noun
הָאָדָם אָדָם	the man/human/humanity *hā·ʾā·**dām***	ABS W/ DEF. ART.	noun

מִן־ from מִן *min-*		---	prep
הַבְּהֵמָה the beast/animal בְּהֵמָה *hab·bə·hē·**mâ***		ABS W/ DEF. ART.	noun
אָיִן there is not אַיִן *ʾā·yin*		---	particle

מוֹתָר ("advantage") is closely related to a word we have seen before in Ecclesiastes: יִתְרוֹן ("profit"). Both nouns derive from the root יתר ("to remain, be left over"). As we have seen, Qoheleth argues that work produces no "profit" or "leftover portion" and thus makes a lousy foundation for building one's legacy. Here he argues that the mere fact of being human produces no "advantage" over animals because in the end both end up in the same place: the ground.

19g כִּי הַכֹּל הָבֶל׃

Indeed, everything is Abel.

כִּי indeed/thus/so/because כִּי ***kî***	---	conj
הַכֹּל the whole/all/everything כֹּל *hak·**kōl***	ABS W/ DEF. ART.	noun
הָבֶל׃ Abel/mist/vapor/breath הֶבֶל ***hā**·vel*	ABS	noun

The shared fate of humans and animals leads Qoheleth to this declaration that "Indeed, everything is Abel." That is, everything, like Abel, is a "breath." Everything—humans and animals alike—dies. He is not stating that the death of all the living is "vanity" or "meaningless," as some translations indicate. Rather, he is acknowledging the reality of the world in which we live—death marks *everything*, just like it marked Abel so long ago.

20a	הַכֹּל הוֹלֵךְ אֶל־מָקוֹם אֶחָד

All go to one place.

הַכֹּל כֹּל	the all/whole *hak·kōl*	ABS W/ DEF. ART.	noun
הוֹלֵךְ הלך	going/walking *hô·lēḵ*	QAL PTCP MS	verb
אֶל־ אֶל	to/toward *ʾel-*	---	prep
מָקוֹם מָקוֹם	place *mā·qôm*	ABS	noun
אֶחָד אֶחָד	one *ʾe·ḥād*	ABS	cardinal number

20b	הַכֹּל הָיָה מִן־הֶעָפָר

All are from the dust,

הַכֹּל כֹּל	the all/whole *hak·kōl*	ABS W/ DEF. ART.	noun
הָיָה היה	(he/it) is *hā·yâ*	QAL PF 3MS	verb
מִן־ מִן	from *min-*	---	prep
הֶעָפָר עָפָר	the dust *he·ʿā·fār*	ABS W/ DEF. ART.	noun

20c	וְהַכֹּל שָׁב אֶל־הֶעָפָר׃

and all return to the dust.

וְהַכֹּל כֹּל	and the all/whole *wə·hak·kōl*	ABS W/ CONJ וְ + DEF. ART.	noun
שָׁב שׁוּב	return *šāv*	QAL PF 3MS	verb

אֶל־ אֶל	to *'el-*	---	prep
הֶעָפָר׃ עָפָר	the dust *he·'ā·**fār***	ABS W/ DEF. ART.	noun

This verse includes another key allusion to the book of Genesis. In Gen 1:27 we read that God created humans from "dust [עָפָר] of the ground," and in 3:19 God states that because of Adam's sin, "you will return to the ground from which you were taken, for dust you are and to dust you will return [כִּי־עָפָר אַתָּה וְאֶל־עָפָר תָּשׁוּב]." This last phrase in particular indicates Qoheleth's use of Genesis, as he repeats three terms from Gen 3:19 ("dust," "return," and "to") and inverts their order, a key marker of allusion (Fishbane 1985:291). This use of Genesis helps strengthen our understanding of Qoheleth's use of "under the sun" to describe his—and our—experience of life. It is the post-fall, Abelish life, the life after which humans have been cursed to return to the dust from which we came. Qoheleth will pick up this same "dust" language again in ch. 12. In the "From Text to Sermon" section below we will explore more fully the theological significance of 3:18–21 and its use of Genesis.

21a מִי יוֹדֵעַ רוּחַ בְּנֵי הָאָדָם הָעֹלָה הִיא לְמָעְלָה

Who knows? Does the spirit of humans ascend upwards?

מִי מִי	who ***mî***	---	interr pron
יוֹדֵעַ ידע	knows *yô·**dē**·a'*	QAL PTCP MS	verb
רוּחַ רוּחַ	spirit/breath of ***rû**·aḥ*	CST	noun
בְּנֵי בֵּן	sons/children of *bə·**nê***	CST	noun
הָאָדָם אָדָם	the man/human/humanity *hā·'ā·**dām***	ABS W/ DEF. ART.	noun
הָעֹלָה עלה	does [it] ascend/go up? *hā·'ō·**lâ***	QAL PTCP FS W/ INTERR הֲ	verb
הִיא הִיא	it/she ***hî'***	---	personal pron

לְמַ֫עְלָה מַ֫עַל	to/toward upward *lə · **mā**ʿ · lâ*	--- W/ PREP לְ + LOCATIVE ה	prep

21b **וְר֣וּחַ הַבְּהֵמָ֔ה הַיֹּרֶ֥דֶת הִ֖יא לְמַ֥טָּה לָאָֽרֶץ׃**

And does the spirit of beasts descend to the earth beneath?"

וְר֣וּחַ רוּחַ	and spirit/breath of *wə · **rû** · aḥ*	CST W/ CONJ וְ	noun
הַבְּהֵמָ֔ה בְּהֵמָה	the beast/animal *hab · bə · hē · **mâ***	ABS W/ DEF. ART.	noun
הַיֹּרֶ֥דֶת ירד	does [it] descend/go down? *hay · yō · **re** · det*	QAL PTCP FS W/ INTERR הַ	verb
הִ֖יא הִיא	it/she ***hî***	---	personal pron
לְמַ֥טָּה מַ֫טָּה	to/toward beneath/downward *lə · **maṭ** · ṭâ*	--- W/ PREP לְ	adv
לָאָֽרֶץ׃ אֶרֶץ	to the earth *lā · **ʾā** · reṣ*	ABS W/ PREP לְ + DEF. ART.	noun

In a book filled with existential questions that cause us to confront evil, injustice, death, and the general frustrations of life "under the sun," this question in particular will resonate with many of Qoheleth's readers—if we are being honest with ourselves. Rather than provide a quick response that will alleviate the discomfort this question causes, Qoheleth leaves it hanging in the air for the rest of the book, until he finally answers it in 12:7. Again discussing humanity's dusty end, there he affirms that "the spirit returns to the God who gave it."

3:22

22a וְרָאִ֙יתִי֙ כִּ֣י אֵ֥ין טוֹב֙ מֵאֲשֶׁ֨ר יִשְׂמַ֤ח הָֽאָדָם֙ בְּמַעֲשָׂ֔יו

wərāʾîtî kî ʾên ṭôv mēʾăšer yiśmaḥ hāʾādām bəmaʿăśāyw

So I saw that there is nothing better than that humans take joy in their work

22b כִּי־ה֖וּא חֶלְק֑וֹ

kî-hûʾ ḥelqô

because that is their portion.

22c כִּ֣י מִ֤י יְבִיאֶ֙נּוּ֙ לִרְא֔וֹת בְּמֶ֖ה שֶׁיִּהְיֶ֥ה אַחֲרָֽיו׃

kî mî yəvîʾennû lirʾôt bəme šeyyihye ʾaḥărāyw.

Who can bring them to see what will be after them?

22a וְרָאִ֙יתִי֙ כִּ֣י אֵ֥ין טוֹב֙ מֵאֲשֶׁ֨ר יִשְׂמַ֤ח הָֽאָדָם֙ בְּמַעֲשָׂ֔יו

So I saw that there is nothing better than that humans take joy in their work

וְרָאִ֙יתִי֙ ראה	and/so I saw/observed *wə·rā·ʾî·tî*	QAL PF 1CS W/ CONJ וְ	verb
כִּ֣י כִּי	that *kî*	---	conj
אֵ֥ין אַ֫יִן	there is nothing *ʾên*	---	particle
טוֹב֙ טוֹב	good/better *ṭôv*	MS PRED	adj
מֵאֲשֶׁ֨ר אֲשֶׁר	than/from that *mē·ʾă·šer*	--- W/ PREP מִן	relative pron

יִשְׂמַח שׂמח	(he) will rejoice/be glad/ take joy *yiś·**maḥ***	QAL IMPF 3MS	verb
הָאָדָם אָדָם	the man/human/humanity *hā·ʾā·**dām***	ABS W/ DEF. ART.	noun
בְּמַעֲשָׂיו מַעֲשֶׂה	in his work/product/ achievement *bə·ma·ʿă·**śāyw***	CST W/ PREP בְּ + 3MS SX	noun

22b כִּי־הוּא חֶלְקוֹ

because that is their portion.

כִּי־ כִּי	because/for *kî-*	---	conj
הוּא הוא	that ***hûʾ***	---	personal pron
חֶלְקוֹ חֵלֶק	his portion/reward *ḥel·**qô***	CST W/ 3MS SX	noun

Here Qoheleth returns once again to the question of work and what role it should play in the lives of humans. Above he lamented that work offers no "profit" or "left-over portion." Here, though, he affirms that joy in work is humanity's "portion" or "reward." That is, work is not meant to satisfy any sort of longing for legacy or ultimate meaning in life; it does not and cannot fulfill humans because it was not ever meant to. However, by pointing to the inherent joy in the work itself, Qoheleth casts our vision back to the garden of Eden before the fall. There the man and woman were created and placed the garden in order "to work it and to guard it" (Gen 2:15). In that paradise before sin—and before Abelness—entered into human life, the man and the woman were given work as a gift. Thus, taking joy in work now is good and right, a means of pushing back against the sin that envelops the world, and therefore a means of pointing backward to Eden.

22c כִּ֣י מִ֤י יְבִיאֶ֙נּוּ֙ לִרְא֔וֹת בְּמֶ֖ה שֶׁיִּהְיֶ֥ה אַחֲרָֽיו׃

Who can bring them to see what will be after them?

כִּ֣י כִּי	for/because/thus *kî*	---	conj
מִ֤י מִי	who? *mî*	---	interr pron
יְבִיאֶ֙נּוּ֙ בוא	(he) will bring him *yə·vî·ʾen·nû*	HIPH IMPF 3MS W/ 3MS SX	verb
לִרְא֔וֹת ראה	to see/observe *lir·ʾôt*	QAL INF CST W/ PREP לְ	verb
בְּמֶ֖ה מָה	what *bə·me*	--- W/ PREP בְּ	interr pron
שֶׁיִּהְיֶ֥ה היה	that will be *šey·yih·ye*	QAL IMPF 3MS W/ RELATIVE PRON שֶׁ	verb
אַחֲרָֽיו׃ אַחֲרֵי	after him *ʾa·ḥă·rāyw*	--- W/ 3MS SX	prep

Qoheleth concludes this section of his thoughts on the role of work in our lives with a rhetorical question: "Who can bring him to see what will be after him?" The answer, of course, is "no one." Although many of us have visions of grandeur and a longing to be remembered fondly for this achievement or that one, the truth is that most of us do not even know the names of our great-great-grandparents, and our great-great-grandchildren will likely not know our names. We simply do not know what will occur on this earth when we die, and therefore searching for meaning in legacy or what we leave behind is a fool's errand. Again, Qoheleth's insistence is that *there is no left-over portion, no profit in work*. Thus, rather than attempting to achieve the impossible, the better thing is to work for what God *has* given us: joy in the work itself. Will we heed Qoheleth's call to a radically reoriented view of work and its value?

From Text to Sermon

Qoheleth's Meanderings. Given the depth of despair in this passage, it is good to remember that the book of Ecclesiastes is cyclical in nature, like we discussed above, and mimics the human experience. Qoheleth's questions and meanderings do not signal a lack of faith; rather they illustrate how to navigate—with brutal honesty—the questions that often plague humanity. Thus, preaching and teaching these passages offers you an opportunity to show your congregation how to engage in open and honest dialogue with God and one another.

Injustice—and Trust in God's Justice. Children seem to be born with a well-defined sense of justice. "That's not fair" is a favorite refrain among my own three sons, and often it's the most compelling argument they make when trying to convince me to, for example, share my candy with them. We carry this innate sense of justice with us into adulthood, where the stakes are usually much higher than whether our parent shared their candy with us. Ecclesiastes 3:16 offers us the opportunity to talk openly about justice denied or thwarted. You can do this with a more lighthearted example of the child who just wants a piece of candy, or you can wade into deeper waters by addressing something far more serious: sexual abuse, a crime whose survivors are far more numerous than most of us imagine and whose perpetrators most often escape punishment (Morabito, Williams, and Pattavina 2019). Acknowledging and lamenting the injustice, as Qoheleth does here, is a powerful way to help all victims of injustice to feel seen and heard—an important step on the journey of healing. Further, as Qoheleth models articulating injustice in v. 16, in v. 17 he models articulating faith in God's ultimate justice. On its own, v. 17, "the righteous person and the wicked person, God will judge," can come across as an empty platitude at best or as downplaying another's experience at worst, but combined with speaking frankly about injustice, proclaiming the truth of God's just judgment is a healing balm for shattered hearts.

The Same Fate. Our experience confirms Qoheleth's lament in 3:18–20. We know that humans and beasts share the same fate, that eventually all of us will die, and Qoheleth asks the question that maybe we are too afraid to ask: "Who knows? Does the spirit of humans ascend upwards? And does the spirit of beasts descend to the earth beneath?" Later in the book, he answers his question, expressing his trust that "the spirit returns to the

God who gave it" (Eccl 12:7). These verses offer a prime opportunity to transition to the gospel of Jesus Christ, our only hope in life and death.

Echoes of Genesis. Ecclesiastes 3:18–21 echoes both humanity's creation in Gen 2 (in particular, v. 7) and the curse of death that results from sin in Gen 3 (in particular, v. 19). All three passages speak of God creating humans from "dust" (עָפָר), and Gen 3 and Eccl 3 speak of "the human" (הָאָדָם) "returning" (שׁוּב) to "dust" upon death. Additionally, Gen 3:19 reads כִּי־עָפָר אַתָּה וְאֶל־עָפָר תָּשׁוּב ("dust you are and to dust you will return").

Qoheleth's allusions to Genesis here are theologically significant because he uses Genesis to affirm and support the argument he is formulating in ch. 3: (1) God created humanity, (2) humans die, and (3) work is toilsome, even if it is enjoyable. By echoing Gen 2:7, Qoheleth reminds his readers that God is the creator—it is he who formed them from the dust. Yet death is inescapable, which provides the impetus to enjoy the gifts of God while we can. The allusion to Gen 3:19 subtly reminds his readers that the curse has hindered humanity's ability to take pleasure in work. Thus, enjoying work will not come naturally, and in enjoying work we simultaneously look back toward Eden and—with the benefit of New Testament revelation—look forward to the new heavens and new earth, where the curse will be no more.

RELATIONSHIPS MATTER

We often think that work matters above all else; even if we don't voice this sentiment, we live like we believe it, giving the best of our lives to places of work that will barely register our absence when we leave. But what really, truly matters in life are relationships. No one on their deathbed wishes they had spent more time working and less time with their family, and no one laments that they didn't prioritize their most important relationships above everything else. That's because at the end of life, humans have a laser focus on what really mattered—the people God placed around them. In these few verses, Qoheleth addresses the importance of meaningful relationships in contrast to the value we typically place on work. He tells us that envy (or "keeping up with the Joneses") shouldn't cause us to work hard to attain more, and he argues that working to accumulate wealth at the expense of relationships is a foolish task. Wealth at the cost of loneliness, Qoheleth tells us, is "Abelish": it results from and is a symptom of living in an upside-down world with upside-down priorities.

LARGER LITERARY CONTEXT › 4:1–12

4a וְרָאִ֨יתִי אֲנִ֜י אֶת־כָּל־עָמָ֗ל

wərāʾîtî ʾănî ʾet-kol-ʿāmāl

And I myself saw all toil

4b וְאֵת֙ כָּל־כִּשְׁר֣וֹן הַֽמַּעֲשֶׂ֔ה

wəʾēt kol-kišrôn hammaʿăśe

and all the success of work—

4c כִּ֛י הִ֥יא קִנְאַת־אִ֖ישׁ מֵרֵעֵ֑הוּ

kî hîʾ qinʾat-ʾîš mērēʿēhû

that it is from a person's envy of his neighbor.

4d גַּם־זֶ֥ה הֶ֖בֶל וּרְע֥וּת רֽוּחַ׃

gam-ze hevel ûrəʿût rûaḥ.

This also is Abel and striving after wind.

5a הַכְּסִיל֙ חֹבֵ֣ק אֶת־יָדָ֔יו

hakkəsîl ḥōvēq ʾet-yādāyw

The fool clasps his hands

5b וְאֹכֵ֖ל אֶת־בְּשָׂרֽוֹ׃

wəʾōḵēl ʾet-bəśārô.

and eats his own body.

6a ט֕וֹב מְלֹ֥א כַ֖ף נָ֑חַת

ṭôv məlōʾ ḵaf nāḥat

Better is one hand full of rest

6b מִמְּלֹ֥א חָפְנַ֛יִם עָמָ֖ל וּרְע֥וּת רֽוּחַ׃

mimməlōʾ ḥofnayim ʿāmāl ûrəʿût rûaḥ.

than two hands full of toil and striving after wind.

4a

וְרָאִ֫יתִי אֲנִי אֶת־כָּל־עָמָל

And I myself saw all toil

וְרָאִ֫יתִי ראה	and (I) saw/observed *wə·rā·**ʾî**·tî*	QAL PF 1CS W/ CONJ וְ	verb
אֲנִי אֲנִי	I *ʾă·**nî***	---	personal pron
אֶת־ אֵת	*(direct object marker)* *ʾet-*	---	particle
כָּל־ כֹּל	all/every of *kol-*	CST	noun
עָמָל עָמָל	toil/labor *ʿā·**māl***	ABS	noun

Again Qoheleth uses the gratuitous first-person pronoun to emphasize the personal nature of this account. He is expounding on what he has personally observed in life.

4b

וְאֵ֫ת כָּל־כִּשְׁר֣וֹן הַֽמַּעֲשֶׂה

and all the success of work—

וְאֵ֫ת אֵת	and *(direct object marker)* *wə·**ʾēt***	--- W/ CONJ וְ	particle
כָּל־ כֹּל	all of *kol-*	CST	noun
כִּשְׁר֣וֹן כִּשְׁרוֹן	success/profit/skill of *kiš·**rôn***	CST	noun
הַֽמַּעֲשֶׂה מַעֲשֶׂה	the work/product/ achievement *ham·ma·ʿă·**śe***	ABS W/ DEF. ART.	noun

"Success" (כִּשְׁרוֹן) appears only three times in the Hebrew Bible, and all occurrences are in Ecclesiastes (2:21; 4:4; 5:10), all in the context of material wealth and its inability to satisfy a person. In 2:21 the laborer's profits are enjoyed by another person, in 5:10[11] the increase of wealth coincides with the increase of people who consume that wealth, and here Qoheleth laments that the motivation for work is misplaced. Verbs from the same root (כשׁר) are used in Ecclesiastes 10:10 in reference to wisdom's ability to make one's work "succeed"; in 11:6, in reference to the "success" of various business ventures; and in Esth 8:5, in the queen's request for Ahasuerus to save the Jews from Haman ("if the matter *seems right* before the king"). English translations render כִּשְׁרוֹן in various ways: "skill" (ESV, NASB), "skillful" (CSB, NET), "right [work]" (KJV). Whether the term is best understood as "success" or "skill," the basic meaning of "work that is beneficial" is clear.

4c כִּ֣י הִ֔יא קִנְאַת־אִ֖ישׁ מֵרֵעֵ֑הוּ

that it is from a person's envy of his neighbor.

Hebrew	Gloss	Parsing	Part of speech
כִּ֣י כִּי	that/because *kî*	---	conj
הִ֔יא הִיא	it/she *hîʾ*	---	personal pron
קִנְאַת־ קִנְאָה	envy of *qin·ʾat-*	CST	noun
אִ֖ישׁ אִישׁ	man/person *ʾîš*	ABS	noun
מֵרֵעֵ֑הוּ רֵעַ	from his friend/neighbor/ companion *mē·rē·ʿē·hû*	CST W/ PREP מִן + 3MS SX	noun

According to traditional wisdom, hard work should result in wealth (e.g., Prov 10:4), but Qoheleth has already stated that work produces no "profit" or "lasting gain" and that the "reward" or "portion" of humanity is in enjoying the work itself. Now he points out another problem with misusing the gift of work: rather than working because it brings joy, humans work because they are jealous of one another. Long before the Joneses existed, Qoheleth remarks upon this primary motivator of human achievement. This should not be, and Qoheleth tells us in the next clause that it represents another aspect in which life today reflects the life of Abel, whose jealous brother murdered him.

4d	גַּם־זֶה הֶבֶל וּרְעוּת רוּחַ׃			
	This also is Abel and striving after wind.			
גַּם־ גַּם	also/even *gam-*	---	adv
זֶה זֶה	this *ze*	---	demonstr pron
הֶבֶל הֶבֶל	Abel/mist/vapor/breath ***he**·vel*	ABS	noun
וּרְעוּת רְעוּת	and chasing/striving after *û·rə·**ʿût***	CST W/ CONJ וְ	noun
רוּחַ׃ רוּחַ	wind/breath spirit ***rû**·aḥ*	ABS	noun

As noted throughout this commentary, Qoheleth is not stating that work is "meaningless" or that a wrong motivation for work is "vanity." Rather, he is articulating the truth of the world we live in: Like Abel, it is unjust, upside down, and it does not work the way it should because of the sin that now stains all of life. Taking into account the broader discussion of work in Ecclesiastes, the way to press back against the "Abelness" of work—whether that be sinful motivations (envy) or asking work to give us what it cannot (gain)—is to reorient our view of work to align with God's original intent for work.

5a	הַכְּסִיל֙ חֹבֵ֣ק אֶת־יָדָ֔יו			
	The fool clasps his hands			
הַכְּסִיל֙ כְּסִיל	the fool *hak·kə·**sîl***	ABS W/ DEF. ART.	noun
חֹבֵק חבק	folds/clasps *ḥō·**vēq***	QAL PTCP MS	verb
אֶת־ אֵת	*(direct object marker)* *ʾet-*	---	particle
יָדָיו יָד	his hands *yā·**dāyw***	CST W/ 3MS SX	noun

5b	וְאֹכֵ֖ל אֶת־בְּשָׂרֽוֹ׃
	and eats his own body.

וְאֹכֵ֖ל אכל	and eats/consumes *wə·ʾō·kēl*	QAL PTCP MS W/ CONJ וְ	verb
אֶת־ אֵת	*(direct object marker)* *ʾet-*	---	particle
בְּשָׂרֽוֹ׃ בָּשָׂר	his body/flesh *bə·śā·rô*	CST W/ 3MS SX	noun

Qoheleth here likely repeats a proverb that warns his readers against rejecting work altogether. Work will not give us any sort of legacy or lasting reward, and it is often fueled by wrong motivations (jealousy), but to work—and supremely to enjoy work—remains a gift and call from God. Those who do not work end up cannibalizing themselves!

6a	ט֕וֹב מְלֹ֥א כַ֖ף נָ֑חַת
	Better is one hand full of rest

ט֕וֹב טוֹב	good *ṭôv*	MS PRED	adj
מְלֹ֥א מְלֹא	full/fullness of *mə·lōʾ*	CST	noun
כַ֖ף כַּף	hand of *kaf*	CST	noun
נָ֑חַת נַ֫חַת	rest *nā·ḥat*	ABS	noun

6b	מִמְּלֹ֥א חָפְנַ֛יִם עָמָ֖ל וּרְע֥וּת רֽוּחַ׃
	than two hands full of toil and striving after wind.

מִמְּלֹ֥א מְלֹא	from/than fullness of *mim·mə·lōʾ*	CST W/ PREP מִן	noun
חָפְנַ֛יִם חֹ֫פֶן	two handfuls/hollows of hand *ḥof·na·yim*	ABS	noun

עָמָ֖ל עָמָל	toil/labor *ʿā·māl*	ABS	noun
וּרְע֥וּת רְעוּת	and chasing/striving after *û·rə·ʿût*	CST W/ CONJ וְ	noun
רֽוּחַ׃ רוּחַ	wind *rû·aḥ*	ABS	noun

In this second of two proverbs, Qoheleth reflects further on the nature of work. In the first proverb he highlighted the folly of laziness, but here he offers a complementary perspective: a little rest is better than much "toil and striving after wind." Taken with the previous proverb and Qoheleth's reflections on work throughout Ecclesiastes, we should recognize the priorities in life that Qoheleth advocates. Working is vital, but working too much and working for the wrong reasons are disastrous. Rather than "striving after wind," which in this case likely refers to seeking from work something that it cannot give ("profit" or "lasting gain"), we should embrace the better thing—a handful of rest.

4:7–12

7 וְשַׁ֣בְתִּֽי אֲנִ֔י וָאֶרְאֶ֥ה הֶ֖בֶל תַּ֥חַת הַשָּֽׁמֶשׁ׃

*wə**šav**tî ʾă**nî** wāʾer**ʾe** **he**vel **ta**ḥat hašš**ā**meš.*

And I turned, and I myself observed Abelness under the sun.

8a יֵ֣שׁ אֶחָד֩ וְאֵ֨ין שֵׁנִ֜י

*yēš ʾe**ḥād** wəʾ**ên** šē**nî***

There is one without another,

8b גַּ֣ם בֵּ֤ן וָאָח֙ אֵֽין־ל֔וֹ

gam bēn** wā**ʾāḥ** ʾên-**lô

even a son or brother he does not have.

8c וְאֵ֥ין קֵץ֙ לְכָל־עֲמָל֔וֹ גַּם־עֵינ֖וֹ לֹא־תִשְׂבַּ֣ע עֹ֑שֶׁר

*wəʾ**ên qēṣ** ləkol-ʿămā**lô** gam-ʿê**nô** lōʾ-tiś**ba**ʿ **ʿō**šer*

There is no end to all of his toil, and his eye is not sated with wealth.

8d וּלְמִ֣י ׀ אֲנִ֣י עָמֵ֗ל וּמְחַסֵּ֤ר אֶת־נַפְשִׁי֙ מִטּוֹבָ֔ה

*ûlə**mî** ʾă**nî** ʿā**mēl** ûməḥas**sēr** ʾet-naf**šî** miṭṭô**vâ***

“And for whom am I toiling and depriving myself of good?”

8e גַּם־זֶ֥ה הֶ֖בֶל

*gam-**ze** **he**vel*

This also is Abel,

8f וְעִנְיַ֥ן רָ֖ע הֽוּא׃

*wəʿin**yan** **rā**ʿ **hû**ʾ.*

and it is an evil business.

9a טוֹבִ֥ים הַשְּׁנַ֖יִם מִן־הָאֶחָ֑ד

*ṭô**vîm** haššə**na**yim min-hāʾe**ḥād***

Two are better than one

9b אֲשֶׁר יֵשׁ־לָהֶם שָׂכָר טוֹב בַּעֲמָלָם׃

ʾăšer yēš-lāhem śāḵār ṭôv baʿămālām.

because they have a good return on their labor.

10a כִּי אִם־יִפֹּלוּ

kî ʾim-yippōlû hāʾeḥād

For if they fall,

10b הָאֶחָד יָקִים אֶת־חֲבֵרוֹ

yāqîm ʾet-ḥăvērô

the one will lift up his friend.

10c וְאִילוֹ הָאֶחָד שֶׁיִּפּוֹל

wəʾîlô hāʾeḥād šeyyippôl

But woe to him, the one who falls,

10d וְאֵין שֵׁנִי לַהֲקִימוֹ׃

wəʾên šēnî lahăqîmô.

and there is not another to lift him up.

11a גַּם אִם־יִשְׁכְּבוּ שְׁנַיִם

gam ʾim-yiškəvû šənayim

In addition, if two lie down,

11b וְחַם לָהֶם

wəḥam lāhem

they are warm.

11c וּלְאֶחָד אֵיךְ יֵחָם׃

ûləʾeḥād ʾêḵ yēḥām.

But one person—how can he be warm?

12a וְאִם־יִתְקְפוֹ הָאֶחָד

wəʾim-yitqəfô hāʾeḥād

Although someone may overpower the one,

12b הַשְּׁנַיִם יַעַמְדוּ נֶגְדּוֹ

haššənayim yaʿamdû negdô

the two will stand against him.

12c וְהַחוּט הַמְשֻׁלָּשׁ לֹא בִמְהֵרָה יִנָּתֵק׃

wəhaḥûṭ haməšullāš lōʾ vimhērâ yinnātēq.

And the threefold cord will not be snapped quickly.

7 וְשַׁבְתִּי אֲנִי וָאֶרְאֶה הֶבֶל תַּחַת הַשָּׁמֶשׁ׃

And I turned, and I myself observed Abelness under the sun.

וְשַׁבְתִּי שׁוּב	And I turned *wə·šav·tî*	QAL PF 1CS W/ CONJ וְ	verb
אֲנִי אֲנִי	I *ʾă·nî*	---	personal pron
וָאֶרְאֶה ראה	and (I) saw/observed *wā·ʾer·ʾe*	QAL WAYY 1CS	verb
הֶבֶל הֶבֶל	Abel/mist/vapor/breath *he·vel*	ABS	noun
תַּחַת תַּחַת	under *ta·ḥat*	---	prep
הַשָּׁמֶשׁ׃ שֶׁמֶשׁ	the sun *haš·šā·meš*	ABS W/ DEF. ART.	noun

Verse 7 introduces the observations Qoheleth will make in the following few verses. He again relies on personal experience, emphasizing his point of view by including the optional first-person pronoun. His observations relate to life "under the sun," a phrase discussed more fully above at 1:3b. The following observations will expand on the topic of work, introduced with a pair of proverbs in vv. 5 and 6, to include the relationship between work and meaningful relationships with others. The use of הֶבֶל ("Abel-ness") primes readers to expect that Qoheleth will remark on how his topic reflects the injustice common to the human experience ("under the sun") and exemplified in Abel's (הֶבֶל) life in Gen 4.

8a	יֵשׁ אֶחָד וְאֵין שֵׁנִי		
	There is one without another,		
יֵשׁ יֵשׁ	there is *yēš*	---	particle
אֶחָד אֶחָד	one *ʾe·ḥād*	ABS	cardinal number
וְאֵין אַיִן	and there is not *wə·ʾên*	--- W/ CONJ וְ	particle
שֵׁנִי שֵׁנִי	a second/another *šē·nî*	---	ordinal number

8b	גַּם בֵּן וָאָח אֵין־לוֹ		
	even a son or brother he does not have.		
גַּם גַּם	also/even *gam*	---	adv
בֵּן בֵּן	son *bēn*	ABS	noun
וָאָח אָח	and brother *wā·ʾāḥ*	ABS W/ CONJ וְ	noun
אֵין־ אַיִן	there is not *ʾên-*	---	particle
לוֹ לְ	to him *lô*	--- W/ 3MS SX	prep

Qoheleth highlights the lack of two of the most significant relationships in most people's lives: that between siblings and that between a parent and child. Such lack of relationship entails enormous loneliness, but in the male-centered culture of ancient Israel the lack of a son or brother would have had further disastrous consequences. Namely, there would be no one to provide and care for this fellow's family once he died, and with no son as an heir and no brother to perform the duties of a Levirate marriage, there was a real risk that "his name [would be] blotted out of Israel" (Deut 25:6 ESV; see also the narrative of the daughters of Zelophehad in Num 27 and 36).

8c	וְאֵ֣ין קֵץ֮ לְכָל־עֲמָלוֹ֒ גַּם־עֵינ֖וֹ לֹא־תִשְׂבַּ֣ע עֹ֑שֶׁר

There is no end to all of his toil, and his eye is not sated with wealth.

וְאֵ֣ין אַיִן	and there is not *wə·ʾên*	--- W/ CONJ וְ	particle
קֵץ֮ קֵץ	end/limit *qēṣ*	ABS	noun
לְכָל־ כֹּל	to all of *lə·kol-*	CST W/ PREP לְ	noun
עֲמָלוֹ֒ עָמָל	his toil/labor *ʿă·mā·lô*	CST W/ 3MS SX	noun
גַּם־ גַּם	also/even *gam-*	---	adv
עֵינ֖וֹ עַיִן	his eye *ʿê·nô*	CST W/ 3MS SX	noun
לֹא־ לֹא	not *lōʾ-*	---	particle
תִשְׂבַּ֣ע שׂבע	(it) is satisfied/sated/filled *tiś·baʿ*	QAL IMPF 3FS	verb
עֹ֑שֶׁר עֹשֶׁר	wealth/riches *ʿō·šer*	ABS	noun

Just above, Qoheleth cited a proverb arguing that a little rest is better than a lot of toil, and in 1:8 he declared that the "eye is never sated with seeing." Too much work is unequivocally bad, and no matter how much wealth this man—or we—accumulates, it never sates the appetite.

8d	וּלְמִ֣י ׀ אֲנִ֣י עָמֵ֗ל וּמְחַסֵּ֤ר אֶת־נַפְשִׁי֙ מִטּוֹבָ֔ה

"And for whom am I toiling and depriving myself of good?"

וּלְמִ֣י ׀ מִי	and for whom *û·lə·mî*	--- W/ CONJ וְ + PREP לְ	interr

אֲנִי	I	---	personal pron
אֲנִי	*ʾă·nî*		
עָמֵל	am toiling/laboring	MS PRED	adj
עָמֵל	*ʿā·mēl*		
וּמְחַסֵּר	and depriving/causing to lack	PIEL PTCP MS W/ CONJ וְ	verb
חסר	*û·mə·ḥas·sēr*		
אֶת־	*(direct object marker)*	---	particle
אֵת	*ʾet-*		
נַפְשִׁי	my soul/self/life	CST W/ 1CS SX	noun
נֶ֫פֶשׁ	*naf·šî*		
מִטּוֹבָה	from good	ABS W/ PREP מִן	noun
טוֹבָה	*miṭ·ṭô·vâ*		

This question highlights the importance of relationships over the accumulation of wealth and unceasing labor. The term נֶ֫פֶשׁ ("myself") has a broad range of meaning, from the concrete "throat" to the more metaphorical "appetite" and "soul" or "mind." It also is used to refer to a person or people or, as here and in 2:24, to one's "self." The "good" (טוֹבָה) of which he deprives himself reminds readers of Qoheleth's earlier quest to find what is "good" (טוֹב) for humans (2:3) and of his pronouncements of what that "good" actually is: taking joy in eating, drinking, a spouse, and toil (e.g., 2:24; 3:12–13, 22). Such focus on enjoyment in daily activities and relationships envisions a strikingly different life than is typically valued in the West.

8e **גַּם־זֶה הֶבֶל**

This also is Abel,

גַּם־	also/even	---	adv
גַּם	*gam-*		
זֶה	this	---	demonstr pron
זֶה	*ze*		
הֶבֶל	Abel/mist/vapor/breath	ABS	noun
הֶ֫בֶל	*he·vel*		

8f **וְעִנְיַן רָע הוּא׃**

and it is an evil business.

וְעִנְיַן עִנְיָן	and a business/task of *wə·ʿin·**yan***	CST W/ CONJ וְ	noun
רָע רַע	evil/bad ***rāʿ***	ABS	noun
הוּא׃ הוּא	it ***hûʾ***	---	personal pron

9a **טוֹבִים הַשְּׁנַיִם מִן־הָאֶחָד**

Two are better than one

טוֹבִים טוֹב	good *ṭô·**vîm***	MP PRED	adj
הַשְּׁנַיִם שְׁנַיִם	the two *haš·šə·**na**·yim*	ABS W/ DEF. ART.	cardinal number
מִן־ מִן	from *min-*	---	prep
הָאֶחָד אֶחָד	the one *hā·ʾe·**ḥād***	ABS W/ DEF. ART.	cardinal number

9b **אֲשֶׁר יֵשׁ־לָהֶם שָׂכָר טוֹב בַּעֲמָלָם׃**

because they have a good return on their labor.

אֲשֶׁר אֲשֶׁר	who/that/which/because *ʾă·**šer***	---	relative pron
יֵשׁ־ יֵשׁ	there is *yēš-*	---	particle
לָהֶם לְ	to them *lā·**hem***	--- W/ 3MP SX	prep
שָׂכָר שָׂכָר	wages/return *śā·**kār***	ABS	noun

טֹ֖וב טוֹב	good *ṭôv*	MS ATTR	adj
בַּעֲמָלָֽם׃ עָמָל	in/on their toil/labor *ba·ʿă·mā·**lām***	CST W/ PREP בְּ + 3MP SX	noun

"Better-than" proverbs occur several times in Ecclesiastes and frequently in the book of Proverbs. In this proverb, Qoheleth states that it is better to work with another person than alone because working in tandem produces a better return on one's labor. While אֲשֶׁר ("because") is typically translated "who, that, or which," here it functions causally, with the second half of the proverb delineating the reason for the first half. This proverb also helps Qoheleth make his broader point in this section of Ecclesiastes regarding the significance of relationships for human flourishing. Though the argument here is grounded in economics (two workers earn a better return than one), he will develop this line of reasoning with further examples of the value of relationships in the following verses.

10a כִּ֤י אִם־יִפֹּ֔לוּ

For if they fall,

כִּ֤י אִם־ כִּי אִם־	for if ***kî** ʾim-*	---	conj
יִפֹּ֔לוּ נפל	(they) fall *yip·**pō**·lû*	QAL IMPF 3MP	verb

10b הָאֶחָ֖ד יָקִ֣ים אֶת־חֲבֵר֑וֹ

the one will lift up his friend.

הָאֶחָ֖ד אֶחָד	the one *hā·ʾe·**ḥād***	ABS W/ DEF. ART.	cardinal number
יָקִ֣ים קוּם	will raise/lift up *yā·**qîm***	HIPH IMPF 3MS	verb
אֶת־ אֵת	*(direct object marker)* *ʾet-*	---	particle
חֲבֵר֑וֹ חָבֵר	his companion/friend *ḥă·vē·**rô***	CST W/ 3MS SX	noun

10c	וְאִ֣ילוֹ הָֽאֶחָ֗ד שֶׁיִּפּ֔וֹל

But woe to him, the one who falls,

וְאִ֣ילוֹ אִי	but woe to him *wə·ʾî·lô*	--- W/ CONJ וְ + 3MS SX	particle
הָֽאֶחָ֗ד אֶחָד	the one *hā·ʾe·ḥād*	ABS W/ DEF. ART.	cardinal number
שֶׁיִּפּ֔וֹל נפל	who falls *šey·yip·pôl*	QAL IMPF 3MS W/ RELATIVE PRON שֶׁ	verb

10d	וְאֵ֥ין שֵׁנִ֖י לַהֲקִימֽוֹ׃

and there is not another to lift him up.

וְאֵ֥ין אַיִן	and there is not *wə·ʾên*	--- W/ CONJ וְ	particle
שֵׁנִ֖י שֵׁנִי	a second *šē·nî*	---	ordinal number
לַהֲקִימֽוֹ׃ קום	to raise/lift him up *la·hă·qî·mô*	HIPH INF CST W/ PREP לְ + 3MS SX	verb

In addition to the economic value of a greater return on work, Qoheleth supplies another reason for the value of relationships: people help one another during times of trouble. What could be life threatening when one is alone ("woe to him") is manageable with the help of another. This is true in the case of falling down, and it is likewise true in all of the difficulties humans face "under the sun."

11a	גַּ֛ם אִם־יִשְׁכְּב֥וּ שְׁנַ֖יִם

In addition, if two lie down,

גַּ֛ם גַּם	also/even *gam*	---	adv
אִם־ אִם	if *ʾim-*	---	conj
יִשְׁכְּב֥וּ שׁכב	(they) lie down *yiš·kə·vû*	QAL IMPF 3MP	verb

שְׁנַ֫יִם שְׁנַיִם	two *šə·**na**·yim*	ABS	cardinal number

11b	וְחַ֣ם לָהֶ֑ם

they are warm.

וְחַ֣ם חמם	and it is warm *wə·**ḥam***	QAL WEQATAL 3MS W/ CONJ וְ	verb
לָהֶ֑ם לְ	to/for them *lā·**hem***	--- W/ 3MP SX	prep

The word חמם ("be warm") is a stative verb, and the phrase reads woodenly, "it is warm to them." In English we render this as "they are warm."

11c	וּלְאֶחָ֖ד אֵ֥יךְ יֵחָֽם׃

But one person—how can he be warm?

וּלְאֶחָ֖ד אֶחָד	but for one *û·lə·ʾe·**ḥād***	ABS W/ CONJ וְ + PREP לְ	cardinal number
אֵ֥יךְ אֵיךְ	how? ***ʾêḵ***	---	interr adv
יֵחָֽם׃ חמם	will be warm *yē·**ḥām***	QAL IMPF 3MS	verb

To an increased return on work and help when trouble comes, Qoheleth adds the benefit of staying warm on cold nights. Living in relationship with other humans far exceeds living life alone. Though this series of verses lacks a clear allusion to the garden of Eden narrative, Qoheleth's observations echo Yahweh's sentiment in Gen 2:18: "It is not good for the man to be alone."

12a	וְאִם־יִתְקְפוֹ הָאֶחָד		

Although someone may overpower the one,

וְאִם־ אִם	and although/even if *wə·ʾim-*	--- W/ CONJ וְ	conj
יִתְקְפוֹ תקף	(he) may/will overpower him *yit·qə·**fô***	QAL IMPF 3MS W/ 3MS SX	verb
הָאֶחָד אֶחָד	the one *hā·ʾe·**ḥād***	ABS W/ DEF. ART.	cardinal number

אִם ("although") is used here as a concessive particle, not a conditional particle, as is indicated by the next clause. Although תקף ("overpower") appears only four times in the Hebrew Bible (Eccl 4:12; 6:10; Job 14:20; 15:24), in each instance it clearly means "to overpower." In its usage here, the subject is the implied and impersonal "someone," and the third-person suffix attached to the verb anticipates the object, הָאֶחָד ("the one").

12b	הַשְּׁנַיִם יַעַמְדוּ נֶגְדּוֹ		

the two will stand against him.

הַשְּׁנַיִם שְׁנַיִם	the two *haš·šə·**na**·yim*	ABS W/ DEF. ART.	cardinal number
יַעַמְדוּ עמד	(they) will stand/withstand *ya·ʿam·**dû***	QAL IMPF 3MP	verb
נֶגְדּוֹ נֶגֶד	against him *neg·**dô***	--- W/ 3MS SX	prep

12c	וְהַחוּט הַמְשֻׁלָּשׁ לֹא בִמְהֵרָה יִנָּתֵק׃		

And the threefold cord will not be snapped quickly.

וְהַחוּט חוּט	and the cord *wə·ha·**ḥûṭ***	ABS W/ CONJ וְ + DEF. ART.	noun
הַמְשֻׁלָּשׁ שׁלשׁ	the threefold (one) / the divided-in-three (one) *ha·mə·šul·**lāš***	PUAL PTCP MS W/ DEF. ART.	verb

לֹא לֹא	not *lō'*	---	particle
בִּמְהֵרָ֖ה מְהֵרָה	with haste/quickness *vim·hē·**râ***	ABS W/ PREP בְּ	noun
יִנָּתֵֽק׃ נתק	(it) will be snapped/ torn apart *yin·nā·**tēq***	NIPH IMPF 3MS	verb

Throughout this passage, Qoheleth has demonstrated the benefits of "the two" people over "the one," and here he concludes the discussion with a proverb that illustrates the benefit of multiple companions. As Tremper Longman (1998:143) states, "If one is bad, and two is good, how much better is three!" The Gilgamesh Epic includes a similar numerical statement that moves from one to two and concludes with reference to a "three-ply cord," thus indicating that Qoheleth is likely drawing on a well-known ancient Near Eastern proverb (Shaffer 1967; 1969; see discussion in Samet 2015). Although some interpreters have seen in this passage references to Jesus as the Second Person or to the Trinity in the "threefold cord," neither the immediate context of the passage nor the broader context of the book indicate that such is the case. Nevertheless, there remain important theological implications for living in community with others, which is a prominent theme throughout the Old Testament and especially the New.

From Text to Sermon

Working for the Right Reasons. As noted above, Ecclesiastes is circular: the author cycles through various topics throughout the book. In the first part of this passage, vv. 4–6, he returns to the issue of work. This is a particularly important issue in Western culture, as it was for Qoheleth, and it is one that your congregation likely thinks about often. Many of us become frustrated and disillusioned with the work we do for any number of reasons. This passage gives you the opportunity to reorient your congregation to confront a primary reason that we work—the desire for more—as well as the opportunity to address the true value of work (joy) and the more important matters of life (relationships).

Qoheleth has already said that work produces no ultimate "gain" or "profit," but rather its value is in the joy it brings—if God allows it. In this passage, Qoheleth laments that so much of the toil he observes "under the sun" results from envy. This, he says, is הֶבֶל, or Abelish. Just as envy led Cain to murder his own brother, so "envy of [one's] neighbor" (4:4) too often motivates work. We know this is true; we see it in those around us and in our own hearts, and yet still we struggle to align our motives with Scripture. Working because of envy is problematic on a few levels. First, it indicates that we do not trust God to care for us, for we think that his provision is insufficient. Second, working from envy prevents us from the "reward" or "portion" of work, which is to enjoy the work itself. Finally, it creates conflict between us and our fellow humans and robs us of what truly matters in life: relationships, to which Qoheleth turns in 4:7–12.

Relationships Matter. I grew up going to Vacation Bible School at Bethany Missionary Baptist Church. It was the highlight of my summer—the red Kool-Aid, oatmeal raisin cookies, and crafts made with pasta. In addition to the crafts and Bible stories told using felt and poster board, we sang. Boy did we sing! "Father Abraham" was a fan favorite, what with its arm motions and head nodding. I particularly enjoyed "You Can't Get to Heaven." Ms. Pam let us kids shout out different methods of transportation that would not take us to heaven—it was a blast. The more serious message of those songs, which I didn't understand then and maybe not fully even now, is that Abraham *is* our father if we are in Christ, nothing but faith alone in Christ alone will get us to heaven, and we have to leave that pickup truck or skateboard or stinky socks at the pearly gates. In other words, all that we accumulate in this life is ultimately for naught;

there is no "gain" in it. Yet in American culture—and perhaps in *human* culture—we work tirelessly to accumulate wealth, often at the expense of what actually matters in life: relationships with other human beings.

Ecclesiastes 4:7–12 opens with Qoheleth observing an Abelish situation in life: the person who toils tirelessly, working constantly and accumulating wealth, but he has no one with whom to share life. He finally asks, "For whom am I toiling and depriving myself of good?" The answer, of course, is no one. Though he has "arrived" in the sense of enjoying success and wealth, this man is utterly alone in the world—a state of being with which many of us can identify. In American culture we even valorize the sort of work ethic Qoheleth describes, often not stopping to ask that all-important question until it is too late: "Why am I doing this?" I have never actually thought that my early-nineties pickup is going to get me to heaven, but I have often lived as if achievement is what matters in life, as if earning more money, publishing more books, and "succeeding" in my career matters more than my wife, my children, and the church community God has put me in.

Qoheleth's point in this passage confronts such wrongheaded thinking. What matters in life, says Qoheleth, is relationships. They matter more than any amount of wealth we could accumulate, more than any amount of honor or fame we could amass through working hard, climbing the ladder, hustling—name your metaphor. Work is good—God gave it to Adam and Eve in the garden, and Qoheleth names it as one of the unique gifts God has given all of humanity to enjoy. But work is not *ultimate*, and it certainly does not and cannot imbue humans with the meaning we so deeply crave. We pursue work at the expense of meaningful relationships to our own peril, says Qoheleth: "This is Abel, and it is an evil business."

ECCLESIASTES 5:12–19 [13–20]

WHAT MAKES US "RICH"?

Qoheleth returns to continue his discussion of wealth, relationships, and what really matters in life, and invites us to imagine our own lives in comparison to two scenarios. In the first scenario, he highlights the inherent unpredictability of riches and the harm of selfishness with the story of a miser who lost everything and thus left no inheritance to his son. This man lacked the joy of sitting around a table with the people he loved, instead eating his meals alone, accompanied only by illness and anger. In the second scenario, Qoheleth presents what is "good," where true riches lie. God's gift is found not in selfish accumulation but in eating, drinking, and enjoying one's work; the person who enjoys this "portion" or "reward" will live a full life that is "occupied with the joy of his heart" (Eccl 5:19). The question we must respond to is, What makes us "rich"?

LARGER LITERARY CONTEXT › 5:7–20 [8–20]

5:12–16 [13–17]

12a[13a] יֵ֚שׁ רָעָ֣ה חוֹלָ֔ה רָאִ֖יתִי תַּ֣חַת הַשָּׁ֑מֶשׁ

*yēš rā**ʿâ** ḥô**lâ** rā**ʾî**tî **ta**ḥat haš**šā**meš*

There is a sickening evil I have observed under the sun:

12b[13b] עֹ֛שֶׁר שָׁמ֥וּר לִבְעָלָ֖יו לְרָעָתֽוֹ׃

*ʿō**šer** šā**mûr** livʿā**lāyw** lərāʿā**tô**.*

wealth kept to its owner's harm.

13a[14a] וְאָבַ֛ד הָעֹ֥שֶׁר הַה֖וּא בְּעִנְיַ֣ן רָ֑ע

*wəʾā**vad** hā**ʿō**šer ha**hûʾ** bəʿin**yan** **rāʿ***

That wealth vanished in an evil business,

13b[14b] וְהוֹלִ֣יד בֵּ֔ן

*wəhô**lîd** **bēn***

then he had a son,

13c[14c] וְאֵ֥ין בְּיָד֖וֹ מְאֽוּמָה׃

*wəʾ**ên** bəyā**dô** məʾ**û**mâ.*

but there's nothing in his hand.

14a[15a] כַּאֲשֶׁ֤ר יָצָא֙ מִבֶּ֣טֶן אִמּ֔וֹ

*kaʾă**šer** yā**ṣā**ʾ mib**be**ṭen ʾim**mô***

As he departed from his mother's womb—

14b[15b] עָר֛וֹם יָשׁ֥וּב לָלֶ֖כֶת כְּשֶׁבָּ֑א

*ʿā**rôm** yā**šûv** lā**le**ḵet kəšeb**bāʾ***

naked—he will again go as he came.

14c[15c] וּמְא֙וּמָה֙ לֹא־יִשָּׂ֣א בַעֲמָל֔וֹ שֶׁיֹּלֵ֖ךְ בְּיָדֽוֹ׃

*ûmə**ʾû**mâ lōʾ-yiś**śā**ʾ vaʿămā**lô** šeyyō**lēḵ** bəyā**dô**.*

He will not carry anything from his toil that he may take in his hand.

15a[16a] וְגַם־זֹה רָעָה חוֹלָה

*wəgam-**zō** rā**ʿâ** ḥô**lâ***

This also is a sickening evil.

15b[16b] כָּל־עֻמַּת שֶׁבָּא

*kol-ʿum**mat** šeb**bā**ʾ*

Just as he came,

15c[16c] כֵּן יֵלֵךְ

kēn** yē**lēḵ

so he goes.

15d[16d] וּמַה־יִּתְרוֹן לוֹ שֶׁיַּעֲמֹל לָרוּחַ׃

*ûmah-yit**rôn lô** šeyyaʿă**mōl** lā**rû**aḥ.*

And what profit does he have that he should toil for wind?

16a[17a] גַּם כָּל־יָמָיו בַּחֹשֶׁךְ יֹאכֵל

gam** kol-yā**māyw** ba**ḥō**šeḵ yōʾ**ḵēl

Indeed, all his days he eats in darkness,

16b[17b] וְכָעַס הַרְבֵּה וְחָלְיוֹ וָקָצֶף׃

*wəḵā**ʿas** har**bē** wəḥol**yô** wā**qā**ṣef.*

with great grief, sickness, and anger.

12a[13a] יֵשׁ רָעָה חוֹלָה רָאִיתִי תַּחַת הַשָּׁמֶשׁ

There is a sickening evil I have observed under the sun:

יֵשׁ יֵשׁ	there is *yēš*	---	particle
רָעָה רָעָה	evil/wickedness *rā · ʿâ*	ABS	noun

חוֹלָ֖ה חלה	is sickening/painful/grievous *ḥô·lâ*	QAL PTCP FS	verb
רָאִ֣יתִי ראה	I have seen/observed *rā·ʾî·tî*	QAL PF 1CS	verb
תַּ֣חַת תַּחַת	under *ta·ḥat*	---	prep
הַשָּׁ֑מֶשׁ שֶׁמֶשׁ	the sun *haš·šā·meš*	ABS W/ DEF. ART.	noun

As previously, "under the sun" refers to the life we live on earth. Qoheleth is not alluding to "worldly wisdom" but rather indicating that his observations relate to human life. The phrase "sickening evil" (רָעָה חוֹלָה) indicates that what Qoheleth has observed is particularly tragic and causes him no small amount of grief.

12b[13b]	עֹ֛שֶׁר שָׁמ֥וּר לִבְעָלָ֖יו לְרָעָתֽוֹ׃
	wealth kept to its owner's harm.

עֹ֛שֶׁר עֹשֶׁר	riches/wealth *ʿō·šer*	ABS	noun
שָׁמ֥וּר שׁמר	kept/guarded *šā·mûr*	QAL PASS PTCP MS	verb
לִבְעָלָ֖יו בַּעַל	to/for its owner/master *liv·ʿā·lāyw*	CST W/ PREP לְ + 3MS SX	noun
לְרָעָתֽוֹ׃ רָעָה	for his harm/evil *lə·rā·ʿā·tô*	CST W/ PREP לְ + 3MS SX	noun

The tragedy, the "sickening evil," is that someone accumulates wealth and simply stores it up for himself—to his harm. Ironically, the "master" (בַּעַל; translated "owner") is mastered by his possessions, and rather than enabling one to live a good life—to enjoy one's work, wine, food, and spouse—the wealth causes its owner harm (Bollhagen 2011:204). Although Qoheleth does not specify the nature of the harm, we can imagine any number of personal situations in which we have observed exactly what he refers to. In Luke 12:16–21, Jesus develops this theme: A rich man builds an extra barn to store his abundant harvest, to which God responds, "Fool! This night your soul is required of you, and the things you have prepared, whose will they be?" (ESV). Whatever wealth is for, it is certainly not to be simply heaped up for its owner's "security."

13a[14a]	וְאָבַד הָעֹשֶׁר הַהוּא בְּעִנְיַן רָע		
	That wealth vanished in an evil business,		
וְאָבַד אבד	and (it) vanished/perished/ was lost *wə·ʾā·**vad***	QAL PF 3MS	verb
הָעֹשֶׁר עֹשֶׁר	the wealth *hā·ʿō·šer*	ABS W/ DEF. ART.	noun
הַהוּא הוא	that *ha·**hûʾ***	--- W/ DEF. ART.	demonstr pron
בְּעִנְיַן עִנְיָן	in business of *bə·ʿin·**yan***	CST W/ PREP בְּ	noun
רָע רַע	evil/bad ***rāʿ***	ABS	noun

The phrase עִנְיַן רָע ("evil business") occurs three times in the Hebrew Bible, every time in Ecclesiastes. It is used in 1:13 in reference to the human task of examining "all that is done under the sun," which according to Qoheleth is an "evil business that God gave humans to occupy them." In 4:8, it describes the man who toils ceaselessly and lives in isolation, with no one with whom to share his wealth. Here, a man has likewise acquired wealth, but it "vanished in an evil business," leaving him with nothing with which to provide for his son and no inheritance to pass on. Qoheleth does not specify the "evil business" that caused the man's wealth to evaporate, but ancient and modern readers alike will have no trouble identifying comparable scenarios in their own lives.

13b[14b]	וְהוֹלִיד בֵּן		
	then he had a son,		
וְהוֹלִיד ילד	and he fathered/begat *wə·hô·**lîd***	HIPH WEQATAL 3MS	verb
בֵּן בֵּן	son ***bēn***	ABS	noun

13c[14c]	וְאֵין בְּיָדוֹ מְאוּמָה׃

but there's nothing in his hand.

וְאֵין אַיִן	and there is not *wə·ʾên*	--- W/ CONJ וְ	particle
בְּיָדוֹ יָד	in his hand *bə·yā·dô*	CST W/ PREP בְּ + 3MS SX	noun
מְאוּמָה׃ מְאוּמָה	anything *mə·ʾû·mâ*	---	indef pron

It is not clear if the third-person suffix on "hand" (בְּיָדוֹ, "in his hand") refers to the father or the son. The closest antecedent is son, but the focus throughout the passage has been on the "owner" (בַּעַל) of the wealth, thus I take it to refer not to the son without an inheritance but rather to the father who must grapple with his inability to provide for his son or to leave him an inheritance. The son surely will suffer due to the poverty in which he will be raised and the lack of any inheritance, but the father will suffer enormously for his inability to care for his family well, which is a, if not *the*, primary function of wealth.

14a[15a]	כַּאֲשֶׁר יָצָא מִבֶּטֶן אִמּוֹ

As he departed from his mother's womb—

כַּאֲשֶׁר אֲשֶׁר	like/as *ka·ʾă·šer*	--- W/ PREP כְּ	relative
יָצָא יצא	he came out/departed *yā·ṣāʾ*	QAL PF 3MS	verb
מִבֶּטֶן בֶּטֶן	from the womb/belly of *mib·be·ṭen*	CST W/ PREP מִן	noun
אִמּוֹ אֵם	his mother *ʾim·mô*	CST W/ 3MS SX	noun

As in v. 13[14], there is some ambiguity as to the referent. However, as above, since the subject of this section has been the "owner" of the vanished wealth, here the subject of the verb "departed" (יצא) remains the same. The father will depart life "under the sun" just as he entered it.

14b[15b] עָרוֹם יָשׁוּב לָלֶכֶת כְּשֶׁבָּא

naked—he will again go as he came.

עָרוֹם עָרוֹם	naked *ā·**rôm***	MS PRED	adj
יָשׁוּב שׁוב	he will return *yā·**šûv***	QAL IMPF 3MS	verb
לָלֶכֶת הלך	to go/walk *lā·**le**·ḵet*	QAL INF CST W/ PREP לְ	verb
כְּשֶׁבָּא בוא	as he came *kə·šeb·**bā’***	QAL PF 3MS W/ PREP כְּ + RELATIVE PRON שֶׁ	verb

The root שׁוב ("return"), when used in conjunction with another verb, often means to repeat an action (Schoors 2013:435). Thus, the man is not "returning to go," but rather he is "again" going back to where he came from; i.e., he is dying. The root הלך ("go") is used similarly in 1:4 to describe the "going" of generations from life to death and back again, and in 3:20 Qoheleth uses the verb again to describe death: "All go [הלך] to one place."

14c[15c] וּמְאוּמָה לֹא־יִשָּׂא בַעֲמָלוֹ שֶׁיֹּלֵךְ בְּיָדוֹ׃

He will not carry anything from his toil
that he may take in his hand.

וּמְאוּמָה מְאוּמָה	and anything/nothing *û·mə·**’û**·mâ*	--- W/ CONJ וְ	indef pron
לֹא־ לֹא	not *lō’-*	---	particle
יִשָּׂא נשׂא	he lifts/carries/takes *yiś·**śā’***	QAL IMPF 3MS	verb
בַעֲמָלוֹ עָמָל	in his toil/labor *va·‘ă·mā·**lô***	CST W/ PREP בְּ + 3MS SX	noun
שֶׁיֹּלֵךְ הלך	which/that he may take/ cause to go *šey·yō·**lēḵ***	HIPH JUSS 3MS W/ RELATIVE PRON שֶׁ	verb
בְּיָדוֹ׃ יָד	in his hand *bə·yā·**dô***	CST W/ PREP בְּ + 3MS SX	noun

The tragedy of this man's wealth continues to pile up. The wealth he worked so hard to attain vanished in an "evil business," leaving him with no ability to provide for his son or leave an inheritance, and now death renders void any hope of lasting gain from his work. Just as the man entered the world with nothing, he will also depart the world with nothing, unable to take anything with him.

15a[16a] וְגַם־זֹה רָעָה חוֹלָה

This also is a sickening evil.

וְגַם־ / גַּם	and also/even *wə·gam-*	--- W/ CONJ וְ	adv
זֹה / זֹה	this *zō*	---	demonstr pron
רָעָה / רָעָה	evil/harm *rā·ʿâ*	ABS	noun
חוֹלָה / חלה	is sickening/painful/grievous *ḥô·lâ*	QAL PTCP FS	verb

"Sickening evil" (רָעָה חוֹלָה) is the same phrase Qoheleth used in 1:12 to refer to "wealth kept to its owners harm." Here it refers to fact that there is no "profit" (יִתְרוֹן, 5:15d [16d]) from one's labor.

15b[16b] כָּל־עֻמַּת שֶׁבָּא

Just as he came,

כָּל־ / לְ	just *kol-*	--- W/ PREP כְּ	prep
עֻמַּת / עֻמָּה	as *ʿum·mat*	---	prep
שֶׁבָּא / בוא	he came *šeb·bāʾ*	QAL PF 3MS W/ RELATIVE PRON שֶׁ	verb

There is an enormous amount of discussion over the meaning of כָּל־עֻמַּת. Most translations and commentators take the phrase as the inseparable preposition כְּ ("like" or "as") plus the insperable preposition לְ ("to" or "for") plus עֻמַּת (a construct form of the noun עֻמָּה), thus the translation "just as he came." The form עֻמַּת appears thirty-two times in the Hebrew Bible, and in thirty-one of those instances (including in Eccl 7:14) it has a prefixed לְ; the only exception is this instance here. Thus, the translation above follows other translations and commentaries in understanding this instance as עֻמַּת prefixed with both the prepositions לְ and כְּ rather than with the word כֹּל ("all").

15c[16c]	כֵּ֥ן יֵלֵֽךְ׃			
	so he goes.			
כֵּ֥ן כֵּן	thus/so *kēn*	---		adv
יֵלֵֽךְ׃ הלך	he goes/walks *yē·lēḵ*	QAL IMPF 3MS		verb

15d[16d]	וּמַה־יִּתְר֣וֹן ל֔וֹ שֶׁיַּעֲמֹ֖ל לָרֽוּחַ׃		
	And what profit does he have that he should toil for wind?		
וּמַה־ מָה	and what *û·mah-*	--- W/ CONJ וְ	interr pron
יִּתְר֣וֹן יִתְרוֹן	profit/gain/surplus/advantage *yit·rôn*	ABS	noun
ל֔וֹ לְ	to/for him *lô*	--- W/ 3MS SX	prep
שֶׁיַּעֲמֹ֖ל עמל	that he toils/labors *šey·ya·ʿă·mōl*	QAL IMPF 3MS W/ RELATIVE PRON שֶׁ	verb
לָרֽוּחַ׃ רוּחַ	for the wind/breath *lā·rû·aḥ*	ABS W/ PREP לְ + DEF. ART.	noun

Qoheleth returns to a theme he introduced at the book's outset: "What profit is there for the human in all of his toil at which he toils under the sun?" (1:3). In 1:11 he answered the question for us: "There is no profit under the sun." Here the story of the man who gained and then lost drives home his point. Toiling for "profit" or "gain" or some "leftover portion" is folly, because that profit simply does not exist. It will do us well to face this question honestly now rather than realize the truth at end of life, as happens to the "master" (בַּעַל; translated "owner") of wealth in this narrative.

16a[17a]	גַּם כָּל־יָמָיו בַּחֹשֶׁךְ יֹאכֵל		
	Indeed, all his days he eats in darkness,		
גַּם גַּם	also/even/indeed *gam*	---	adv
כָּל־ כֹּל	all of *kol-*	CST	noun
יָמָיו יוֹם	his days *yā·māyw*	CST W/ 3MS SX	noun
בַּחֹשֶׁךְ חֹשֶׁךְ	in darkness *ba·ḥō·šek*	ABS W/ PREP בְּ + DEF. ART.	noun
יֹאכֵל אכל	he eats *yō'·kēl*	QAL IMPF 3MS	verb

16b[17b]	וְכָעַס הַרְבֵּה וְחָלְיוֹ וָקָצֶף׃		
	with great grief, sickness, and anger.		
וְכָעַס כַּעַס	and vexation/anger/grief *wə·kā·'as*	ABS W/ CONJ וְ	noun
הַרְבֵּה רבה	to be many/much *har·bē*	HIPH INF ABS	verb
וְחָלְיוֹ חֳלִי	and his sickness *wə·ḥol·yô*	CST W/ CONJ וְ + 3MS SX	noun
וָקָצֶף׃ קֶצֶף	and anger *wā·qā·ṣef*	ABS W/ CONJ וְ	noun

This description of the "owner" (5:12b [13b]) eating in darkness with "great grief, sickness, and anger" forms a stark contrast to Eccl 9:7–10, where Qoheleth urges his readers to celebrate with joyful eating, drinking, and time with one's spouse. The image perhaps reminds us of someone we know—and maybe even of ourselves. Without saying so explicitly, the brief, emotionally charged depiction of the conclusion to this man's life urges readers to choose wisely the objects of our affection and devotion.

5:17–19 [18–20]

17a[18a] הִנֵּה אֲשֶׁר־רָאִיתִי אָנִי טוֹב

hinnē ʾăšer-rāʾîtî ʾānî ṭôv

Behold, I have seen what is good!

17b[18b] אֲשֶׁר־יָפֶה לֶאֱכוֹל־וְלִשְׁתּוֹת

ăšer-yāfe leʾekôl-wəlištôt wəlirʾôt ṭôvâ

What is beautiful is eating, drinking,

17c[18c] וְלִרְאוֹת טוֹבָה בְּכָל־עֲמָלוֹ ׀ שֶׁיַּעֲמֹל תַּחַת־הַשֶּׁמֶשׁ

bəkol-ʿămālô šeyyaʿămōl taḥat-haššemeš

and experiencing good in all his toil
at which he toils under the sun

17d[18d] מִסְפַּר יְמֵי־חַיָּיו

mispar yəmê-ḥayyāyw

the few days of his life

17e[18e] אֲשֶׁר־נָתַן־לוֹ הָאֱלֹהִים

ăšer-nātan-lô hāʾĕlōhîm

that God has given him

17f[18f] כִּי־הוּא חֶלְקוֹ׃

kî-hûʾ ḥelqô.

because this is his reward.

18a[19a] גַּם כָּל־הָאָדָם אֲשֶׁר נָתַן־לוֹ הָאֱלֹהִים

gam kol-hāʾādām ʾăšer nātan-lô hāʾĕlōhîm

What's more, every person to whom God gives

18b[19b] עֹשֶׁר וּנְכָסִים וְהִשְׁלִיטוֹ לֶאֱכֹל מִמֶּנּוּ

ʿōšer ûnəkāsîm wəhišlîṭô leʾĕkōl mimmennû

wealth and riches and he enables them to eat from it

18c[19c] וְלָשֵׂ֣את אֶת־חֶלְק֔וֹ וְלִשְׂמֹ֖חַ בַּעֲמָל֑וֹ
wəlāśēʾt ʾet-ḥelqô wəliśmōaḥ baʿămālô

and to take up their portion and to take joy in their toil—

18d[19d] זֹ֕ה מַתַּ֥ת אֱלֹהִ֖ים הִֽיא׃
zō mattat ʾĕlōhîm hîʾ.

this, *this* is the gift of God.

19a[20a] כִּ֚י לֹ֣א הַרְבֵּ֔ה יִזְכֹּ֖ר אֶת־יְמֵ֣י חַיָּ֑יו
kî lōʾ harbē yizkōr ʾet-yəmê ḥayyāyw

For such a person does not dwell too much on the days of their life

19b[20b] כִּ֧י הָאֱלֹהִ֛ים מַעֲנֶ֖ה בְּשִׂמְחַ֥ת לִבּֽוֹ׃
kî hāʾĕlōhîm maʿăne bəśimḥat libbô.

because God occupies them with joy in their hearts.

17a[18a] הִנֵּ֞ה אֲשֶׁר־רָאִ֣יתִי אָ֗נִי ט֣וֹב

Behold, I have seen what is good!

הִנֵּ֞ה הִנֵּה	behold *hin·nē*	---	particle
אֲשֶׁר־ אֲשֶׁא	what/that which *ʾă·šer-*	---	relative pron
רָאִ֣יתִי ראה	I saw/have seen *rā·ʾî·tî*	QAL PF 1CS	verb
אָ֗נִי אֲנִי	I/myself *ʾā·nî*	---	personal pron
ט֣וֹב טוֹב	good/right *ṭôv*	MS PRED	adj

17b[18b] אֲשֶׁר־יָפֶה לֶאֱכוֹל־וְלִשְׁתּוֹת

What is beautiful is eating, drinking,

Hebrew	Gloss	Parsing	Part of speech
אֲשֶׁר־ אֲשֶׁר	what/that which *'ă·šer-*	---	relative pron
יָפֶה יָפֶה	beautiful/appropriate *yā·**fe***	MS PRED	adj
לֶאֱכוֹל־ אכל	to eat ***le**·'e·ḵôl-*	QAL INF CST W/ PREP לְ	verb
וְלִשְׁתּוֹת שׁתה	and to drink *wə·liš·**tôt***	QAL INF CST W/ CONJ וְ + PREP לְ	verb

In 3:11, Qoheleth used יָפֶה ("beautiful") to describe the timing of God's creation: "He made everything beautiful in its [or his] time." Here he applies the term to what is "beautiful" for humans to experience in their lives—namely, eating, drinking, and working (see below on 5:17c). While some English translations render the word as "appropriate" (NET) or "fitting" (ESV), the word almost exclusively refers to physical people and objects that are attractive to the eyes. The translation here aims to retain the connotation of something pleasant to observe.

17c[18c] וְלִרְאוֹת טוֹבָה בְּכָל־עֲמָלוֹ | שֶׁיַּעֲמֹל תַּחַת־הַשָּׁמֶשׁ

and experiencing good in all his toil
at which he toils under the sun

Hebrew	Gloss	Parsing	Part of speech
וְלִרְאוֹת ראה	and to experience/see/observe *wə·lir·**'ôt***	QAL INF CST W/ CONJ וְ + PREP לְ	verb
טוֹבָה טוֹבָה	good *ṭô·**vâ***	ABS	noun
בְּכָל־ כֹּל	in all of *bə·ḵol-*	CST W/ PREP בְּ	noun
עֲמָלוֹ | עָמָל	his toil/labor *'ă·mā·**lô***	CST W/ 3MS SX	noun
שֶׁיַּעֲמֹל עמל	that/at which he toils *šey·ya·'ă·**mōl***	QAL IMPF 3MS W/ RELATIVE PRON שֶׁ	verb

תַּ֣חַת־ תַּחַת	under *ta·ḥat-*	---	prep
הַשָּׁ֑מֶשׁ שֶׁ֫מֶשׁ	the sun *haš·**še**·meš*	ABS W/ DEF. ART.	noun

Again Qoheleth uses the more negative term "toil" (עָמָל) to describe the work that humans do "under the sun," or during this life. However, this more negative view of work—that it is indeed difficult—is balanced by the joy that God allows humans to experience in their work. Along with eating and drinking, this is humanity's "portion" or "reward." That is, the enjoyment of these mundane activities is what God has given us—and it is "beautiful."

17d[18d] מִסְפַּ֥ר יְמֵי־חַיָּ֛ו

the few days of his life

מִסְפַּ֥ר מִסְפָּר	few/number of *mis·**par***	CST	noun
יְמֵי־ יוֹם	days of *yə·mê-*	CST	noun
חַיָּ֛ו חַיִּים	his life *ḥay·**yāyw***	CST W/ 3MS SX	noun

מִסְפָּר ("few") is literally "number"; "number of days" is an idiomatic expression for "few days," as translated here (see Num 9:20, in reference to God's presence at the tabernacle in the wilderness). Qoheleth emphasizes throughout his book that human life is brief, and death is the great equalizer that comes for all of us. The "few days of life" make Qoheleth's call to enjoyment all the more urgent: we must grasp the "beautiful" while we can, because it will be gone all too soon.

17e[18e] אֲשֶׁר־נָֽתַן־ל֥וֹ הָאֱלֹהִ֖ים

that God has given him

אֲשֶׁר־ אֲשֶׁר	that *'ă·šer-*	---	relative pron

נָתַן־ נתן	(he) gave *nā·tan-*	QAL PF 3MS	verb
ל֖וֹ לְ	to him *lô*	--- W/ 3MS SX	prep
הָאֱלֹהִ֑ים אֱלֹהִים	the God *hā·'ĕ·lō·hîm*	ABS W/ DEF. ART.	noun

The definite article on הָאֱלֹהִים ("God") is strange to our ears and is left untranslated here, but thirty-two of the forty (80 percent) occurrences of אֱלֹהִים in Ecclesiastes have the definite article attached.

17f[18f] כִּי־ה֥וּא חֶלְקֽוֹ׃

because this is his reward.

כִּי־ כִּי	because/for *kî-*	---	conj
ה֥וּא הוּא	this *hû'*	---	personal pron
חֶלְקֽוֹ׃ חֵ֫לֶק	his reward/portion *ḥel·qô*	CST W/ 3MS SX	noun

As he has done and will do several more times in the book, Qoheleth invites readers to "see" life from his perspective. Just as he saw or experienced injustice in 3:16, so in this section he sees what is beautiful and good. And just as he has previously discussed the "portion" or "reward" of humans, in this section he returns to the theme, reminding readers that this life is short and work is difficult, yet there is something uniquely "beautiful" about life: enjoying the gifts of God. The days we have on earth are themselves a gift, Qoheleth tells us, and the ability to enjoy eating, drinking, and working are likewise a gift. This message, repeated throughout the book, is particularly significant for a culture that struggles with healthy patterns of working, eating, and drinking, like ours today. Qoheleth confirms that these things are intended for our good, but all too often we make them ultimate, seeking "gain" in what God intended only as "reward" (see further discussion at 1:3a; 2:10b; and 5:14c).

18a[19a] גַּ֣ם כָּל־הָאָדָ֡ם אֲשֶׁ֣ר נָֽתַן־ל֣וֹ הָאֱלֹהִ֡ים

What's more, every person to whom God gives

Hebrew	Gloss	Parsing	Part of speech
גַּ֣ם	also/even	---	adv
גַּם	*gam*		
כָּל־	each/every/all of	CST	noun
כֹּל	*kol-*		
הָאָדָ֡ם	the man/human/humanity	ABS	noun
אָדָם	*hā·ʾā·**dām***	W/ DEF. ART.	
אֲשֶׁ֣ר	who/that/which	---	relative pron
אֲשֶׁר	*ʾă·**šer***		
נָֽתַן־	(he) gave/has given/gives	QAL PF 3MS	verb
נתן	***nā**·tan-*		
ל֣וֹ	to him	---	prep
לְ	***lô***	W/ 3MS SX	
הָאֱלֹהִ֡ים	the God	ABS	noun
אֱלֹהִים	*hā·ʾĕ·lō·**hîm***	W/ DEF. ART.	

Though Qoheleth's use of the term הָאָדָם could be translated woodenly as "the man," in this verse it is translated "person" in keeping with the universal nature of the book's discussion of human life. This statement is not limited to men only but rather refers to humans in general, as throughout the book. See further the note at 6:1b.

18b[19b] עֹ֜שֶׁר וּנְכָסִ֗ים וְהִשְׁלִיטוֹ֙ לֶאֱכֹ֣ל מִמֶּ֔נּוּ

wealth and riches and he enables them to eat from it

Hebrew	Gloss	Parsing	Part of speech
עֹ֜שֶׁר	riches/wealth	ABS	noun
עֹשֶׁר	*ʿ**ō**·šer*		
וּנְכָסִ֗ים	and riches/wealth	ABS	noun
נֶכֶס	*û·nə·ḵā·**sîm***	W/ CONJ וְ	
וְהִשְׁלִיטוֹ֙	and he enables/empowers him	HIPH PF 3MS	verb
שׁלט	*wə·hiš·lî·**ṭô***	W/ CONJ וְ + 3MS SX	
לֶאֱכֹ֣ל	to eat	QAL INF CST	verb
אכל	*le·ʾĕ·**ḵōl***	W/ PREP לְ	

מִמֶּ֑נּוּ מִן	from it *mim·**men**·nû*	--- W/ 3MS SX	prep

In the previous section, Qoheleth emphasized that God gives wealth and riches. Though we may think we deserve what we have worked for, we must remember that all good things are a gift from God (cf. Jas 1:17). In this clause, Qoheleth reminds us that enjoying one's wealth, or eating from it (לֶאֱכֹ֣ל מִמֶּ֑נּוּ), is likewise from the hand of God.

18c[19c] וְלָשֵׂ֣את אֶת־חֶלְק֔וֹ וְלִשְׂמֹ֖חַ בַּעֲמָל֑וֹ

and to take up their portion and to take joy in their toil—

וְלָשֵׂ֣את נשׂא	and to lift/bear/carry *wə·lā·**śēʾt***	QAL INF CST W/ CONJ וְ + PREP לְ	verb
אֶת־ אֵת	*(direct object marker)* *ʾet-*	---	particle
חֶלְק֔וֹ חֵ֫לֶק	his portion/reward *ḥel·**qô***	CST W/ 3MS SX	noun
וְלִשְׂמֹ֖חַ שׂמח	and to take joy/rejoice *wə·liś·**mō**·aḥ*	QAL INF CST W/ CONJ וְ + PREP לְ	verb
בַּעֲמָל֑וֹ עָמָל	in his toil/labor *ba·ʿă·mā·**lô***	CST W/ PREP בְּ + 3MS SX	noun

The word translated "take up" (נשׂא) often means to "carry" or to "bear," as in a burden or heavy load. In this context, it refers to embracing one's portion, or reward, in life, which is the (necessarily temporary) enjoyment of God's gifts.

18d[19d] זֹ֕ה מַתַּ֥ת אֱלֹהִ֖ים הִֽיא׃

this, *this* is the gift of God.

זֹ֕ה זֹה	this ***zō***	---	demonstr pron
מַתַּ֥ת מַתַּת	gift of *mat·**tat***	CST	noun

אֱלֹהִ֑ים אֱלֹהִים	God *ʾĕ·lō·**hîm***	ABS	noun
הִֽיא׃ הִיא	it ***hîʾ***	---	personal pron

This final clause both summarizes and emphasizes the clauses before it. God gives, God enables enjoyment, and all of this is indeed the gift of God.

19a[20a] כִּ֚י לֹ֣א הַרְבֵּ֔ה יִזְכֹּ֖ר אֶת־יְמֵ֣י חַיָּ֑יו

For such a person does not dwell too much on the days of their life

כִּ֚י כִּי	because/for ***kî***	---	conj
לֹ֣א לֹא	no/not ***lōʾ***	---	particle
הַרְבֵּ֔ה רבה	to make much/multiply *har·**bē***	HIPH INF ABS	verb
יִזְכֹּ֖ר זכר	(he) remembers *yiz·**kōr***	QAL IMPF 3MS	verb
אֶת־ אֵת	*(direct object marker)* *ʾet-*	---	particle
יְמֵ֣י יוֹם	days of *yə·**mê***	CST	noun
חַיָּ֑יו חַיִּים	his life *ḥay·**yāyw***	CST W/ 3MS SX	noun

19b[20b] כִּ֧י הָאֱלֹהִ֛ים מַעֲנֶ֖ה בְּשִׂמְחַ֥ת לִבּֽוֹ׃

because God occupies them with joy in their hearts.

כִּ֧י כִּי	because/for ***kî***	---	conj
הָאֱלֹהִ֛ים אֱלֹהִים	the God *hā·ʾĕ·lō·**hîm***	ABS W/ DEF. ART.	noun
מַעֲנֶ֖ה ענה	makes attentive/occupies *ma·ʿă·**ne***	HIPH PTCP MS	verb

בְּשִׂמְחַ֥ת שִׂמְחָה	with joy/pleasure/ gladness of *bə·śim·**ḥat***	CST W/ PREP בְּ	noun
לִבּֽוֹ׃ לֵב	his heart/mind *lib·**bô***	CST W/ 3MS SX	noun

Qoheleth does not indicate in this verse that a person should blithely traverse life in a sort of "ignorance is bliss" state. Qoheleth makes clear that there are many dark parts of life—and he urges readers to engage such darkness with eyes wide open. Here he is emphasizing that the darkness of life will pale as one is occupied with God's gifts of joy in eating, drinking, working, and being with one's spouse.

From Text to Sermon

What Is Money For? Popular-level discussions of Ecclesiastes typically frame the book as teaching that life is meaningless . . . without God. If your congregation has this general view of the book, then they may be surprised that Qoheleth spends so much time talking about "worldly" issues such as money and eating and drinking. But Ecclesiastes isn't trying to convince readers that life is meaningless without God, nor is it attempting to encourage readers to take some heavenly perspective that jettisons life on planet Earth. Rather, the book aims to show readers how to navigate the "Abelish" life we live under the sun—which is through living in relationship with God and fully embracing the earthly realities of working, eating, drinking, and living in community. A key piece of his argument is that we must radically reorient our perspective regarding work and wealth. We've seen already that work is not meant to give us some sort of "legacy" or "meaning" in life. There is no "gain" or "left-over portion" in work. The benefit of work, rather, is in enjoying the work itself. Similarly—and counterculturally—money offers no real satisfaction or meaning or purpose in life. That is, if we view wealth as an end in itself, as something to be kept. All of us will exit this life just as naked as we came, so we hoard wealth to our great detriment. The real benefit of wealth, Qoheleth tells us in this passage, is its enjoyment.

The Sovereignty and Goodness of God—in This Life and the Next. In the two sections of this passage (5:12–16 and 5:17–19), Qoheleth paints contrasting pictures. The first is of the person who accumulates wealth with no regard for the pleasure it may bring. They then lose their wealth and their children are left without an inheritance. In contrast is the person whom God allows to enjoy their wealth through eating, drinking, and joy in their work. "Such a person," Qoheleth tells us, "does not dwell too much on the days of their life because God occupies them with joy in their hearts." God's goodness and sovereignty extend over both the gifts he gives and the ability to enjoy those gifts. Discussing these aspects of God's work in the world that allow us joy in the present opens a clear pathway for explaining the goodness of God in giving the ultimate gift—namely, redemption in Christ that makes it possible for us to one day return to Eden. The transition from discussion of life in the here and now to life eternal may seem a bit overwrought and cheesy, but remember that Ecclesiastes is concerned primarily with what it means to live in relationship with God and enjoy the gifts he gives. Though the book's author lacked a fully developed eschatology, the New Testament reveals in no uncertain terms that resurrection awaits all of us—some to life and some to death. Thus, while we must resist the urge to flatten the message of Ecclesiastes to something akin to "live with eternity in mind" or "life is meaningless without God," we must also integrate Qoheleth's picture of the good life with the New Testament's eschatological picture of the good life.

GOD IS SOVEREIGN OVER HIS GIFTS AND THE ABILITY TO ENJOY THEM

This passage returns to a theme Qoheleth has already covered and will cover again: the importance of enjoying the gifts of God, and the tragedy that occurs when one cannot enjoy such gifts. As we have seen before, Qoheleth emphasizes that (1) wealth is itself a gift of God and, perhaps more importantly, (2) enjoyment of that wealth is itself a gift of God. The tragedy of a person's inability to enjoy God's gifts is an easy enough concept to understand and communicate in the modern West, where we are acutely attuned to ceaseless striving for more. His frank assessment of the horror of such striving without satisfaction will hopefully shake up modern readers, forcing us to reevaluate what we value in life. Do we really enjoy what God has given us? Or are we more like the man who has a hundred children, many years of life, and yet true joy slips through his fingers? And if the latter, what can and should we do?

LARGER LITERARY CONTEXT › 6:1–12

6:1–6

1a יֵ֣שׁ רָעָ֔ה אֲשֶׁ֥ר רָאִ֖יתִי תַּ֣חַת הַשָּׁ֑מֶשׁ

*yēš rā**ʿâ** ʾă**šer** rā**ʾîtî** **ta**ḥat hašš**ā**meš*

Here's an evil that I've observed under the sun,

1b וְרַבָּ֥ה הִ֖יא עַל־הָאָדָֽם׃

*wərab**bâ** **hîʾ** ʿal-hāʾā**dām**.*

and it is significant upon humanity:

2a אִ֣ישׁ אֲשֶׁ֣ר יִתֶּן־ל֣וֹ הָאֱלֹהִ֗ים

ʾîš** ʾă**šer** yitten-**lô** hāʾĕlō**hîm

God gives a person

2b עֹ֠שֶׁר וּנְכָסִ֣ים וְכָב֞וֹד

*ʿō**šer** ûnəḵā**sîm** wəḵā**vôd***

wealth, riches, and honor,

2c וְֽאֵינֶ֨נּוּ חָסֵ֥ר לְנַפְשׁ֣וֹ ׀

*wəʾê**nen**nû ḥā**sēr** lənaf**šô***

and his appetite lacks nothing

2d מִכֹּ֣ל אֲשֶׁר־יִתְאַוֶּ֔ה

*mik**kōl** ʾăšer-yitʾaw**we***

of all that he could crave.

2e וְלֹֽא־יַשְׁלִיטֶ֤נּוּ הָֽאֱלֹהִים֙ לֶאֱכֹ֣ל מִמֶּ֔נּוּ

*wəlōʾ-yašlîṭ**en**nû hāʾĕlō**hîm** leʾĕ**ḵōl** mim**men**nû*

Yet God does not enable him to eat from it,

2f כִּ֛י אִ֥ישׁ נָכְרִ֖י יֹאכְלֶ֑נּוּ

***kî** **ʾîš** nok**rî** yōʾḵā**len**nû*

for a foreigner will eat it.

2g זֶה הֶבֶל וָחֳלִי רָע הוּא׃

ze hevel woḥŏlî rāʿ hûʾ.

This is Abelish; it's a sick evil.

3a אִם־יוֹלִיד אִישׁ מֵאָה

ʾim-yôlîd ʾîš mēʾâ

If a man fathers a hundred children

3b וְשָׁנִים רַבּוֹת יִחְיֶה

wəšānîm rabbôt yiḥye

and lives a great many years,

3c וְרַב | שֶׁיִּהְיוּ יְמֵי־שָׁנָיו

wərav šeyyihyû yəmê-šānāyw

and the days of his years are many,

3d וְנַפְשׁוֹ לֹא־תִשְׂבַּע מִן־הַטּוֹבָה

wənafšô lōʾ-tiśbaʿ min-haṭṭôvâ

but his appetite is not sated from the good,

3e וְגַם־קְבוּרָה לֹא־הָיְתָה לּוֹ

wəgam-qəvûrâ lōʾ-hāyətâ lô

and he doesn't even receive a proper burial—

3f אָמַרְתִּי טוֹב מִמֶּנּוּ הַנָּפֶל׃

āmartî ṭôv mimmennû hannāfel.

I say that a stillborn child is better than him.

4a כִּי־בַהֶבֶל בָּא

kî-vahevel bāʾ

For a stillborn child enters into Abelness,

4b וּבַחֹשֶׁךְ יֵלֵךְ

ûvaḥōšek̲ yēlēk̲

and into the darkness he walks,

4c וּבַחֹ֖שֶׁךְ שְׁמ֥וֹ יְכֻסֶּֽה׃

*ûva**ḥō**šek̲ šə**mô** yək̲u**sse**.*

and in the darkness his name is covered.

5a גַּם־שֶׁ֥מֶשׁ לֹא־רָאָ֖ה

*gam-**še**meš lō’-rā’**â***

He hasn't even seen the sun,

5b וְלֹ֣א יָדָ֑ע

*wə**lō**’ yā**dā**‘*

nor has he known anything,

5c נַ֥חַת לָזֶ֖ה מִזֶּֽה׃

***na**ḥat lā**ze** mizze.*

yet the stillborn child has more rest than the unsated person.

6a וְאִלּ֣וּ חָיָ֗ה אֶ֤לֶף שָׁנִים֙ פַּעֲמַ֔יִם

*wə’il**lû** ḥā**yâ** ’**e**lef šā**nîm** pa‘ă**ma**yim*

And even if he lived a thousand years—twice!—

6b וְטוֹבָ֖ה לֹ֣א רָאָ֑ה

*wəṭô**vâ** **lō**’ rā’**â***

but didn't experience good,

6c הֲלֹ֛א אֶל־מָק֥וֹם אֶחָ֖ד הַכֹּ֥ל הוֹלֵֽךְ׃

*hă**lō**’ ’el-mā**qôm** ’e**ḥād** hak**kōl** hô**lēk̲**.*

are not all going to one place?

1a	יֵשׁ רָעָה אֲשֶׁר רָאִיתִי תַּחַת הַשָּׁמֶשׁ

Here's an evil that I've observed under the sun,

יֵשׁ יֵשׁ	there is/are *yēš*	---	particle
רָעָה רָעָה	evil/wicked (thing) *rā·ʿâ*	ABS	noun
אֲשֶׁר אֲשֶׁר	that/which *ʾă·šer*	---	relative pron
רָאִיתִי ראה	I have seen/observed *rā·ʾî·tî*	QAL PF 1CS	verb
תַּחַת תַּחַת	under *ta·ḥat*	---	prep
הַשָּׁמֶשׁ שֶׁמֶשׁ	the sun *haš·šā·meš*	ABS W/ DEF. ART.	noun

1b	וְרַבָּה הִיא עַל־הָאָדָם׃

and it is significant upon humanity:

וְרַבָּה רַב	and much/great *wə·rab·bâ*	FS PRED W/ CONJ וְ	adj
הִיא הִיא	it *hîʾ*	---	personal pron
עַל־ עַל	on/upon *ʿal-*	---	prep
הָאָדָם׃ אָדָם	the man/human/humanity *hā·ʾā·dām*	ABS W/ DEF. ART.	noun

Note that as previously, Qoheleth again relies on his personal experience—what he has seen or observed himself—of life "under the sun," which again is his way of speaking of the life we experience on earth. We will find out in the next verse what bothers him so, but here he impresses upon his readers that this "evil" or "wicked thing" (רָעָה) is significant (רַבָּה), or as some translators have it, "heavy" upon humanity (e.g., ESV). Note also that, as is his custom, Qoheleth uses the masculine הָאָדָם, literally "the man," to refer to all of humanity.

2a	אִ֣ישׁ אֲשֶׁ֣ר יִתֶּן־ל֣וֹ הָאֱלֹהִ֡ים		
	God gives a person		
אִ֣ישׁ אִישׁ	man/person *ʾîš*	ABS	noun
אֲשֶׁ֣ר אֲשֶׁר	whom *ʾă·šer*	---	relative pron
יִתֶּן־ נתן	(he) gives *yit·ten-*	QAL IMPF 3MS	verb
ל֣וֹ לְ	to him *lô*	--- W/ 3MS SX	prep
הָאֱלֹהִ֡ים אֱלֹהִים	the God *hā·ʾĕ·lō·hîm*	ABS W/ DEF. ART.	noun

2b	עֹשֶׁר֩ וּנְכָסִ֨ים וְכָב֜וֹד		
	wealth, riches, and honor,		
עֹשֶׁר֩ עֹשֶׁר	wealth/riches *ʿō·šer*	ABS	noun
וּנְכָסִ֨ים נֶכֶס	and riches/wealth *û·nə·kā·sîm*	ABS W/ CONJ וְ	noun
וְכָב֜וֹד כָּבוֹד	and honor/respect *wə·kā·vôd*	ABS W/ CONJ וְ	noun

The repetition of "riches" and "wealth" connects this passage to 5:18–19, inviting readers to compare this "evil" situation with the "good" situation Qoheleth describes in the previous passage. They are polar opposites of each other, with the main difference being a person's ability to enjoy what God has given.

2c	וְֽאֵינֶ֨נּוּ חָסֵ֥ר לְנַפְשׁ֣וֹ ׀		
	and his appetite lacks nothing		
וְֽאֵינֶ֨נּוּ אַיִן	and there is not to him *wə·ʾê·nen·nû*	--- W/ CONJ וְ + 3MS SX	particle

חָסֵר חָסֵר	lacking/missing *ḥā·sēr*	MS PRED	adj
לְנַפְשׁוֹ ׀ נֶפֶשׁ	to/for his appetite/soul *lə·naf·šô*	CST W/ PREP לְ + 3MS SX	noun

נֶפֶשׁ can be translated as "soul" or "self," such that Qoheleth refers to a person who "lacks nothing his soul/self desires." However, the word also refers to one's "appetite," which seems to be appropriate in this context, where Qoheleth invites readers to consider a person who has access to all good things God gives, yet he lacks the ability to enjoy, or "eat" (6:2e), those things. That is, his "appetite" is not sated (see below).

2d מִכֹּל אֲשֶׁר־יִתְאַוֶּה

of all that he could crave.

מִכֹּל כֹּל	from all *mik·kōl*	ABS W/ PREP מִן	noun
אֲשֶׁר־ אֲשֶׁר	that *ʾă·šer-*	---	relative pron
יִתְאַוֶּה אוה	he will desire/crave *yit·ʾaw·we*	HITH IMPF 3MS	verb

2e וְלֹא־יַשְׁלִיטֶנּוּ הָאֱלֹהִים לֶאֱכֹל מִמֶּנּוּ

Yet God does not enable him to eat from it,

וְלֹא־ לֹא	and no/not *wə·lō-*	--- W/ CONJ וְ	particle
יַשְׁלִיטֶנּוּ שׁלט	(he) enables/empowers him *yaš·lî·ṭen·nû*	HIPH IMPF 3MS W/ 3MS SX	verb
הָאֱלֹהִים אֱלֹהִים	the God *hā·ʾĕ·lō·hîm*	ABS W/ DEF. ART.	noun
לֶאֱכֹל אכל	to eat *le·ʾĕ·kōl*	QAL INF CST W/ PREP לְ	verb
מִמֶּנּוּ מִן	from it *mim·men·nû*	--- W/ 3MS SX	prep

Again Qoheleth piles up terms used in 5:17–19, causing readers to reflect on the difference between the person in that passage and the person here.

2f	כִּי אִישׁ נָכְרִי יֹאכְלֶנּוּ

for a foreigner will eat it.

כִּי כִּי	for/because *kî*	---	conj
אִישׁ אִישׁ	man *ʾîš*	ABS	noun
נָכְרִי נָכְרִי	stranger/foreigner *nok·rî*	MS ATTR	adj
יֹאכְלֶנּוּ אכל	(he) will eat/consume it *yō'·kă·len·nû*	QAL IMPF 3MS W/ 3MS SX	verb

The "foreigner" (אִישׁ נָכְרִי) or "stranger" in the Hebrew Bible "denotes either an undefined someone else, a member of another family or a member of another nation or community" (Schoors 2013:462). Whatever exact referent Qoheleth has in mind, it is clear that the person who enjoys the "wealth, riches, and honor" is a complete stranger, thus piling onto the "evil" of a person's inability to enjoy. Note that Qoheleth does not here connect the inability to enjoy to a person's moral disposition, as in Eccl 2:26. The issue is not whether a person is wicked or righteous but simply whether God chooses to enable one to enjoy the riches, wealth, and honor he bestows as he sees fit.

2g	זֶה הֶבֶל וָחֳלִי רָע הוּא׃

This is Abelish; it's a sick evil.

זֶה זֶה	this *ze*	---	demonstr pron
הֶבֶל הֶבֶל	Abel/mist/vapor/breath *he·vel*	ABS	noun
וָחֳלִי חֳלִי	sickness/affliction *wo·ḥŏ·lî*	ABS W/ CONJ וְ	noun
רָע רַע	evil/wicked *rāʿ*	MS ATTR	adj

הוּא׃ הוא	it *hûʾ*	---	personal pron

Just as Abel was unable to enjoy the fruit of his labor because his brother murdered him, so this situation is a "sick evil" (וְחֳלִי רָע) that simply should not be.

3a אִם־יוֹלִיד אִישׁ מֵאָה

If a man fathers a hundred children

אִם־ אִם	if *ʾim-*	---	conj
יוֹלִיד ילד	(he) begets/fathers *yô·lîd*	HIPH IMPF 3MS	verb
אִישׁ אִישׁ	man *ʾîš*	ABS	noun
מֵאָה מֵאָה	hundred *mē·ʾâ*	ABS	cardinal number

Though Qoheleth typically refers to humans in a general sense (i.e., "person, human, humanity"), here the verbal form (Hiphil) of "fathers" indicates he has in mind specifically a man. "A hundred" (מֵאָה) is of course hyperbolic and causes readers to imagine a man blessed beyond measure, for progeny represents Yahweh's blessing (e.g., Gen 17:2; Ps 127:3–5). Abel had no such blessing.

3b וְשָׁנִים רַבּוֹת יִחְיֶה

and lives a great many years,

וְשָׁנִים שָׁנָה	and years *wə·šā·nîm*	ABS W/ CONJ וְ	noun
רַבּוֹת רַב	many/much/numerous *rab·bôt*	FP ATTR	adj
יִחְיֶה חיה	(he) lives *yiḥ·ye*	QAL IMPF 3MS	verb

As with progeny, long life represents Yahweh's blessing (e.g., Prov 16:31).

3c	וְרַ֣ב ׀ שֶׁיִּהְי֣וּ יְמֵֽי־שָׁנָ֗יו

and the days of his years are many,

וְרַ֣ב ׀ רַב	and many *wə·rav*	MS PRED W/ CONJ וְ	adj
שֶׁיִּהְי֣וּ היה	that/which will be *šey·yih·yû*	QAL IMPF 3MP W/ RELATIVE PRON שֶׁ	verb
יְמֵֽי־ יוֹם	days of *yə·mê-*	CST	noun
שָׁנָ֗יו שָׁנָה	his years *šā·nāyw*	CST W/ 3MS SX	noun

3d	וְנַפְשׁוֹ֙ לֹא־תִשְׂבַּ֣ע מִן־הַטּוֹבָ֔ה

but his appetite is not sated from the good,

וְנַפְשׁוֹ֙ נֶ֫פֶשׁ	but/and his appetite/soul *wə·naf·šô*	CST W/ CONJ וְ + 3MS SX	noun
לֹא־ לֹא	not *lō᾽-*	---	particle
תִשְׂבַּ֣ע שׂבע	(it) is sated/satisfied *tiś·baʿ*	QAL IMPF 3FS	verb
מִן־ מִן	from *min*	---	prep
הַטּוֹבָ֔ה טוֹבָה	the good (thing) *haṭ·ṭô·vâ*	ABS W/ DEF. ART.	noun

Though speaking in terms of one's "appetite" being "sated," Qoheleth is not limiting his discussion to literal food and drink alone, yet we should not exclude those, for we know from other contexts in Ecclesiastes that God's gifts are food, wine, work, and relationships.

3e	וְגַם־קְבוּרָ֖ה לֹא־הָ֣יְתָה לּ֑וֹ

and he doesn't even receive a proper burial—

וְגַם־ גַּם	and also/even *wə·gam-*	--- W/ CONJ וְ	adv

קְבוּרָה קְבוּרָה	burial *qə·vû·**râ***	ABS	noun
לֹא־ לֹא	not *lō'-*	---	particle
הָיְתָה היה	(it) was ***hā**·yə·tâ*	QAL PF 3FS	verb
לּוֹ לְ	to him ***lô***	--- W/ 3MS SX	prep

The inability to enjoy "the good" (הַטּוֹבָה) extends even to his death.

3f אָמַרְתִּי טוֹב מִמֶּנּוּ הַנָּפֶל׃

I say that a stillborn child is better than him.

אָמַרְתִּי אמר	I said *'ā·**mar**·tî*	QAL PF 1CS	verb
טוֹב טוֹב	good ***ṭôv***	MS PRED	adj
מִמֶּנּוּ מִן	from him *mim·**men**·nû*	--- W/ 3MS SX	prep
הַנָּפֶל׃ נֵפֶל	miscarriage/stillborn child *han·**nā**·fel*	ABS W/ DEF. ART.	noun

Qoheleth's intent—which he accomplishes—is to shock his readers. With over-the-top, hyperbolic language he drives home his point that enjoyment of God's gifts is of utmost importance, and the inability to enjoy what God gives is indeed a "sick evil." Readers will remember this theme from 4:2–4.

4a כִּי־בַהֶבֶל בָּא

For a stillborn child enters into Abelness,

כִּי־ כִּי	for/although/because *kî-*	---	conj

בַּהֶבֶל הֶבֶל	in the Abel/mist/ vapor/breath *va·**he**·vel*	ABS W/ PREP בְּ + DEF. ART.	noun
בָּא בוא	coming/entering ***bā'***	QAL PF 3MS	verb

4b וּבַחֹשֶׁךְ יֵלֵךְ

and into the darkness he walks,

וּבַחֹשֶׁךְ חֹשֶׁךְ	and in/into/with the darkness *û·va·**ḥō**·šek̠*	ABS W/ CONJ וְ + PREP בְּ + DEF. ART.	noun
יֵלֵךְ הלך	he walks/goes *yē·**lēk̠***	QAL IMPF 3MS	verb

4c וּבַחֹשֶׁךְ שְׁמוֹ יְכֻסֶּה׃

and in the darkness his name is covered.

וּבַחֹשֶׁךְ חֹשֶׁךְ	and in the darkness *û·va·**ḥō**·šek̠*	ABS W/ CONJ וְ + PREP בְּ + DEF. ART.	noun
שְׁמוֹ שֵׁם	his name *šə·**mô***	CST W/ 3MS SX	noun
יְכֻסֶּה׃ כסה	(it) was covered/clothed *yə·k̠us·**se***	PUAL IMPF 3MS	verb

The author piles up phrases to emphasize that premature death—death in the womb, even—is preferable to living devoid of God's enablement to enjoy his gifts. Darkness is a common biblical metaphor with a range of referents, including sin, the inability to perceive spiritual things, and, as here, death.

5a גַּם־שֶׁ֫מֶשׁ לֹא־רָאָה

He hasn't even seen the sun,

גַּם־	also/even	---	adv
גַּם	*gam-*		
שֶׁ֫מֶשׁ	sun	ABS	noun
שֶׁ֫מֶשׁ	***še***·*meš*		
לֹא־	not	---	particle
לֹא	*lō'-*		
רָאָה	he saw/has seen	QAL PF 3MS	verb
ראה	*rā*·***'â***		

Seeing the sun is a metaphorical way of speaking of experiencing life. Qoheleth uses the same metaphor in 11:7 to extol the value of enjoying life. There, as in 6:4, he again uses the metaphor of darkness, warning his readers to "remember the days of darkness, for they will be many."

5b וְלֹא יָדָע

nor has he known anything,

וְלֹא	and not	---	particle
לֹא	*wə*·***lō'***	W/ CONJ וְ	
יָדָע	he knew/has known	QAL PF 3MS	verb
ידע	*yā*·***dā'***		

5c נַחַת לָזֶה מִזֶּה׃

yet the stillborn child has more rest than the unsated person.

נַחַת	rest	ABS	noun
נַ֫חַת	***na***·*ḥat*		
לָזֶה	to this (one)	---	demonstr
זֶה	*lā*·***ze***	W/ PREP לְ	pron
מִזֶּה׃	from this (one)	---	demonstr
זֶה	*miz*·***ze***	W/ PREP מִן	pron

The translation here makes explicit the two people (the stillborn child and the unsated person) that the Hebrew represents with the pronoun "this" (לָזֶה מִזֶּה, lit., "to this from this"). Above, Qoheleth emphasized the importance of enjoyment from wealth—rather than its accumulation—and here he draws out another implication of enjoyment: namely, rest. As we have seen several times above, work and wealth are both gifts from God, but a flourishing human life prioritizes rest. All the money in the world amounts to nothing for the person who, like the Rolling Stones, "can't get no satisfaction."

6a וְאִלּוּ חָיָה אֶלֶף שָׁנִים פַּעֲמַיִם

And even if he lived a thousand years—twice!—

Hebrew	Gloss	Parsing	Part of speech
וְאִלּוּ אִלּוּ	and even if/even *wə·ʾil·lû*	--- W/ CONJ וְ	conj
חָיָה חיה	he lived *ḥā·yâ*	QAL PF 3MS	verb
אֶלֶף אֶלֶף	thousand *ʾe·lef*	ABS	cardinal number
שָׁנִים שָׁנָה	years *šā·nîm*	ABS	noun
פַּעֲמַיִם פַּעַם	two times/twice *pa·ʿă·ma·yim*	ABS	noun

The conjunction אִלּוּ is rare in the Hebrew Bible, appearing only here and in Esth 7:4. The term is used widely in later Hebrew, however, and its meaning is not in question (Schoors 2013:473). Qoheleth is using "thousand" (אֶלֶף) hyperbolically to represent a large number. He uses the word one other time, in 7:28, in the same way.

6b וְטוֹבָה לֹא רָאָה

but didn't experience good,

Hebrew	Gloss	Parsing	Part of speech
וְטוֹבָה טוֹבָה	but good *wə·ṭô·vâ*	ABS W/ CONJ וְ	noun
לֹא לֹא	not *lōʾ*	---	particle

רָאָה ראה	(he) saw/experienced *rā·ʾâ*	QAL PF 3MS	verb

As with uses of רָאָה ("experience") throughout this section, though the term literally means "to see," it indicates what a person experiences in life. And as above, the "good" Qoheleth has in mind is the satisfaction or satiation from the gifts God gives.

6c הֲלֹא אֶל־מָקוֹם אֶחָד הַכֹּל הוֹלֵךְ׃

are not all going to one place?

הֲלֹא לֹא	do/does/is/are not? *hă·lōʾ*	--- W/ INTERR הֲ	particle
אֶל־ אֶל	to/toward *ʾel-*	---	prep
מָקוֹם מָקוֹם	place *mā·qôm*	ABS	noun
אֶחָד אֶחָד	one/same *ʾe·ḥād*	ABS	cardinal number
הַכֹּל כֹּל	the all/whole *hak·kōl*	ABS W/ DEF. ART.	noun
הוֹלֵךְ׃ הלך	walking/going *hō·lek̲*	QAL PTCP MS	verb

The "one place" to which everything goes is, of course, death. We have seen this phrasing already in 3:20, where Qoheleth states that "all go to one place" (הַכֹּל הוֹלֵךְ אֶל־מָקוֹם אֶחָד), rather than asking a question as he does here. In 3:18–21 he argues that humans and beasts share the same fate—both ultimately die. That, he said, was Abelish (הָבֶל), and just as the shared fate of humans and beasts caused him great consternation, so does the possibility that a person may live without enjoying the good God gives.

7a כָּל־עֲמַל הָאָדָם לְפִיהוּ
*kol-ʿă**mal** hāʾā**dām** ləfîhû*

All of humanity's toil is for their mouth,

7b וְגַם־הַנֶּפֶשׁ לֹא תִמָּלֵא׃
*wəgam-han**ne**feš **lōʾ** timmā**lēʾ**.*

but the appetite will not be filled.

8a כִּי מַה־יּוֹתֵר לֶחָכָם מִן־הַכְּסִיל
kî** mah-yô**tēr** leḥā**ḵām** min-hakkə**sîl

So what advantage does the wise have over the fool?

8b מַה־לֶּעָנִי יוֹדֵעַ לַהֲלֹךְ נֶגֶד הַחַיִּים׃
*mah-leʿā**nî** yô**dē**aʿ lahă**lōḵ** **ne**ged haḥay**yîm**.*

What advantage does the poor get
from knowing how to walk among the living?

9a טוֹב מַרְאֵה עֵינַיִם מֵהֲלָךְ־נָפֶשׁ
***ṭôv** mar**ʾē** ʿê**na**yim **mē**hălo**ḵ**-**nā**feš*

Sight of the eyes is better than a wandering appetite.

9b גַּם־זֶה הֶבֶל וּרְעוּת רוּחַ׃
*gam-**ze** **he**vel ûrəʿ**ût** **rû**aḥ.*

This also is Abel and striving after wind.

7a	כָּל־עֲמַל הָאָדָם לְפִיהוּ		
	All of humanity's toil is for their mouth,		
כָּל־ כֹּל	each/every/all of *kol-*	CST	noun
עֲמַל עָמָל	toil/labor of *ʿă·**mal***	CST	noun
הָאָדָם אָדָם	the man/human/humanity *hā·ʾā·**dām***	ABS W/ DEF. ART.	noun
לְפִיהוּ פֶּה	to/for his mouth *lə·**fî**·hû*	CST W/ PREP לְ + 3MS SX	noun

The purpose of all labor, Qoheleth states, is to fill one's mouth—that is, so that a person can eat. Put in more modern terms, we work so that we can live. Of course, Qoheleth argues throughout that such a view of toil is misguided, for joy in the work itself is a gift from God, as is experiencing joy in the things he gives to sate us (food, wine, and companionship).

7b	וְגַם־הַנֶּפֶשׁ לֹא תִמָּלֵא׃		
	but the appetite will not be filled.		
וְגַם־ גַּם	and/but also/even *wə·gam-*	--- W/ CONJ וְ	adv
הַנֶּפֶשׁ נֶפֶשׁ	the soul/appetite *han·**ne**·feš*	ABS W/ DEF. ART.	noun
לֹא לֹא	not *lōʾ*	---	particle
תִמָּלֵא׃ מלא	(it) will be filled *tim·mā·**lēʾ***	NIPH IMPF 3FS	verb

Similar language was used in the book's opening poem to illustrate the cyclic nature of the world. There, Qoheleth observed that "the sea is never full" (1:7), despite the rivers constantly running to it, and the "ear is never full of hearing" (1:8). Like the sea and the ear, one's appetite is a gaping maw that swallows everything it can reach.

8a	כִּ֣י מַה־יּוֹתֵ֥ר לֶחָכָ֖ם מִֽן־הַכְּסִ֑יל

So what advantage does the wise have over the fool?

כִּ֣י כִּי	for/thus/so *kî*	---	conj
מַה־ מָה	what? *mah-*	---	interr pron
יּוֹתֵ֥ר יוֹתֵר	advantage/profit *yô·tēr*	ABS	noun
לֶחָכָ֖ם חָכָם	to/for wise *le·ḥā·kām*	MS SUBST W/ PREP לְ + DEF. ART.	adj
מִֽן־ מִן	from *min-*	---	prep
הַכְּסִ֑יל כְּסִיל	the fool *hak·kə·sîl*	ABS W/ DEF. ART.	noun

The wise and the fool are contrasted throughout the book of Proverbs. The wise person fears the Lord, whereas the fool turns away from Yahweh. Since both end up dead, as Qoheleth lamented in ch. 3, he asks what "advantage" or "profit" exists for the wise. (Remember that Qoheleth is concerned throughout the book with the "profit" in work.) He withholds an answer here, but in 8:12 he states that "I know that it will be good for the ones who fear God."

8b	מַה־לֶּעָנִ֣י יוֹדֵ֔עַ לַהֲלֹ֖ךְ נֶ֥גֶד הַחַיִּֽים׃

What advantage does the poor get
from knowing how to walk among the living?

מַה־ מָה	what *mah-*	---	interr pron
לֶּעָנִ֣י עָנִי	to/for the poor/humble/ afflicted *le·ʿā·nî*	MS SUBST W/ PREP לְ + DEF. ART.	adj
יוֹדֵ֔עַ ידע	knows *yô·dē·aʿ*	QAL PTCP MS	verb
לַהֲלֹ֖ךְ הלך	to walk/go *la·hă·lōḵ*	QAL INF CST W/ PREP לְ	verb

נֶ֫גֶד נֶ֫גֶד	before/in front of/opposite *ne·ged*	---	prep
הַחַיִּֽים׃ חַי	the living/life *ha·ḥay·yîm*	MP SUBST W/ DEF. ART.	adj

This entire second clause of v. 8 is difficult to translate and has resulted in multiple interpretations among commentators. The term "poor" (עָנִי) could also mean "humble" or "afflicted"; the term "the living" (הַחַיִּים) could also mean "life"; and נֶגֶד ("among") could mean "before, in front of" or "against, opposite." Scholars disagree on how to understand each of these terms. Further, a literal translation makes little sense: "What for the poor, knowing to walk before the living?" Following Longman, the translation here assumes "advantage" from the previous clause (see Longman 1998:173; see also the discussion in Seow 1997:214 and Schoors 2013:477–80). Despite the lack of clarity, the context indicates that Qoheleth is making a comparison between the wealthy person discussed throughout the passage and an economically poor person (rather than "humble" or "afflicted").

9a טֹ֛וב מַרְאֵ֥ה עֵינַ֖יִם מֵֽהֲלָךְ־נָ֑פֶשׁ

Sight of the eyes is better than a wandering appetite.

טֹ֛וב טוֹב	good *ṭôv*	MS PRED	adj
מַרְאֵ֥ה מַרְאֶה	from sight/appearance of *mar·ʾē*	CST	noun
עֵינַ֖יִם עַ֫יִן	eyes *ʿê·na·yim*	ABS	noun
מֵֽהֲלָךְ־ הלך	from walking/going *mē·hă·lok-*	QAL INF CST W/ PREP מִן	verb
נָ֑פֶשׁ נֶ֫פֶשׁ	soul/appetite *nā·feš*	ABS	noun

This sentence is a better-than proverb, common in Israelite wisdom literature, in which one thing is declared better than another. Here, the idea is that what one can see or experience is better than that which is never satisfied—namely, one's appetite—as Qoheleth has already explored in this passage.

9b	גַּם־זֶה הֶבֶל וּרְעוּת רוּחַ׃

This also is Abel and striving after wind.

גַּם־ / גַּם	also/even / *gam-*	---	adv
זֶה / זֶה	this / ***ze***	---	demonstr pron
הֶבֶל / הֶ֫בֶל	Abel/mist/vapor/breath / ***he***·*vel*	ABS	noun
וּרְעוּת / רְעוּת	and chasing/striving after / *û*·*rə*·***ʿût***	CST W/ CONJ וְ	noun
רוּחַ׃ / רוּחַ	wind / ***rû***·*aḥ*	ABS	noun

Qoheleth concludes this section with his programmatic statement of "life under the sun." This statement could refer to the immediate context (i.e., 6:9a), but it more likely refers to the entire situation that this passage describes: the wealthy person who is unable to enjoy the gifts of God. Abel, because of his untimely death at the hands of Cain, was unable to enjoy God's gifts and represents the premier Old Testament example of the world turned upside down. So the inability to enjoy what God has given is another example of the Abelness experienced by many in this life under the sun.

From Text to Sermon

God's Sovereignty and a Sick Evil. Throughout Ecclesiastes thus far we have heard the author's clarion call to enjoy the gifts of God. He's stated repeatedly that enjoying God's gifts of food, work, wine, and a spouse is what really and truly matters in life. They are a balm to ease the pain of living in a world marked by Abelness—by injustice and death and the lack of congruence between actions and rewards. Here Qoheleth invites us into a thought experiment that asks us to consider the wealthy person who lacks nothing at all. Imagine that such a person has meaningful work, children, a long life, all the best food and wine, and yet God does not enable him to enjoy these things. There is no indication that God's withholding joy results from this person's moral disposition. We have no reason to believe he is a rank sinner bent on evil all of his days. We simply know that God, in his mysterious sovereignty, has withheld the satisfaction that comes from enjoying his gifts. This is a tragedy, Qoheleth tells us, "a sick evil," and in fact the stillborn child has a preferable fate.

This thought experiment doesn't make for a very encouraging sermon, does it? Yet it does highlight a few key themes in Ecclesiastes that speak to modern readers. First, Qoheleth acknowledges God's sovereignty. God gives the person in our thought experiment all of the good things they have. Especially in American culture, we like to think that we make our way with our own sweat and tears, that the key to success is a strong work ethic and refusal to accept help from the people around us. This passage—and Ecclesiastes as a whole—confronts our modern idolatry of thinking that we have earned everything we have, that all good gifts come from our own hands.

Second, Qoheleth wrestles honestly with the reality of life. I would venture to guess that everyone knows someone like the person in our thought experiment. At the very least, we're likely familiar with F. Scott Fitzgerald's Jay Gatsby, the titular character of *The Great Gatsby*. Sometimes a person has everything and still God does not give him the gift of enjoying those things. This lack of enjoyment coalesces with the previous point, for it forces us to recognize that not only are the gifts themselves from God, but even (especially?) the ability to enjoy those gifts comes from God. Sometimes God withholds such joy; sometimes he doesn't. Sometimes the inability to enjoy stems from our own sin; sometimes it doesn't. The ways of God are mysterious, and Qoheleth gives his readers the gifts of modeling how to wrestle with such mystery—namely, by honestly acknowledging it for what it is: "a sick evil," "a striving after wind," "Abel." Though Qoheleth's sharp language and rhetoric may make us uncomfortable, in the darkest night we all crave the freedom to be honest with God and one another.

Thus, while this passage is certainly difficult to preach, it also a gift to the modern church. It confronts the idolatry that elevates our own will and determination above the Creator of the universe, and it gives us language to wrestle with the mysteries of God and our own finiteness in his presence. Qoheleth refuses easy answers, but he does unshackle us from the worship of self and gives voice to the often unspeakable tragedy of life under the sun.

PROVERBIAL REFLECTIONS

This next section is a series of proverbs, or short, pithy sayings that encapsulate a broader truth. The sayings may seem more at home in the book of Proverbs, but they also fit with the larger program of Ecclesiastes, which aims to explore how best to navigate this upside-down, fallen world in which we live. The topics addressed here range from bribery to death to anger, but all are connected by the theme of how best to get along "under the sun." As in the book of Proverbs, interpreting these individual sayings requires that readers sit with them, rolling them around in their minds (that is, meditating on them), and trying to understand how best to apply the advice to various situations in life. As with all proverbial literature, the proverbs here are not applicable across the board—wisdom is in knowing *when* to apply *which* proverb.

7:1–14

1a טֹ֥וב שֵׁ֖ם מִשֶּׁ֣מֶן טֹ֑וב

ṭôv šēm miššemen ṭôv

A good reputation is better than fine oil,

1b וְי֣וֹם הַמָּ֔וֶת מִיּ֖וֹם הִוָּלְדֽוֹ׃

wəyôm hammāwet miyyôm hiwwālədô.

and the day of death is better than the day of his birth.

2a טוֹב֩ לָלֶ֨כֶת אֶל־בֵּֽית־אֵ֜בֶל

ṭôv lāleḵet ʾel-bêt-ʾēvel

It's better to go to a house of mourning

2b מִלֶּ֙כֶת֙ אֶל־בֵּ֣ית מִשְׁתֶּ֔ה

milleḵet ʾel-bêt mište

than to go to a house of feasting

2c בַּאֲשֶׁ֕ר ה֖וּא ס֣וֹף כָּל־הָאָדָ֑ם

baʾăšer hûʾ sôf kol-hāʾādām

because that is the end of all humans.

2d וְהַחַ֖י יִתֵּ֥ן אֶל־לִבּֽוֹ׃

wəhaḥay yittēn ʾel-libbô.

May the living take it to heart.

3a ט֥וֹב כַּ֖עַס מִשְּׂחֹ֑ק

ṭôv kaʿas miśśəḥōq

Sorrow is better than laughter,

3b כִּֽי־בְרֹ֥עַ פָּנִ֖ים יִ֥יטַב לֵֽב׃

kî vərōaʿ pānîm yîṭav lēv.

for by a scowl, the heart becomes well.

4a לֵ֤ב חֲכָמִים֙ בְּבֵ֣ית אֵ֔בֶל

lēv ḥăḵāmîm bəvêt ʾēvel

The heart of the wise is in the house of mourning,

4b וְלֵ֥ב כְּסִילִ֖ים בְּבֵ֥ית שִׂמְחָֽה׃

wəlēv kəsîlîm bəvêt śimḥâ.

but the heart of fools is in the house of joy.

5a ט֕וֹב לִשְׁמֹ֖עַ גַּעֲרַ֣ת חָכָ֑ם

ṭôv lišmōaʿ gaʿărat ḥāḵām

It is better to listen to the rebuke of the wise

5b מֵאִ֕ישׁ שֹׁמֵ֖עַ שִׁ֥יר כְּסִילִֽים׃

mēʾîš šōmēaʿ šîr kəsîlîm.

than to be a man who listens to the song of fools.

6a כִּ֣י כְק֤וֹל הַסִּירִים֙ תַּ֣חַת הַסִּ֔יר

kî ḵəqôl hassîrîm taḥat hassîr

For like the sound of thorns beneath a pot—

6b כֵּ֖ן שְׂחֹ֣ק הַכְּסִ֑יל

kēn śəḥōq hakkəsîl

thus is the fool's laughter.

6c וְגַם־זֶ֖ה הָֽבֶל׃

wəgam-ze hāvel.

And this is also Abelish.

7a כִּ֥י הָעֹ֖שֶׁק יְהוֹלֵ֣ל חָכָ֑ם

kî hāʿōšeq yəhôlēl ḥāḵām

Surely extortion makes a fool of the wise,

7b וִֽיאַבֵּ֥ד אֶת־לֵ֖ב מַתָּנָֽה׃

wîʾabbēd ʾet-lēv mattānâ.

and a bribe destroys the heart.

8a טוֹב אַחֲרִית דָּבָר מֵֽרֵאשִׁיתוֹ

ṭôv ʾaḥărît dāvār mērēʾšîtô

The end of a matter is better than its beginning.

8b טוֹב אֶֽרֶךְ־רוּחַ מִגְּבַהּ־רֽוּחַ׃

*ṭôv ʾereḵ-**rûaḥ** miggəvah-**rûaḥ**.*

A patient spirit is better than a proud spirit.

9a אַל־תְּבַהֵל בְּרֽוּחֲךָ לִכְעוֹס

*ʾal-təva**hēl** bərûḥăḵā likʿôs*

Don’t rush in your spirit to be angry,

9b כִּי כַעַס בְּחֵיק כְּסִילִים יָנֽוּחַ׃

kî ḵaʿas bəḥêq kəsîlîm yānûaḥ.

for anger reposes in the bosom of fools.

10a אַל־תֹּאמַר

*ʾal-tōʾ**mar***

Do not say,

10b מֶה הָיָה שֶׁהַיָּמִים הָרִאשֹׁנִים הָיוּ טוֹבִים מֵאֵלֶּה

*me hāyâ šehayyā**mîm** hāriʾšō**nîm** hāyû ṭôvîm mēʾēlle*

“What has happened, that the old days were better than these?”

10c כִּי לֹא מֵחָכְמָה שָׁאַלְתָּ עַל־זֶֽה׃

*kî lōʾ mēḥoḵ**mâ** šāʾ**al**tā ʿal-ze.*

Because you don’t ask this from wisdom.

11a טוֹבָה חָכְמָה עִם־נַחֲלָה

*ṭôvâ ḥoḵ**mâ** ʿim-naḥă**lâ***

Wisdom with an inheritance is a good thing;

11b וְיֹתֵר לְרֹאֵי הַשָּֽׁמֶשׁ׃

*wəyō**tēr** lərōʾê haššāmeš.*

it’s an advantage to those who see the sun.

12a כִּי בְּצֵל הַחָכְמָה בְּצֵל הַכָּסֶף

*__kî__ bə**ṣēl** haḥoḵ**mâ** bə**ṣēl** hak**kā**sef*

For being in the shade of wisdom is being in the shade of money,

12b וְיִתְרוֹן דַּעַת הַחָכְמָה תְּחַיֶּה בְעָלֶיהָ׃

*wəyit**rôn** **da**ʿat haḥoḵ**mâ** təḥay**ye** vəʿā**lê**hā.*

and the profit of knowledge is that wisdom preserves its owner’s life.

13a רְאֵה אֶת־מַעֲשֵׂה הָאֱלֹהִים

*rəʾ**ē** ʾet-maʿă**śē** hāʾĕlō**hîm***

Observe the work of God!

13b כִּי מִי יוּכַל לְתַקֵּן אֵת אֲשֶׁר עִוְּתוֹ׃

*__kî__ **mî** yû**ḵal** lətaq**qēn** **ʾēt** ʾă**šer** ʿiwwə**tô**.*

Indeed, who can straighten what he has bent?

14a בְּיוֹם טוֹבָה הֱיֵה בְטוֹב

*bə**yôm** ṭô**vâ** hĕ**yē** və**ṭôv***

On a good day, enjoy the good,

14b וּבְיוֹם רָעָה רְאֵה

*ûvə**yôm** rā**ʿâ** rə**ʾē***

and on a bad day—take note:

14c גַּם אֶת־זֶה לְעֻמַּת־זֶה עָשָׂה הָאֱלֹהִים

*__gam__ ʾet-**ze** ləʿummat-**ze** ʿā**śâ** hāʾĕlō**hîm***

this one alongside that one—God made both

14d עַל־דִּבְרַת שֶׁלֹּא יִמְצָא הָאָדָם אַחֲרָיו מְאוּמָה׃

*ʿal-div**rat** šel**lōʾ** yim**ṣāʾ** hāʾā**dām** ʾaḥă**rāyw** məʾ**û**mâ.*

so that humans cannot discover anything after them.

1a	טוֹב שֵׁם מִשֶּׁמֶן טוֹב

A good reputation is better than fine oil,

טוֹב טוב	good *ṭôv*	MS ATTR	adj
שֵׁם שֵׁם	name/reputation *šēm*	ABS	noun
מִשֶּׁמֶן שֶׁמֶן	from oil/ointment *miš·še·men*	ABS W/ PREP מִן	noun
טוֹב טוב	good *ṭôv*	MS ATTR	adj

This verse is often compared with Prov 22:1: "A good name is to be chosen rather than great riches, and favor is better than silver or gold" (ESV). The wordplay of this line comes across clearly in Hebrew. The first and last words are the same (טוֹב), though translated differently here ("good" and "fine"). The middle two words sound similar to one another: *shēm* and *shemen*. Fine oil was a luxurious item used in both burials and in setting a person apart for service to the Lord (e.g., the anointing of kings). Better than luxury, though, is a good reputation.

1b	וְיוֹם הַמָּוֶת מִיּוֹם הִוָּלְדוֹ׃

and the day of death is better than the day of his birth.

וְיוֹם יוֹם	and day of *wə·yôm*	CST W/ CONJ וְ	noun
הַמָּוֶת מָוֶת	the death *ham·**mā**·wet*	ABS W/ DEF. ART.	noun
מִיּוֹם יוֹם	from day of *miy·**yôm***	CST W/ PREP מִן	noun
הִוָּלְדוֹ׃ ילד	his being born *hiw·wā·lə·**dô***	NIPH INF CST W/ 3MS SX	verb

This part of the proverb trends against what we would typically expect, but it is consistent with some of Qoheleth's previous statements on death, most notably in 6:3. However, Qoheleth also bemoans death as one of the Abelish features of life under the sun. Perhaps the connection between the two lines is that one's reputation is only secured at the end of life (so Gordis 1945:256–57), or perhaps the day of death is preferable to the day of birth because many dark days await us at the beginning of life (so Schoors 2013:502; Fredericks and Estes 2010:166).

2a	טֹ֗וב לָלֶ֜כֶת אֶל־בֵּֽית־אֵ֗בֶל		
	It's better to go to a house of mourning		
טֹ֗וב טוֹב	good *ṭôv*	MS PRED	adj
לָלֶ֜כֶת הלך	to walk/go *lā·**le**·ḵet*	QAL INF CST W/ PREP לְ	verb
אֶל־ אֶל	to *ʾel-*	---	prep
בֵּֽית־ בַּ֫יִת	house of *bêt-*	CST	noun
אֵ֗בֶל אֵ֫בֶל	mourning *ʾ**ē**·vel*	ABS	noun

2b	מִלֶּ֙כֶת֙ אֶל־בֵּ֣ית מִשְׁתֶּ֔ה		
	than to go to a house of feasting		
מִלֶּ֙כֶת֙ הלך	from to go/walk *mil·**le**·ḵet*	QAL INF CST W/ PREP מִן	verb
אֶל־ אֶל	to *ʾel-*	---	prep
בֵּ֣ית בַּ֫יִת	house of *bêt*	CST	noun
מִשְׁתֶּ֔ה מִשְׁתֶּה	feasting *miš·**te***	ABS	noun

2c	בַּאֲשֶׁר הוּא סוֹף כָּל־הָאָדָם

because that is the end of all humans.

Hebrew	Gloss	Parsing	Part of speech
בַּאֲשֶׁר אֲשֶׁר	for/that/because *ba·ʾă·šer*	--- W/ PREP בְּ	relative pron
הוּא הוּא	he/it/that *hûʾ*	---	personal pron
סוֹף סוֹף	end/conclusion *sôf*	CST	noun
כָּל־ כֹּל	all of *kol-*	CST	noun
הָאָדָם אָדָם	the man/human/humanity *hā·ʾā·dām*	ABS W/ DEF. ART.	noun

2d	וְהַחַי יִתֵּן אֶל־לִבּוֹ׃

May the living take it to heart.

Hebrew	Gloss	Parsing	Part of speech
וְהַחַי חַי	and the living *wə·ha·ḥay*	MS SUBST W/ CONJ וְ + DEF. ART.	adj
יִתֵּן נתן	may (he) give/place *yit·tēn*	QAL JUSSIVE 3MS	verb
אֶל־ אֶל	to *ʾel-*	---	prep
לִבּוֹ׃ לֵב	his heart/mind *lib·bô*	CST W/ 3MS SX	noun

The last sentence in this verse explains the reasoning of the better-than proverb. Since all human life ends in death, it is much better to face it while alive than to spend one's time at a "house of feasting" (Alter 2010:367). Though death is the "end of all humans" (v. 2c), in 12:13 Qoheleth will state, at the "end of the matter" (סוֹף דָּבָר), that fearing God is the "whole of humanity" (כָּל־הָאָדָם; see the comments on 12:13 below for further discussion). Taken together, these two statements give important insight into the book's overall theology: (1) death is humanity's "end," and (2) humanity's "whole" is living in right relationship with God. Confronting the first reality stimulates us to more fully embrace the second.

3a	טֹ֣וב כַּ֖עַס מִשְּׂחֹ֑ק

Sorrow is better than laughter,

טֹ֣וב טוֹב	good *ṭôv*	MS PRED	adj
כַּ֖עַס כַּ֫עַס	anger/vexation/grief ***ka*·*ʿas***	ABS	noun
מִשְּׂחֹ֑ק שְׂחֹק	from laughter *miś·śə·**ḥōq***	ABS W/ PREP מִן	noun

The word translated "sorrow" here (כַּעַס) most often means "anger," but in at least two other places it clearly refers to grief or sorrow (Pss 6:8 [7]; 10:14). Some commentators understand laughter in this context to have a negative connotation (e.g., Ogden 2007:111; Curtis 2013:64), in the sense of foolish laughter or frivolity. Qoheleth uses "laughter" (שְׂחֹק) three other times in the book (2:2; 7:6; 10:19), once calling it "madness" (2:2), once referring explicitly to the laughter of "fools" (7:6), and once using it to describe a feast where "wine makes the living joyful" (10:19). Given the range of contexts in which the author uses "laughter" and the book's broader concern with embracing joy, there is no compelling reason to understand the term negatively here. While this statement may on the surface seem to contradict Qoheleth's admonition to live joyfully, we must take care not to totalize proverbial statements.

3b	כִּֽי־בְרֹ֥עַ פָּנִ֖ים יִ֥יטַב לֵֽב׃

for by a scowl, the heart becomes well.

כִּֽי־ כִּי	for/because ***kî***	---	conj
בְרֹ֥עַ רֹעַ	in evil/bad of *və·**rō**·aʿ*	CST W/ PREP בְּ	noun
פָּנִ֖ים פָּנֶה	face *pā·**nîm***	ABS	noun
יִ֥יטַב יטב	(it) is good/goes well/ is pleasing ***yî**·ṭav*	QAL IMPF 3MS	verb
לֵֽב׃ לֵב	heart/mind ***lēv***	ABS	noun

"Scowl" follows Alter (2010:369) in translating בְּרֹעַ פָּנִים, which is woodenly "in an evil face." The translation offered here implies that a person's inward life ("heart") is improved by rebuke, or a scowl (e.g., Prov 27:5). However, the meaning of the verse is unclear. Whybray (1989:114) takes the clause to mean that "appearances can be deceiving." Longman (1998:184) argues that it indicates the value of facing life as it really is. Similarly, Brown (2011:73–74) contends that the Qoheleth's meaning is that true joy "emerges from sorrow."

4a לֵ֤ב חֲכָמִים֙ בְּבֵ֣ית אֵ֔בֶל

The heart of the wise is in the house of mourning,

לֵ֤ב לֵב	heart/mind of *lēv*	CST	noun
חֲכָמִים֙ חָכָם	wise ones *ḥă·kā·**mîm***	MP SUBST	adj
בְּבֵ֣ית בַּ֫יִת	in a house of *bə·**vêt***	CST W/ PREP בְּ	noun
אֵ֔בֶל אֵ֫בֶל	mourning *ʾē·vel*	ABS	noun

4b וְלֵ֥ב כְּסִילִ֖ים בְּבֵ֥ית שִׂמְחָֽה׃

but the heart of fools is in the house of joy.

וְלֵ֥ב לֵב	but a heart/mind of *wə·**lēv***	CST W/ CONJ וְ	noun
כְּסִילִ֖ים כְּסִיל	fools *kə·sî·**lîm***	ABS	noun
בְּבֵ֥ית בַּ֫יִת	in a house of *bə·**vêt***	CST W/ PREP בְּ	noun
שִׂמְחָֽה׃ שִׂמְחָה	joy/happiness *śim·**ḥâ***	ABS	noun

Verse 4 repeats the sentiment expressed above in v. 2, though in this verse, rather than a better-than proverb, he compares the dwelling place of fools with the dwelling place of the wise. As mentioned regarding v. 3, we should avoid the mistake of totalizing this proverb such that it introduces a contradiction into Qoheleth's thought. By their nature, proverbs encapsulate general truths that require wisdom to apply to specific situations. Thus, we should not think that this proverb means that all the time and in all situations the wise live in a "house of sorrow" while fools live in a "house of joy."

5a טוֹב לִשְׁמֹעַ גַּעֲרַת חָכָם

It is better to listen to the rebuke of the wise

Hebrew	Gloss	Parsing	Part of speech
טוֹב טוֹב	good *ṭôv*	MS PRED	adj
לִשְׁמֹעַ שׁמע	to hear/listen/heed *liš·mō·aʿ*	QAL INF CST W/ PREP לְ	verb
גַּעֲרַת גְּעָרָה	rebuke of *ga·ʿă·rat*	CST	noun
חָכָם חָכָם	wise (one) *ḥā·ḵām*	MS SUBST	adj

5b מֵאִישׁ שֹׁמֵעַ שִׁיר כְּסִילִים׃

than to be a man who listens to the song of fools.

Hebrew	Gloss	Parsing	Part of speech
מֵאִישׁ אִישׁ	from/than a man *mē·ʾîš*	ABS W/ PREP מִן	noun
שֹׁמֵעַ שׁמע	listening (one) *šō·mē·aʿ*	QAL PTCP MS	verb
שִׁיר שִׁיר	song of *šîr*	CST	noun
כְּסִילִים׃ כְּסִיל	fools *kə·sî·lîm*	ABS	noun

This proverb is consistent with material from the book of Proverbs that extols the value of hearing rebuke (e.g., Prov 18:24; 27:5–6). Truly loving one's neighbor, as Jesus commanded, sometimes entails rebuke. Likewise, hearing correction from a friend signals that they truly love you.

6a	כִּ֤י כְקֹ֨ול הַסִּירִים֙ תַּ֣חַת הַסִּ֔יר

For like the sound of thorns beneath a pot—

Hebrew	Gloss	Form	Part of speech
כִּ֤י	for/thus/because	---	conj
כִּי	*kî*		
כְקֹ֨ול	like sound/voice of	CST	noun
קֹול	*kə·qôl*	W/ PREP כְּ	
הַסִּירִים֙	the thorns	ABS	noun
סִיר	*has·sî·rîm*	W/ DEF. ART.	
תַּ֣חַת	under/beneath	---	prep
תַּחַת	*ta·ḥat*		
הַסִּ֔יר	the pot	ABS	noun
סִיר	*has·sîr*	W/ DEF. ART.	

6b	כֵּ֖ן שְׂחֹ֣ק הַכְּסִ֑יל

thus is the fool's laughter.

Hebrew	Gloss	Form	Part of speech
כֵּ֖ן	thus/so	---	adv
כֵּן	*kēn*		
שְׂחֹ֣ק	laughter of	CST	noun
שְׂחֹק	*śə·ḥōq*		
הַכְּסִ֑יל	the fool	ABS	noun
כְּסִיל	*hak·kə·sîl*	W/ DEF. ART.	

6c	וְגַם־זֶ֖ה הָֽבֶל׃

And this is also Abelish.

Hebrew	Gloss	Form	Part of speech
וְגַם־	and also/even	---	adv
גַּם	*wə·gam-*	W/ CONJ וְ	
זֶ֖ה	this	---	demonstr pron
זֶה	*ze*		
הָֽבֶל׃	Abel/mist/vapor/breath	ABS	noun
הֶ֫בֶל	*hā·vel*		

Once ignited, thorns burst into flames. They burn bright and incredibly fast—so is the laughter of fools. It dies out as quickly as it erupts, and in this way the fool's laughter is like Abel—altogether brief, a mere breath or vapor that vanishes in the wind.

7a	כִּי הָעֹשֶׁק יְהוֹלֵל חָכָם		
	Surely extortion makes a fool of the wise,		
כִּי כִּי	thus/so/surely *kî*	---	conj
הָעֹשֶׁק עֹשֶׁק	the oppression/extortion *hā·ʿō·šeq*	ABS W/ DEF. ART.	noun
יְהוֹלֵל הלל	(it) makes foolish/a fool of *yə·hô·**lēl***	POEL IMPF 3MS	verb
חָכָם חָכָם	wise (one) *ḥā·**ḵām***	MS SUBST	adj

עֹשֶׁק ("extortion") most often refers to "oppression," but the parallelism with "bribe" in the next clause makes the meaning "extortion" more likely here (see also Lev 5:23 [6:4]; Ezek 18:18). The idea is that extortion causes a wise person to be a fool in the same way that a bribe corrupts one's heart (see v. 7b).

7b	וִיאַבֵּד אֶת־לֵב מַתָּנָה׃		
	and a bribe destroys the heart.		
וִיאַבֵּד אבד	and (it) destroyed/killed *wî·ʾab·**bēd***	PIEL IMPF 3MS W/ CONJ וְ	verb
אֶת־ אֵת	*(direct object marker)* *ʾet-*	---	particle
לֵב לֵב	heart/mind ***lēv***	ABS	noun
מַתָּנָה׃ מַתָּנָה	a gift *mat·tā·**nâ***	ABS	noun

8a טֹ֛וב אַחֲרִ֥ית דָּבָ֖ר מֵֽרֵאשִׁית֑וֹ

The end of a matter is better than its beginning.

Hebrew	Gloss	Parsing	Part of speech
טֹ֛וב טוֹב	good *ṭôv*	MS PRED	adj
אַחֲרִ֥ית אַחֲרִית	end/result of *ʾa·ḥă·rît*	CST	noun
דָּבָ֖ר דָּבָר	word/matter/thing *dā·vār*	ABS	noun
מֵֽרֵאשִׁית֑וֹ רֵאשִׁית	from/than its beginning *mē·rē'·šî·tô*	CST W/ PREP מִן + 3MS SX	noun

8b טֹ֥וב אֶֽרֶךְ־ר֖וּחַ מִגְּבַהּ־רֽוּחַ׃

A patient spirit is better than a proud spirit.

Hebrew	Gloss	Parsing	Part of speech
טֹ֥וב טוֹב	good *ṭôv*	MS PRED	adj
אֶֽרֶךְ־ אֶרֶךְ	long of *ʾe·reḵ-*	MS CST	adj
ר֖וּחַ רוּחַ	spirit *rû·aḥ*	ABS	noun
מִגְּבַהּ־ גָּבֹהַּ	from/than height of *mig·gə·vah-*	MS CST W/ PREP מִן	adj
רֽוּחַ׃ רוּחַ	spirit *rû·aḥ*	ABS	noun

Length and height are physical terms that Hebrew uses to describe one's emotional or psychological disposition. Here, "height of spirit" (מִגְּבַהּ־רוּחַ) refers to one who is proud or haughty, and "long of spirit" (אֶרֶךְ־רוּחַ) refers to one who is patient or longsuffering. In Exod 34:6, Yahweh describes himself as "long of nose," or "slow to anger."

9a	אַל־תְּבַהֵ֣ל בְּרוּחֲךָ֣ לִכְע֑וֹס

Don’t rush in your spirit to be angry,

אַל־ אַל	no/not *'al-*	---	particle
תְּבַהֵ֣ל בהל	(you) rush/hasten/be quick *tə·va·**hēl***	PIEL IMPF 2MS	verb
בְּרוּחֲךָ֣ ר֫וּחַ	in your spirit *bə·rû·ḥă·**ḵā***	CST W/ PREP בְּ + 2MS SX	noun
לִכְע֑וֹס כעס	to be angry *liḵ·**'ôs***	QAL INF CST W/ PREP לְ	verb

9b	כִּ֣י כַ֔עַס בְּחֵ֥יק כְּסִילִ֖ים יָנֽוּחַ׃

for anger reposes in the bosom of fools.

כִּ֣י כִּי	for/thus/so ***kî***	---	conj
כַ֔עַס כַּ֫עַס	anger ***ka**·'as*	ABS	noun
בְּחֵ֥יק חֵיק	in a bosom/lap of *bə·**ḥêq***	CST W/ PREP בְּ	noun
כְּסִילִ֖ים כְּסִיל	fools *kə·sî·**lîm***	ABS	noun
יָנֽוּחַ׃ נוח	(it) will rest/repose/ settle down *yā·**nû**·aḥ*	QAL IMPF 3MS	verb

The term translated “bosom” (חֵיק) refers to the “fold of garment above belt” (*DCH*, s.v. חֵיק), thus the NET translates it as “lap.” Other translations, such as the CSB and ESV, opt for “heart” because “metaphorically it also signifies the inner self of a person, the seat of passions” (Schoors 2013:519).

10a	אַל־תֹּאמַר

Do not say,

אַל־ / אַל	no/not / *'al-*	---	particle
תֹּאמַר / אמר	(you) say / *tō'·**mar***	QAL IMPF 2MS	verb

10b	מֶה הָיָה שֶׁהַיָּמִים הָרִאשֹׁנִים הָיוּ טוֹבִים מֵאֵלֶּה

"What has happened, that the old days were better than these?"

מֶה / מָה	what? / ***me***	---	interr pron
הָיָה / היה	(it) was / *hā·**yâ***	QAL PF 3MS	verb
שֶׁהַיָּמִים / יוֹם	that the days of / *še·hay·yā·**mîm***	ABS W/ RELATIVE PRON שֶׁ + DEF. ART.	noun
הָרִאשֹׁנִים / רִאשׁוֹן	the former/earlier/previous / *hā·ri'·šō·**nîm***	MP ATTR W/ DEF. ART.	adj
הָיוּ / היה	(they) were / *hā·**yû***	QAL PF 3CP	verb
טוֹבִים / טוֹב	good / *ṭô·**vîm***	MP PRED	adj
מֵאֵלֶּה / אֵלֶּה	from/than these / *mē·**'ēl**·le*	--- W/ PREP מִן	demonstr pron

10c	כִּי לֹא מֵחָכְמָה שָׁאַלְתָּ עַל־זֶה׃

Because you don't ask this from wisdom.

כִּי / כִּי	for/thus/so / ***kî***	---	conj
לֹא / לֹא	not / ***lō'***	---	particle

מֵחָכְמָה חָכְמָה	from wisdom *mē·ḥok·mâ*	ABS W/ PREP מִן	noun
שָׁאַלְתָּ שׁאל	that you asked *šā·'al·tā*	QAL PF 2MS	verb
עַל־ עַל	concerning/about *'al-*	---	prep
זֶה׃ זֶה	this *ze*	---	demonstr pron

Qoheleth drives home his previous point that a thing's end is better than its beginning by highlighting the folly of nostalgia about the "good ole days." The human inclination toward such nostalgia has remained remarkably consistent in the millennia since he first penned these words. This advice is the obverse of his concern that humans not look to the future for some "profit" or "gain" from the work. Humanity's "portion" or "reward" is life in the moment, which requires that we jettison the allure of both a "legacy" and the "way things used to be."

11a טוֹבָה חָכְמָה עִם־נַחֲלָה

Wisdom with an inheritance is a good thing;

טוֹבָה טוֹב	good (thing) *ṭô·vâ*	FS PRED	adj
חָכְמָה חָכְמָה	wisdom *ḥok·mâ*	ABS	noun
עִם־ עִם	with *'im-*	---	prep
נַחֲלָה נַחֲלָה	inheritance *na·ḥă·lâ*	ABS	noun

נַחֲלָה ("inheritance") refers most often to the patrimonial land that is passed down generationally, but it is also used to describe the tithes that support the Levites, who have no family land (Num 18:21), as well as Yahweh himself, who is the Levite's "inheritance" (Num 18:20).

11b וְיֹתֵר לְרֹאֵי הַשָּׁמֶשׁ׃

it's an advantage to those who see the sun.

Hebrew	Gloss	Parsing	Part of speech
וְיֹתֵר יוֹתֵר	and an advantage/abundance *wə·yō·**tēr***	ABS W/ CONJ וְ	noun
לְרֹאֵי ראה	to seeing (ones) of *lə·rō·ʾê*	Q (CST) PTCP MP W/ PREP לְ	verb
הַשָּׁמֶשׁ׃ שֶׁמֶשׁ	the sun *haš·**šā**·meš*	ABS W/ DEF. ART.	noun

Qoheleth appears quite fond of the words from the root יתר. We've seen before that there is no "advantage" or "gain" (יִתְרוֹן) in work; there is only a "reward" or "portion." In 3:19 he stated that "humans have no advantage [מוֹתַר] over beasts!" And in 6:8 he asks, "So what advantage [יֹּתֵר] does the wise have over the fool?" Here he argues that wisdom combined with an "inheritance" is advantageous for the living, or "those who see the sun." That is, it is better to be poor and wise than rich and foolish, but better still to possess both wisdom and wealth.

12a כִּי בְּצֵל הַחָכְמָה בְּצֵל הַכָּסֶף

For being in the shade of wisdom is being in the shade of money,

Hebrew	Gloss	Parsing	Part of speech
כִּי כִּי	for/so/because *kî*	---	conj
בְּצֵל צֵל	in shade/shadow of *bə·**ṣēl***	CST W/ PREP בְּ	noun
הַחָכְמָה חָכְמָה	wisdom *ha·ḥok·**mâ***	ABS W/ DEF. ART.	noun
בְּצֵל צֵל	in shade/shadow of *bə·**ṣēl***	CST W/ PREP בְּ	noun
הַכָּסֶף כֶּסֶף	the silver/money *hak·**kā**·sef*	ABS W/ DEF. ART.	noun

The Hebrew term translated "shade" can also mean "shadow," as in the beloved Ps 91:1: "The one who lives under the protection of the Most High dwells in the shadow [בְּצֵל] of the Almighty" (CSB). Both here and in Ps 91:1, the "shade" or "shadow" indicates protection.

12b	וְיִתְר֣וֹן דַּ֔עַת הַֽחָכְמָ֖ה תְּחַיֶּ֥ה בְעָלֶֽיהָ׃

and the profit of knowledge is that wisdom preserves its owner's life.

וְיִתְר֣וֹן יִתְרוֹן	and profit/gain/surplus/ advantage of *wə·yit·**rôn***	CST W/ CONJ וְ	noun
דַּ֔עַת דַּעַת	knowledge ***da**·'at*	ABS	noun
הַֽחָכְמָ֖ה חָכְמָה	the wisdom *ha·ḥok·**mâ***	ABS W/ DEF. ART.	noun
תְּחַיֶּ֥ה חיה	(it) keeps alive/ causes to live *tə·ḥay·**ye***	PIEL IMPF 3FS	verb
בְעָלֶֽיהָ׃ בַּעַל	its owner/master *və·'ā·**lê**·hā*	CST W/ 3FS SX	noun

13a	רְאֵ֖ה אֶת־מַעֲשֵׂ֣ה הָאֱלֹהִ֑ים

Observe the work of God!

רְאֵ֖ה ראה	(you) see/observe *rə·'**ē***	QAL IMPV MS	verb
אֶת־ אֵת	*(direct object marker)* *'et-*	---	particle
מַעֲשֵׂ֣ה מַעֲשֶׂה	work/deed of *ma·'ă·**śē***	CST	noun
הָאֱלֹהִ֑ים אֱלֹהִים	the God *hā·'ĕ·lō·**hîm***	ABS W/ DEF. ART.	noun

The verb ראה ("observe") has been translated above as "see" and "experience." Qoheleth often uses the word to describe what he has personally observed in his life "under the sun." Here he calls readers to slow down a bit and consider the work that God does. Unlike human work, God's work is effective and unassailable; what he does cannot be undone.

13b	כִּ֥י מִ֤י יוּכַל֙ לְתַקֵּ֔ן אֵ֖ת אֲשֶׁ֥ר עִוְּתֽוֹ׃

Indeed, who can straighten what he has bent?

כִּ֥י כִּי	thus/so/indeed *kî*	---	conj
מִ֤י מִי	who *mî*	---	interr pron
יוּכַל֙ יכל	(he) can/is able *yû·kal*	QAL IMPF 3MS	verb
לְתַקֵּ֔ן תקן	to straighten/make straight *lə·taq·qēn*	PIEL INF CST W/ PREP לְ	verb
אֵ֖ת אֵת	*(direct object marker)* *ʾēt*	---	particle
אֲשֶׁ֥ר אֲשֶׁר	that/which *ʾă·šer*	---	relative pron
עִוְּתֽוֹ׃ עות	he bent/made crooked *ʿiw·wə·tô*	PIEL PF 3MS W/ 3MS SX	verb

14a	בְּי֤וֹם טוֹבָה֙ הֱיֵ֣ה בְט֔וֹב

On a good day, enjoy the good,

בְּי֤וֹם יוֹם	on a day of *bə·yôm*	CST W/ PREP בְּ	noun
טוֹבָה֙ טוֹבָה	good/prosperity *ṭô·vâ*	ABS	noun
הֱיֵ֣ה היה	be *hĕ·yē*	QAL IMPV MS	verb
בְט֔וֹב טוֹב	in good *və·ṭôv*	ABS W/ PREP בְּ	noun

Due to its proverbial nature, the Hebrew here is truncated. There are only four words in this clause, and two of them are from the same root. טוֹבָה ("good"), the feminine form of טוֹב ("good"), refers often to prosperity, success, or goodness. The translation here uses "good" for both forms in the verse to highlight the similarity of the words in Hebrew.

14b	וּבְי֥וֹם רָעָ֖ה רְאֵ֑ה		
	and on a bad day—take note:		
וּבְי֥וֹם י֫וֹם	and in day of *û·və·yôm*	CST W/ CONJ וְ + PREP בְּ	noun
רָעָ֖ה רָעָה	evil/wickedness *rā·ʿâ*	ABS	noun
רְאֵ֑ה ראה	(you) see/observe *rə·ʾē*	QAL IMPV MS	verb

14c	גַּ֣ם אֶת־זֶ֤ה לְעֻמַּת־זֶה֙ עָשָׂ֣ה הָֽאֱלֹהִ֔ים		
	this one alongside that one—God made both		
גַּ֣ם גַּם	also/even *gam*	---	adv
אֶת־ אֵת	*(direct object marker)* *ʾet-*	---	particle
זֶ֤ה זֶה	this *ze*	---	demonstr pron
לְעֻמַּת־ לְעֻמַּת	alongside/next to/as well as *lə·ʿum·mat-*	---	prep
זֶה֙ זֶה	this *ze*	---	demonstr pron
עָשָׂ֣ה עשׂה	(he) made *ʿā·śâ*	QAL PF 3MS	verb
הָֽאֱלֹהִ֔ים אֱלֹהִים	the God *hā·ʾĕ·lō·hîm*	ABS W/ DEF. ART.	noun

Qoheleth's high view of God's sovereignty is on display in this verse, as he attributes to God both the good days and the bad days. Though acknowledging God's sovereignty over even the "bad" or "evil" (רָעָה) does not necessarily make the bad any less bad, it does help humans put into perspective the reality of life. In short, humans are human and God is God. Though we lack power over life, death, and the vagaries that come with both, God does not lack such power. We can and must rest in that truth.

14d	עַל־דִּבְרַ֗ת שֶׁלֹּ֨א יִמְצָ֧א הָאָדָ֛ם אַחֲרָ֖יו מְאֽוּמָה׃

so that humans cannot discover anything after them.

Hebrew	Gloss	Parsing	Part of speech
עַל־ עַל	concerning/upon *'al-*	---	prep
דִּבְרַת דִּבְרָה	cause/matter *div·**rat***	CST	noun
שֶׁלֹּא לֹא	that which no/not *šel·**lō'***	--- W/ RELATIVE PRON שֶׁ	particle
יִמְצָא מצא	(he) will find/discover *yim·**ṣā'***	QAL IMPF 3MS	verb
הָאָדָם אָדָם	the man/human/humanity *hā·'ā·**dām***	ABS W/ DEF. ART.	noun
אַחֲרָיו אַחֲרֵי	after him *'a·ḥă·**rāyw***	--- W/ 3MS SX	prep
מְאוּמָה׃ מְאוּמָה	anything/nothing *mə·**'û**·mâ*	---	indef pron

The primary interpretive issue in this clause is how to understand the phrase עַל־דִּבְרַת. The phrase could indicate result, as translated here ("so that"). In this case, the phrase relates to the work of God in creating both good days and bad days. That is, the result of God's creation of good days and bad days is that humans are unable to perceive what the future holds. Alternatively, it could indicate cause ("for, because") and thus relate to 14a–b, indicating that humans should (1) enjoy the good days and (2) consider God's creation of both *because* they cannot see into the future. In either case, this final clause strengthens Qoheleth's point that God is sovereign and humans are not. God creates each day, and we cannot even see what will come tomorrow.

From Text to Sermon

The Timing of Wisdom. Readers must take care to interpret proverbial literature correctly, as with all of Scripture. What makes proverbs particularly difficult, though, is the tendency to read them as promises or statements of what is always true all the time. However, that is not how proverbs work. Rather, proverbs apply to particular contexts in particular times, and the primary function of proverbs is to inculcate wisdom in their readers. The key to such wisdom is timing (see also Qoheleth's famous poem on this in ch. 3). Doing the wrong thing is always wrong, but doing the right thing at the wrong time is also wrong. Imagine building a home—it does no good to frame in its walls before laying its foundation. Indeed, it would be folly to do so. In the same way, wisdom means applying a proverb to the right situation at the right time. And in order to do that, we must ingest these sayings, marinate in them, allow them to roll around in our hearts and minds. They must be considered deeply, and then we must determine which situation is appropriate for which piece of wisdom. Thus, while a saying that extols sorrow above pleasure (7:4) seems to contradict Qoheleth's view that joy in God's gifts is humanity's reward, the contradiction is illusory. There is a time when it is good and right to dwell in the house of mourning, and there is also a time for enjoying God's gifts. Wisdom lies in discerning when is the right time for each.

The House of Mourning. Every time I read Eccl 7:2—"It's better to go to a house of mourning than to go to a house of feasting, because that is the end of all humans. May the living take it to heart."—I'm transported back in time to the summer my grandmother died. I remember crumpling to the floor in the hallway outside her hospital room. I remember a nurse trying to comfort me as I wept. I remember the funeral in Tinsman, Arkansas, where my grandmother grew up (current population: 54). I remember the sound of wailing bouncing around the chapel walls at Watson Cemetery. When I looked toward the sound, I was shocked to see a grown man in blue jean overalls with no shirt underneath. My mimi's cousin. They grew up together.

It seems trite to say it, but death is hard. It's hard to think about the death of those we love, and it's hard to imagine that one day we also will face that great equalizer. The anti-aging industry is a multi-billion-dollar juggernaut because it taps into the human desire *not to die*. However, Qoheleth tells us that wisdom lies not in avoiding death but rather in spending time where we feel its power most. Mourning my grandmother's death—or thinking about that experience now—does not make her death any less painful, but it does orient my heart and mind toward "the end of all humans," which naturally makes me consider what comes next. This passage therefore offers wise advice both to those who know Christ and those who do not.

Those who have experienced the forgiveness of Jesus know for certain that Christ has conquered death, that being in Christ means looking forward to resurrected bodies and life eternal in the new heavens and the new earth, and therefore we "do not grieve like the rest who have no hope" (1 Thess 4:13 NET). There is enormous hope for the Christian who spends time in the house of mourning. For those who do not yet know Christ, there is great urgency, because we know that those who die in sin are destined to eternal punishment (Matt 25:21–46)—they truly have no hope. Thus, we must also warn unbelievers all the more and urge them to repent of sin and turn to Jesus for forgiveness.

COPING WITH INJUSTICE

In this passage, Qoheleth speaks frankly about an apparent inconsistency in life that all people have likely struggled with at some point: the prosperity and success of wicked people. This situation, Qoheleth says, is like Abel, the first instance where we see the consequences of righteousness and wickedness flipped upside down. Despite what we see with our eyes, Qoheleth affirms that life ultimately will go better for those who fear God, or live in right relationship with him. In addition, he commends enjoying the gifts of God. Thus, this passage succinctly outlines the entire message of Ecclesiastes:

(1) Life under the sun is upside down—like Abel.
(2) Therefore, fear God
(3) And enjoy his gifts.

LARGER LITERARY CONTEXT › 8:10–17

8:10–13

10a וּבְכֵ֡ן רָאִיתִי֩ רְשָׁעִ֨ים קְבֻרִ֜ים

ûvəkēn rā'ītî rəšā'îm qəvurîm

And so I saw wicked people buried.

10b וָבָ֗אוּ וּמִמְּק֤וֹם קָדוֹשׁ֙ יְהַלֵּ֔כוּ

wāvā'û ûmimməqôm qādôš yəhallēkû

They spent time at the holy place,

10c וְיִֽשְׁתַּכְּח֥וּ בָעִ֖יר אֲשֶׁ֣ר כֵּן־עָשׂ֑וּ

wəyištakkəḥû vā'îr 'ăšer kēn-'āśû

and they received praise in the city because they did this.

10d גַּם־זֶ֖ה הָֽבֶל׃

gam-ze hāvel.

This is also Abelish.

11a אֲשֶׁר֙ אֵין־נַעֲשָׂ֣ה פִתְגָ֔ם מַעֲשֵׂ֥ה הָרָעָ֖ה מְהֵרָ֑ה

'ăšer 'ên-na'ăśâ fitgām ma'ăśē hārā'â məhērâ

Because the sentence for an evil deed is not carried out quickly—

11b עַל־כֵּ֡ן מָלֵ֞א לֵ֧ב בְּֽנֵי־הָאָדָ֛ם בָּהֶ֖ם לַעֲשׂ֥וֹת רָֽע׃

'al-kēn mālē' lēv bənê-hā'ādām bāhem la'ăśôt rā'.

therefore human hearts are filled within them to do evil.

12a אֲשֶׁ֣ר חֹטֶ֗א עֹשֶׂ֥ה רָ֛ע מְאַ֖ת וּמַאֲרִ֣יךְ ל֑וֹ

'ăšer ḥōṭe' 'ōśe rā' mə'at ûma'ărîk lô

For a sinner does evil a hundred times and lives a long time,

12b כִּ֚י גַּם־יוֹדֵ֣עַ אָ֔נִי

kî gam-yôdēa' 'ānî

yet I also know

12c אֲשֶׁר יִהְיֶה־טּוֹב לְיִרְאֵי הָאֱלֹהִים אֲשֶׁר יִירְאוּ מִלְּפָנָיו׃

ʾăšer yihye-ṭôv ləyirʾê hāʾĕlōhîm ʾăšer yîrəʾû milləfānāyw.

that it will be good for those who fear God, who fear in his presence.

13a וְטוֹב לֹא־יִהְיֶה לָרָשָׁע

wəṭôv lōʾ-yihye lārāšāʿ

And it will not be good for the evil person,

13b וְלֹא־יַאֲרִיךְ יָמִים כַּצֵּל

wəlōʾ-yaʾărîḵ yāmîm kaṣṣēl

and he will not lengthen his days like a shadow

13c אֲשֶׁר אֵינֶנּוּ יָרֵא מִלִּפְנֵי אֱלֹהִים׃

ʾăšer ʾênennû yārēʾ millifnê ʾĕlōhîm.

because he does not fear in God's presence.

10a וּבְכֵן רָאִיתִי רְשָׁעִים קְבֻרִים

And so I saw wicked people buried.

וּבְכֵן כֵּן	and thus/so/in this regard/then *û·və·ḵēn*	--- W/ CONJ וְ + PREP בְּ	adv
רָאִיתִי ראה	I saw/observed *rā·ʾî·tî*	QAL PF 1CS	verb
רְשָׁעִים רָשָׁע	wicked/guilty (ones) *rə·šā·ʿîm*	MP SUBST	adj
קְבֻרִים קבר	buried *qə·vu·rîm*	QAL PASS PTCP MP	verb

10b **וָבָ֫אוּ וּמִמְּקֹ֤ום קָדֹושׁ֙ יְהַלֵּ֔כוּ**

They spent time at the holy place,

וָבָ֫אוּ בוא	and they entered/came/went *wā·vā·'û*	QAL PF 3CP W/ CONJ וְ	verb
וּמִמְּקֹ֤ום מָקוֹם	and from place *û·mim·mə·qôm*	ABS W/ CONJ וְ + PREP מִן	noun
קָדֹושׁ֙ קָדוֹשׁ	holy *qā·dôš*	MS ATTR	adj
יְהַלֵּ֔כוּ הלך	(they) went/walked about *yə·hal·lē·ḵû*	PIEL IMPF 3MP	verb

10c **וְיִֽשְׁתַּכְּח֥וּ בָעִ֖יר אֲשֶׁ֣ר כֵּן־עָשׂ֑וּ**

and they received praise in the city because they did this.

וְיִֽשְׁתַּכְּח֥וּ שׁכח	and they were forgotten *wə·yiš·tak·kə·ḥû*	HITH IMPF 3MP W/ CONJ וְ	verb
בָעִ֖יר עִיר	in the city *vā·'îr*	ABS W/ PREP בְּ + DEF. ART.	noun
אֲשֶׁ֣ר אֲשֶׁר	who/that/which *'ă·šer*	---	relative pron
כֵּן־ כֵּן	thus/so/because *kēn-*	---	adv
עָשׂ֑וּ עשׂה	they made/did/worked *'ā·śû*	QAL PF 3CP	verb

The syntax of this verse presents unique problems for interpretation, and commentators have offered multiple solutions to the problem of determining exactly what it says. James Crenshaw (1987:154) has aptly noted that "interpretations of this verse have one thing in common: tentativeness." Miller (2002:137) has summarized the four primary readings of this text: (1) S. R. Driver suggests that the wicked "walk about and boast in the city that they have done right." (2) Following ancient Greek versions, the text indicates that the wicked were buried and praised. (3) Reading it as "and they forgot in the city that they had done thus," the text indicates that "the wicked were buried and their wickedness forgotten." (4) Reading it as "and they forgot in the city those who had done justly," the wicked received a burial and the righteous were forgotten. The translation here coheres with the second option by following the Greek translations of Ecclesiastes, which read ἐπῃνέθησαν, ("they were praised"), representing a slight difference in the Hebrew letters: rather than וְיִשְׁתַּכְּחוּ ("and they were forgotten"), these versions read וְיִשְׁתַּבְּחוּ ("and they were praised")—a change from a *kaph* (כ) to a *bet* (ב), letters that look very similar in Hebrew.

10d	גַּם־זֶה הָֽבֶל׃		
	This is also Abelish.		
גַּם־ *gam-* (גַּם)	also/even	---	adv
זֶה *ze* (זֶה)	this	---	demonstr pron
הָֽבֶל׃ *hā·vel* (הֶבֶל)	Abel/mist/vapor/breath	ABS	noun

Continuing the sentiment expressed in 7:15, Qoheleth highlights the injustice of wicked people receiving the rewards of the righteous, as was seen in the Cain and Abel narrative. Here he uses הֶבֶל ("Abelish") to describe the situation wherein a wicked person receives a burial, access to the holy place, and praise in the very place where they practiced their wickedness. Each of these honors should be reserved for the righteous, but that is not the case in Qoheleth's experience. Observing these things leads Qoheleth to deem this a הֶבֶל ("Abelish") situation—that is, a situation in which the normal order has been reversed, resulting in injustice in the world.

11a	אֲשֶׁר אֵין־נַעֲשָׂה פִתְגָם מַעֲשֵׂה הָרָעָה מְהֵרָה		
	Because the sentence for an evil deed is not carried out quickly—		
אֲשֶׁר *ʾă·šer* (אֲשֶׁר)	who/that/which/because	---	relative pron
אֵין־ *ʾên-* (אַיִן)	there is not	---	particle

נַעֲשָׂה עשׂה	(it) was done/carried out *na·ʿă·**śâ***	NIPH PF 3MS	verb
פִתְגָם פִּתְגָם	sentence/verdict/decree of *fit·**gām***	CST	noun
מַעֲשֵׂה מַעֲשֶׂה	deed/action of *ma·ʿă·**śē***	CST	noun
הָרָעָה רָעָה	the evil/wicked *hā·rā·**ʿâ***	ABS W/ DEF. ART.	noun
מְהֵרָה מְהֵרָה	hastily/speedily/quickly *mə·hē·**râ***	---	adv

Qoheleth leaves it up to interpretation whether the sentence against evil he has in mind is divine or human. Either way, the lack of swift punishment leads to further evil. One of the graces that God gives people is therefore the quick uncovering of their sin. In the moment, discipline is certainly unpleasant, but exposure of sin (hopefully) deters us from doing even greater evil.

11b עַל־כֵּ֗ן מָלֵ֛א לֵ֥ב בְּנֵי־הָאָדָ֖ם בָּהֶ֑ם לַעֲשׂ֥וֹת רָֽע׃

therefore human hearts are filled within them to do evil.

עַל־כֵּ֗ן עַל־כֵּן	thus/so/therefore *ʿal-**kēn***	---	adv
מָלֵ֛א מלא	(it) is full of/filled with *mā·**lēʾ***	QAL PF 3MS	verb
לֵ֥ב לֵב	heart/mind of ***lēv***	CST	noun
בְּנֵי־ בֵּן	sons of *bə·nê-*	CST	noun
הָאָדָ֖ם אָדָם	the man/human/humanity *hā·ʾā·**dām***	ABS W/ DEF. ART.	noun
בָּהֶ֑ם בְּ	in them *bā·**hem***	--- W/ 3MP SX	prep
לַעֲשׂ֥וֹת עשׂה	to do *la·ʿă·**śôt***	QAL INF CST W/ PREP לְ	verb
רָֽע׃ רַע	evil ***rāʿ***	ABS	noun

The phrase מָלֵא לֵב . . . לַעֲשׂוֹת (lit., "filled heart . . . to do") occurs only three times in the Hebrew Bible—here, Exod 35:35, and Esth 7:5. In each case, it refers to a person being characterized by an internal disposition or skill to carry out a particular task. In Exod 35, the hearts of Bezalel and Oholiab are filled with wisdom to do the work of skilled craftsmen on the tabernacle. In Esth 7:5, Haman's heart is filled to attempt to annihilate the Jews in Persia. And here, the human heart is filled to do evil. Jesus will later confront the Pharisees for their hypocrisy using similar imagery: "You brood of vipers! How can you speak good, when you are evil? For out of the abundance of the heart the mouth speaks" (Matt 12:34 ESV).

12a אֲשֶׁר חֹטֶא עֹשֶׂה רָע מְאַת וּמַאֲרִיךְ לוֹ

For a sinner does evil a hundred times and lives a long time,

אֲשֶׁר אֲשֶׁר	who/that/which/for/because *ʾă·šer*	---	relative pron
חֹטֶא חטא	sinning (one) *ḥō·ṭeʾ*	QAL PTCP MS	verb
עֹשֶׂה עשׂה	doing/does *ʿō·śe*	QAL PTCP MS	verb
רָע רַע	evil/wickedness *rāʿ*	ABS	noun
מְאַת מֵאָה	one hundred of *mə·ʾat*	CST	cardinal number
וּמַאֲרִיךְ ארך	and prolonging/enduring *û·ma·ʾă·rîḵ*	HIPH PTCP MS W/ CONJ וְ	verb
לוֹ לְ	to/for him *lô*	--- W/ 3MS SX	prep

Translators are required to supply a few words in this verse. The term מְאַת ("one hundred") is in construct, but there is no absolute noun included. NASB and ESV supply "times," while NET and NIV supply "crimes." The meaning is clear: an evil person multiplying evil deeds and yet living a long time. Long life is a blessing from the Lord that results from righteousness (e.g., Exod 20:12; Deut 5:33; Prov 10:27), yet here Qoheleth recognizes that such is not always the case. Just as sometimes the wicked are praised (8:10), sometimes a sinner multiplies evil deeds and yet prolongs his life.

12b כִּ֣י גַּם־יוֹדֵ֣עַ אָ֔נִי

yet I also know

כִּ֣י	although/rather/yet	---	conj
כִּי	*kî*		
גַּם־	even/also	---	adv
גַּם	*gam-*		
יוֹדֵ֣עַ	know/knowing	QAL PTCP MS	verb
ידע	*yô·**dē**·aʿ*		
אָ֔נִי	I	---	personal pron
אֲנִי	*ʾ**ā**·nî*		

12c אֲשֶׁ֤ר יִהְיֶה־טּוֹב֙ לְיִרְאֵ֣י הָאֱלֹהִ֔ים אֲשֶׁ֥ר יִֽירְא֖וּ מִלְּפָנָֽיו׃

that it will be good for those who fear God,
who fear in his presence.

אֲשֶׁ֤ר	who/that/which	---	relative pron
אֲשֶׁר	*ʾă·**šer***		
יִהְיֶה־	it will be	QAL IMPF 3MS	verb
היה	*yih·ye-*		
טּוֹב֙	good	MS PRED	adj
טוֹב	*ṭôv*		
לְיִרְאֵ֣י	for ones who fear	QAL (CST) PTCP MP W/ PREP לְ	verb
ירא	*lə·yir·**ʾê***		
הָאֱלֹהִ֔ים	the God	ABS W/ DEF. ART.	noun
אֱלֹהִים	*hā·ʾĕ·lō·**hîm***		
אֲשֶׁ֥ר	who/that/which	---	relative pron
אֲשֶׁר	*ʾă·**šer***		
יִֽירְא֖וּ	(they) fear	QAL IMPF 3MP	verb
ירא	*yî·rə·**ʾû***		
מִלְּפָנָֽיו׃	before him/in his presence	--- W/ PREP מִן + 3MS SX	prep
לִפְנֵי	*mil·lə·fā·**nāyw***		

Despite what Qoheleth observes—the prosperity of evildoers—he "knows" that it will be "good" for those who fear the Lord. We should not see this as a contradiction in his thought or an attempt by a later editor to "baptize" his work. Rather, v. 12 illustrates the tension that all people of faith experience at one point or another. As the apostle will later say to the believers at Corinth: "We live by faith, not by sight" (2 Cor 5:7 NET).

13a וְטוֹב לֹֽא־יִהְיֶ֣ה לָֽרָשָׁ֗ע

And it will not be good for the evil person,

וְטוֹב טוֹב	and good *wə·ṭôv*	MS PRED W/ CONJ וְ	adj
לֹֽא־ לֹא	not *lōʾ-*	---	particle
יִהְיֶ֣ה היה	it will be *yih·ye*	QAL IMPF 3MS	verb
לָֽרָשָׁ֗ע רָשָׁע	to/for the evil (one) *lā·rā·šāʿ*	MS SUBST W/ PREP לְ + DEF. ART.	adj

13b וְֽלֹא־יַאֲרִ֣יךְ יָ֭מִים כַּצֵּ֑ל

and he will not lengthen his days like a shadow

וְֽלֹא־ לֹא	and not *wə·lōʾ-*	--- W/ CONJ וְ	particle
יַאֲרִ֣יךְ ארך	he will prolong/lengthen *ya·ʾă·rîḵ*	HIPH IMPF 3MS	verb
יָ֭מִים יוֹם	days *yā·mîm*	ABS	noun
כַּצֵּ֑ל צֵל	like a shadow *kaṣ·ṣēl*	ABS W/ PREP כְּ + DEF. ART.	noun

13c אֲ֭שֶׁר אֵינֶ֥נּוּ יָרֵ֗א מִלִּפְנֵ֥י אֱלֹהִֽים׃

because he does not fear in God's presence.

אֲ֭שֶׁר אֲשֶׁר	for/because *ʾă·šer*	---	relative pron

אֵינֶ֫נּוּ אַ֫יִן	(there is) not to him *ʾê·**nen**·nû*	--- W/ 3MS SX	particle
יָרֵ֥א ירא	he feared *yā·**rēʾ***	QAL PF 3MS	verb
מִלִּפְנֵ֥י לִפְנֵי	before/in the presence of *mil·lif·**nê***	--- W/ PREP מִן	prep
אֱלֹהִֽים׃ אֱלֹהִים	God *ʾĕ·lō·**hîm***	ABS	noun

This verse more fully develops Qoheleth's thought in v. 12 and represents a clear expression of the author's faith and the tension that the book highlights. Despite what Qoheleth "sees" or "experiences," he demonstrates faith that what he knows to be true will ultimately eclipse what appears to be true. In this, he models for believers today how to frankly and truthfully acknowledge what we see around us while also trusting God to be faithful to his word. We are not called to a happy-go-lucky sort of faith that ignores tensions and apparent contradictions, but we are called to trust the Lord despite what we see "under the sun." For further discussion of fearing God as an expression of faith in the Old Testament, see "From Text to Sermon" at 12:9–14.

8:14–15

14a יֶשׁ־הֶבֶל אֲשֶׁר נַעֲשָׂה עַל־הָאָרֶץ

*yeš-**he**vel ʾă**šer** naʿă**śâ** ʿal-hā**ʾā**reṣ*

There is an Abelish thing that is done upon the earth:

14b אֲשֶׁר ׀ יֵשׁ צַדִּיקִים אֲשֶׁר מַגִּיעַ אֲלֵהֶם כְּמַעֲשֵׂה הָרְשָׁעִים

*ʾă**šer** **yēš** ṣaddî**qîm** ʾă**šer** mag**gîa**ʿ ʾălē**hem** kəmaʿă**śē** hārəšā**ʿîm***

there are righteous people who experience the consequences of the wicked,

14c וְיֵשׁ רְשָׁעִים שֶׁמַּגִּיעַ אֲלֵהֶם כְּמַעֲשֵׂה הַצַּדִּיקִים

*wə**yēš** rəšā**ʿîm** šemmag**gîa**ʿ ʾălē**hem** kəmaʿă**śē** haṣṣaddî**qîm***

and there are wicked people who experience the consequences of the righteous.

14d אָמַרְתִּי שֶׁגַּם־זֶה הָבֶל׃

*ʾā**mar**tî šeggam-**ze** **hā**vel.*

I say that this is also Abelish.

15a וְשִׁבַּחְתִּי אֲנִי אֶת־הַשִּׂמְחָה

*wəšib**baḥ**tî ʾă**nî** ʾet haśśim**ḥâ***

So I commend joy

15b אֲשֶׁר אֵין־טוֹב לָאָדָם תַּחַת הַשָּׁמֶשׁ

*ʾă**šer** ʾên-**ṭôv** lāʾā**dām** **ta**ḥat haššemeš*

because there is nothing better for humans under the sun

15c כִּי אִם־לֶאֱכוֹל וְלִשְׁתּוֹת וְלִשְׂמוֹחַ

***kî** ʾim-leʾĕ**ḵôl** wəliš**tôt** wəliś**môa**ḥ*

except to eat and to drink and to rejoice.

15d וְה֛וּא יִלְוֶ֥נּוּ בַעֲמָל֖וֹ יְמֵ֣י חַיָּ֑יו

wəhû' yilwennû va'ămālô yəmê ḥayyāyw

Thus joy will accompany them in their toil during the days of their life

15e אֲשֶׁר־נָֽתַן־ל֥וֹ הָאֱלֹהִ֖ים תַּ֥חַת הַשָּֽׁמֶשׁ׃

'ăšer-nātan-lô hā'ĕlōhîm taḥat haššāmeš.

that God gave them under the sun.

14a יֶשׁ־הֶ֘בֶל֮ אֲשֶׁ֣ר נַעֲשָׂ֣ה עַל־הָאָ֒רֶץ֒

There is an Abelish thing that is done upon the earth:

יֶשׁ־ / יֵשׁ	there is/are / *yeš-*	---	particle
הֶ֘בֶל֮ / הֶבֶל	Abel/mist/vapor/breath / ***he***·*vel*	ABS	noun
אֲשֶׁ֣ר / אֲשֶׁר	who/that/which / *'ă*·***šer***	---	relative pron
נַעֲשָׂ֣ה / עשה	(it) is done/happens / *na*·*'ă*·***śâ***	NIPH PF 3MS	verb
עַל־ / עַל	on/upon / *'al-*	---	prep
הָאָ֒רֶץ֒ / אֶרֶץ	the earth / *hā*·***'ā***·*reṣ*	ABS W/ DEF. ART.	noun

"Upon the earth" is a synonym for Qoheleth's more common "under the sun." Qoheleth is about to describe something that "is done" during human life that is marked by Abel (הֶבֶל, "Abelish thing").

14b אֲשֶׁ֣ר ׀ יֵ֣שׁ צַדִּיקִ֗ים אֲשֶׁ֨ר מַגִּ֤יעַ אֲלֵהֶם֙ כְּמַעֲשֵׂ֣ה הָֽרְשָׁעִ֔ים

there are righteous people who experience
the consequences of the wicked,

Hebrew	Gloss	Parsing	Part of speech
אֲשֶׁ֣ר אֲשֶׁר	who/that which *ʾă·šer*	---	relative pron
יֵ֣שׁ יֵשׁ	there is/are *yēš*	---	particle
צַדִּיקִ֗ים צַדִּיק	righteous (ones) *ṣad·dî·**qîm***	MP SUBT	adj
אֲשֶׁ֨ר אֲשֶׁר	who/that/which *ʾă·šer*	---	relative pron
מַגִּ֤יעַ נגע	(it) happens/befalls *mag·**gî**·aʿ*	HIPH PTCP MS	verb
אֲלֵהֶם֙ אֶל	to them *ʾă·lē·**hem***	--- W/ 3MP SX	prep
כְּמַעֲשֵׂ֣ה מַעֲשֶׂה	according to deeds/ actions of *kə·ma·ʿă·**śē***	CST W/ PREP כְּ	noun
הָֽרְשָׁעִ֔ים רָשָׁע	the wicked *hā·rə·šā·**ʿîm***	MP SUBST W/ DEF. ART.	adj

In this first part of the "Abelish thing" that happens on earth, Qoheleth describes the literal experience of Abel. Though he was righteous and brought an acceptable sacrifice to the Lord, he experienced the consequences of a wicked person—that is, he lacked children, a long life, and (we may assume due to his untimely death) material blessing and prosperity. Instead, his life was cut short by murderous Cain.

14c וְיֵ֣שׁ רְשָׁעִ֗ים שֶׁמַּגִּ֤יעַ אֲלֵהֶם֙ כְּמַעֲשֵׂ֣ה הַצַּדִּיקִ֑ים

and there are wicked people who experience
the consequences of the righteous.

Hebrew	Gloss	Parsing	Part of speech
וְיֵ֣שׁ יֵשׁ	and there is/are *wə·**yēš***	--- W/ CONJ וְ	particle
רְשָׁעִ֗ים רָשָׁע	wicked (ones) *rə·šā·**ʿîm***	MP SUBST	adj

שֶׁמַּגִּיעַ נגע	to whom (it) happens/befalls *šem·mag·**gî**·aʿ*	HIPH PTCP MS W/ RELATIVE PRON שֶׁ	verb
אֲלֵהֶם אֶל	to them *ʾă·lē·**hem***	--- W/ 3MP SX	prep
כְּמַעֲשֵׂה מַעֲשֶׂה	according to deeds/ actions of *kə·ma·ʿă·**śē***	CST W/ PREP כְּ	noun
הַצַּדִּיקִים צַדִּיק	the righteous *haṣ·ṣad·dî·**qîm***	MP SUBST W/ DEF. ART.	adj

Here Qoheleth describes the literal experience of Cain who, though wicked, received a mark of protection from the Lord, lived a long life, fathered children, and founded a city. Though the experiences of the righteous and the wicked are not *always* reversed, it happens often enough to present a significant challenge to people of faith.

14d אָמַרְתִּי שֶׁגַּם־זֶה הָבֶל׃

I say that this is also Abelish.

אָמַרְתִּי אמר	I said/say *ʾā·**mar**·tî*	QAL PF 1CS	verb
שֶׁגַּם־ גַּם	that even/also *šeg·gam-*	--- W/ RELATIVE PRON שֶׁ	adv
זֶה זֶה	this ***ze***	---	demonstr pron
הָבֶל׃ הֶבֶל	Abel/mist/vapor/breath ***hā**·vel*	ABS	noun

This verse is a mini-inclusio, in which parts a and d repeat the same basic sentiment, thus enveloping parts b and c, which form the content of the Abelish situation that Qoheleth observes. Together with v. 13, we can feel—and have likely experienced—the tension between what Qoheleth knows to be ultimately true and what he sees (which is also true). Together these verses both demonstrate and call ancient and modern readers to (1) acknowledge the Abelish reality of life upon the earth, and (2) to lengthen our own perspective of God's justice against wickedness.

15a	וְשִׁבַּ֤חְתִּֽי אֲנִי֙ אֶת־הַשִּׂמְחָ֔ה

So I commend joy

Hebrew	Gloss	Parsing	Part of speech
וְשִׁבַּ֤חְתִּֽי שׁבח	and (I) praised/commended *wə·šib·**baḥ**·tî*	PIEL PF 1CS W/ CONJ וְ	verb
אֲנִי֙ אֲנִי	I *ʾă·**nî***	---	personal pron
אֶת־ אֵת	*(direct object marker)* *ʾet-*	---	particle
הַשִּׂמְחָ֔ה שִׂמְחָה	the joy *haś·śim·**ḥâ***	ABS W/ DEF. ART.	noun

15b	אֲשֶׁ֨ר אֵֽין־ט֤וֹב לָֽאָדָם֙ תַּ֣חַת הַשֶּׁ֔מֶשׁ

because there is nothing better for humans under the sun

Hebrew	Gloss	Parsing	Part of speech
אֲשֶׁ֨ר אֲשֶׁר	who/that/which/because *ʾă·**šer***	---	relative pron
אֵֽין־ אַיִן	there is/are not *ʾên-*	---	particle
ט֤וֹב טוֹב	good ***ṭôv***	MS PRED	adj
לָֽאָדָם֙ אָדָם	for the man *lā·ʾā·**dām***	ABS W/ PREP לְ + DEF. ART.	noun
תַּ֣חַת תַּחַת	under ***ta**·ḥat*	---	prep
הַשֶּׁ֔מֶשׁ שֶׁמֶשׁ	the sun *haš·**še**·meš*	ABS W/ DEF. ART.	noun

15c	כִּ֥י אִם־לֶאֱכ֖וֹל וְלִשְׁתּ֣וֹת וְלִשְׂמ֑וֹחַ

except to eat and to drink and to rejoice.

Hebrew	Gloss	Parsing	Part of speech
כִּ֥י אִם־ כִּי אִם־	except/but ***kî** ʾim-*	---	conj

לֶאֱכוֹל אכל	to eat *le·ʾĕ·kôl*	QAL INF CST W/ PREP לְ	verb
וְלִשְׁתּוֹת שׁתה	and to drink *wə·liš·tôt*	QAL INF CST W/ CONJ וְ + PREP לְ	verb
וְלִשְׂמוֹחַ שׂמח	and to rejoice/be happy *wə·liś·mô·aḥ*	QAL INF CST W/ CONJ וְ + PREP לְ	verb

In light of the Abelish situation that Qoheleth describes in v. 14, he argues that humans should do the very things that Adam and Eve were doing in the garden of Eden: eating, drinking, and (presumably) rejoicing. By fully embracing the gifts God gives, humans both remember the time before the world was turned upside down by sin and look forward to the time when it will be once again turned right side up. We should not understand this *carpe diem* ("seize the day") statement hedonistically. That is, Qoheleth is not advocating for a drunken keg party; that is clear by his consistent calls to fear the Lord (most recently in 8:12–13). Instead, he is arguing that we should acknowledge the Abelish reality of life (v. 14) and then do what God allows us to do: enjoy the gifts he has given. Eating, drinking, and rejoicing do not eradicate life's injustices, but they certainly soften their blow and help us to orient our lives toward what we can actually do (if God allows it).

15d **וְהוּא יִלְוֶנּוּ בַעֲמָלוֹ יְמֵי חַיָּיו**

Thus joy will accompany them in their toil
during the days of their life

וְהוּא הוּא	and it *wə·hûʾ*	--- W/ CONJ וְ	personal pron
יִלְוֶנּוּ לוה	(it) will accompany/join/ stay with him *yil·wen·nû*	QAL IMPF 3MS W/ 3MS SX	verb
בַעֲמָלוֹ עָמָל	in his toil/labor *va·ʿă·mā·lô*	CST W/ PREP בְּ + 3MS SX	noun
יְמֵי יוֹם	days of *yə·mê*	CST	noun
חַיָּיו חַיִּים	his life *ḥay·yāyw*	CST W/ 3MS SX	noun

Though the pronouns in this clause are all third masculine singular ("he"), this translation uses plural pronouns in order to convey the generalized nature of the statement, which is made clear by Qoheleth's use of אָדָם ("human") in v. 15b.

15e אֲשֶׁר־נָתַן־לוֹ הָאֱלֹהִים תַּחַת הַשָּׁמֶשׁ׃

that God gave them under the sun.

אֲשֶׁר־ אֲשֶׁר	who/that/which *ʾă·šer-*	---	relative pron
נָתַן־ נתן	(he) gave ***nā***·*tan-*	QAL PF 3MS	verb
לוֹ לְ	to him ***lô***	--- W/ 3MS SX	prep
הָאֱלֹהִים אֱלֹהִים	the God *hā·ʾĕ·lō·**hîm***	ABS W/ DEF. ART.	noun
תַּחַת תַּחַת	under ***ta***·*ḥat*	---	prep
הַשָּׁמֶשׁ׃ שֶׁמֶשׁ	the sun *haš·**šā**·meš*	ABS W/ DEF. ART.	noun

This closing statement reminds us again that Qoheleth's theology of joy is rooted firmly in God's sovereignty. It is always and only God who sovereignly gives—down to each day of life that humans experience.

From Text to Sermon

The Human Heart. "I don't know what that old Gnag has for planned for you, but you just trust the Maker and . . . and do like your father would have you do. Do like me and yer ma would have you do. Don't just follow your heart. Your heart will betray you" (Peterson 2009:51). Long before Podo Helmar admonished his grandson Janner in the second book of the Wingfeather Saga, the prophet Jeremiah made a similar point: "The heart is deceitful above all things, and desperately sick; who can understand it?" (Jer 17:9 ESV). And before him, the author of Ecclesiastes told us that the lack of justice causes the human heart to be filled with evil (Eccl 8:11) and that "the heart of humans is full of evil, and foolishness is in their hearts during their lives, and afterward to death" (9:3). And before him, the book of Genesis recorded God's similar observation about the human heart, from which Ecclesiastes likely draws (see Meek 2022:23–26). Genesis 6:5 attributes the flood to the wickedness of humans and the evil intent of their heart; in 8:21 Yahweh promises never again to flood the earth, even though "the heart of humans is evil from their youth." The biblical witness is clear: the human heart is not to be trusted.

This passage therefore offers the preacher a few avenues to develop in a sermon. First, working through a biblical theology of the heart may be helpful for people in one's congregation, who have likely more often heard the advice to "follow your heart" than the biblical teaching that it is "desperately sick." Second, and related, this passage could be used as a jumping off point to show your congregation how to fruitfully use inner-biblical allusion as a method for interpreting Scripture. Qoheleth's and Jeremiah's comments on the heart are related to one another by virtue of their common subject matter, but both are likely drawing upon the book of Genesis for their understanding of what is within humans. Further, the New Testament likewise works in the rich soil of the Old Testament to speak to the concept of the heart and inner life.

Living in an Upside-Down World. One need only google "church sexual abuse scandal" to see that we still inhabit the world that Eccl 8:10 describes, a world in which wicked people "spent time at the holy place, and they received praise in the city because they did this." Likewise, 8:14 gives voice to an enduring frustration of life under the sun: "There are righteous people who experience the consequences of the wicked, and there are wicked people who experience the consequences of the righteous."

Both of these situations, says Qoheleth, are הֶבֶל, "Abel," and indeed the narrative of Cain and Abel, as we saw above, is a cipher through which to view the breakdown between actions and rewards that we often see in life. In my personal experience growing up in an evangelical church, acknowledging such realities of life was met with rebuke. I learned in no uncertain terms that sexual abuse in the church and the prosperity of the wicked were not appropriate topics of conversation. Perhaps some in your congregation have similar church experiences. These verses model a different way of dealing with reality. Rather than ignoring the tension or pushing down one's anger over injustice, Qoheleth shows us that we can and should tell the truth about what we see around us. We can and should acknowledge that, yes, Abelish things happen in this life.

Ecclesiastes does not, however, simply leave us there, with the acknowledgement of evil and injustice. Rather, he points us toward two key strategies for navigating life in this upside-down world. The first strategy comes in 8:12–13, where Qoheleth affirms that it is good and right to fear the Lord—that is, to live in right relationship with him. Even though the wicked may prosper for a time, ultimately "it will be good for those who fear God, who fear in his presence" (8:12). Qoheleth's trust in God's justice and judgment calls readers today to demonstrate the same trust in the Lord while acknowledging the reality of our broken world. Second, Qoheleth calls readers (again!) to enjoy the good gifts of God. God's gifts do not eliminate the injustice we see and experience, but they do provide relief, and therefore we must take joy in eating, drinking, and working—as God allows us. As we have seen before in Ecclesiastes, joy in these ephemeral gifts is humanity's "portion" or "reward." In sum, Eccl 8:10–15 summarizes the book's overall theological message and gives you the opportunity to speak honestly and openly about injustice while also commending to your congregation the way through the sin-marred world: fearing God and enjoying his gifts.

DEATH IS COMING, SO ENJOY LIFE

Qoheleth considers again the reality that death is coming for all people. In particular, he laments that the wicked and the righteous suffer the same fate, just as he lamented in ch. 3 that humans and animals share the same fate. In light of this inevitable reality, Qoheleth repeats his admonition for humans to enjoy God's gifts.

9:1–6

1a כִּי אֶת־כָּל־זֶה נָתַתִּי אֶל־לִבִּי וְלָבוּר אֶת־כָּל־זֶה

*kî ʾet-kol-**ze** na**tat**tî ʾel-lib**bî** wəlā**vûr** ʾet-kol-**ze***

Indeed, I put all of this to my heart in order to explain it all:

1b אֲשֶׁר הַצַּדִּיקִים וְהַחֲכָמִים וַעֲבָדֵיהֶם בְּיַד הָאֱלֹהִים

*ʾă**šer** haṣṣaddî**qîm** wəhaḥăkā**mîm** waʿăvādê**hem** bə**yad** hāʾĕlō**hîm***

The righteous and the wise and their works are in the hand of God.

1c גַּם־אַהֲבָה גַם־שִׂנְאָה אֵין יוֹדֵעַ הָאָדָם הַכֹּל לִפְנֵיהֶם׃

*gam-ʾahă**vâ** gam-śin**ʾâ** **ʾên** yô**dē**aʿ hāʾā**dām** hak**kōl** lifnê**hem**.*

Whether love or hate, humans do not know;
everything is in front of them.

2a הַכֹּל כַּאֲשֶׁר לַכֹּל מִקְרֶה אֶחָד

*hak**kōl** kaʾă**šer** lak**kōl** miq**re** ʾe**ḥād***

Everything is as everything else—one fate!

2b לַצַּדִּיק וְלָרָשָׁע

*laṣṣad**dîq** wəlārā**šā**ʿ*

For the righteous and for the wicked,

2c לַטּוֹב וְלַטָּהוֹר וְלַטָּמֵא

*laṭ**ṭôv** wəlaṭṭā**hôr** wəlaṭṭā**mē**ʾ*

for the good, for the ritually pure, and for the ritually impure,

2d וְלַזֹּבֵחַ וְלַאֲשֶׁר אֵינֶנּוּ זֹבֵחַ

*wəlazzō**vē**aḥ wəlaʾă**šer** ʾê**nen**nû zō**vē**aḥ*

for those who offer sacrifices and for those who don't,

2e כַּטּוֹב כַּחֹטֶא

*kaṭ**ṭôv** kaḥō**ṭe**ʾ*

like the good person, so the sinner,

2f הַנִּשְׁבָּ֕ע כַּאֲשֶׁ֖ר שְׁבוּעָ֥ה יָרֵֽא׃

*hanniš**bā‘** ka’**ăšer** šəvû**‘â** yā**rē’**.*

the one who vows, just as the one who shuns swearing a vow.

3a זֶ֣ה ׀ רָ֗ע בְּכֹ֤ל אֲשֶׁר־נַעֲשָׂה֙ תַּ֣חַת הַשֶּׁ֔מֶשׁ

***ze rā‘** bə**ḵōl** ’ăšer-na‘ă**śâ** ta**ḥat** haš**še**meš*

This is an evil in all that is done under the sun:

3b כִּֽי־מִקְרֶ֥ה אֶחָ֖ד לַכֹּ֑ל

*kî-miq**re** ’e**ḥād** lak**kōl***

that the same fate is for everyone,

3c וְגַ֣ם לֵ֣ב בְּֽנֵי־הָ֠אָדָם מָֽלֵא־רָ֨ע

*wə**gam** **lēv** bənê-hā’ă**dām** mā**lē’-rā‘***

and also that the heart of humans is filled with evil,

3d וְהוֹלֵל֤וֹת בִּלְבָבָם֙ בְּחַיֵּיהֶ֔ם

*wəhôlē**lôt** bilvā**vām** bəḥayyê**hem***

and madness resides in their hearts during their lives—

3e וְאַחֲרָ֖יו אֶל־הַמֵּתִֽים׃

*wə’aḥă**rāyw** ’el-hammē**tîm**.*

and after that? To the dead!

4a כִּי־מִי֙ אֲשֶׁ֣ר יְחֻבַּ֔ר אֶ֥ל כָּל־הַחַיִּ֖ים יֵ֣שׁ בִּטָּח֑וֹן

*kî-**mî** ’**ăšer** yəḥub**bar** ’**el** kol-haḥay**yîm** **yēš** biṭṭā**ḥôn***

However, there is hope for whoever is joined to all the living,

4b כִּֽי־לְכֶ֤לֶב חַי֙ ה֣וּא ט֔וֹב מִן־הָאַרְיֵ֖ה הַמֵּֽת׃

*kî-lə**ḵe**lev **ḥay** **hû’** **ṭôv** min-hā’ar**yē** ham**mēt**.*

for even a living dog is better than a dead lion.

5a כִּ֧י הַחַיִּ֛ים יוֹדְעִ֖ים שֶׁיָּמֻ֑תוּ

***kî** ḥaḥay**yîm** yôdə**‘îm** šeyyā**mū**tû*

For the living know that they will die,

5b וְהַמֵּתִ֗ים אֵינָ֤ם יוֹדְעִים֙ מְא֔וּמָה

*wəhammē**tîm** ʾê**nām** yôdə**ʿîm** məʾû**mâ***

but the dead don't know anything,

5c וְאֵֽין־ע֤וֹד לָהֶם֙ שָׂכָ֔ר

*wəʾên-**ʿôd** lā**hem** śā**ḵār***

and there's no longer a return for them

5d כִּ֥י נִשְׁכַּ֖ח זִכְרָֽם׃

***kî** niš**kaḥ** zik**rām**.*

because their memory is forgotten.

6a גַּ֣ם אַהֲבָתָ֤ם גַּם־שִׂנְאָתָם֙ גַּם־קִנְאָתָ֔ם כְּבָ֖ר אָבָ֑דָה

***gam** ʾahăvā**tām** gam-śinʾā**tām** gam-qinʾā**tām** kə**vār** ʾā**vā**dâ*

Also their love, their hate, and their jealousy have already faded away,

6b וְחֵ֨לֶק אֵין־לָהֶ֥ם עוֹד֙ לְעוֹלָ֔ם

*wə**ḥē**leq ʾên-lā**hem** **ʿôd** ləʿô**lām***

and they no longer have a portion—forever—

6c בְּכֹ֥ל אֲשֶׁר־נַעֲשָׂ֖ה תַּ֥חַת הַשָּֽׁמֶשׁ׃

*bə**ḵōl** ʾăšer-naʿă**śâ** **ta**ḥat haš**šā**meš.*

in everything that is done under the sun.

1a כִּ֣י אֶת־כָּל־זֶ֞ה נָתַ֣תִּי אֶל־לִבִּ֗י וְלָב֣וּר אֶת־כָּל־זֶ֔ה

Indeed, I put all of this to my heart in order to explain it all:

כִּי כִּי	indeed/surely/thus/so *kî*	---	conj
אֶת־ אֵת	*(direct object marker)* *ʾet-*	---	particle

כָּל־ כֹּל	all of *kol-*	CST	noun
זֶה זֶה	this *ze*	---	demonstr pron
נָתַתִּי נתן	I set/put/placed/gave *na·**tat**·tî*	QAL PF 1CS	verb
אֶל־ אֶל	to *'el-*	---	prep
לִבִּי לֵב	my heart/mind *lib·**bî***	CST W/ 1CS SX	noun
וְלָבוּר בור	and to explain *wə·lā·**vûr***	QAL INF CST W/ CONJ וְ + PREP לְ	verb
אֶת־ אֵת	*(direct object marker)* *'et-*	---	particle
כָּל־ כֹּל	all of *kol-*	CST	noun
זֶה זֶה	this *ze*	---	demonstr pron

That Qoheleth is putting "all of this" to his heart means that he is setting his mind to think about the issue at hand, which he introduces in the next clause. The term לָבוּר ("to explain") appears only here in the Hebrew Bible, thus its meaning is not altogether clear.

1b אֲשֶׁר הַצַּדִּיקִים וְהַחֲכָמִים וַעֲבָדֵיהֶם בְּיַד הָאֱלֹהִים

The righteous and the wise and their works are in the hand of God.

אֲשֶׁר אֲשֶׁר	who/that/which *'ă·**šer***	---	relative pron
הַצַּדִּיקִים צַדִּיק	the righteous (ones) *haṣ·ṣad·dî·**qîm***	MP SUBST W/ DEF. ART.	adj
וְהַחֲכָמִים חָכָם	and the wise (ones) *wə·ha·ḥă·kā·**mîm***	MP SUBST W/ CONJ וְ + DEF. ART.	adj
וַעֲבָדֵיהֶם עֶבֶד	and their works *wa·'ă·vā·dê·**hem***	CST W/ CONJ וְ + 3MP SX	noun

בְּיַד יָד	in hand of *bə·**yad***	CST W/ PREP בְּ	noun
הָאֱלֹהִים אֱלֹהִים	the God *hā·ʾĕ·lō·**hîm***	ABS W/ DEF. ART.	noun

"Hand" (יָד) is a common expression in the Hebrew Bible for power. In this context, Qoheleth is not speaking of being in God's hand in the sense of being under his protection but rather in the sense that the righteous, the wise, and all that they do are in the power, or control, of God.

1c גַּם־אַהֲבָה גַם־שִׂנְאָה אֵין יוֹדֵעַ הָאָדָם הַכֹּל לִפְנֵיהֶם׃

Whether love or hate, humans do not know;
everything is in front of them.

גַּם־ גַּם	also/even *gam-*	---	adv
אַהֲבָה אַהֲבָה	love *ʾa·hă·**vâ***	ABS	noun
גַם־ גַּם	also/even *gam-*	---	adv
שִׂנְאָה שִׂנְאָה	hate *śin·**ʾâ***	ABS	noun
אֵין אַיִן	there is not ***ʾên***	---	particle
יוֹדֵעַ ידע	knowing *yô·**dē**·aʿ*	QAL PTCP MS	verb
הָאָדָם אָדָם	the man/human/humanity *hā·ʾā·**dām***	ABS W/ DEF. ART.	noun
הַכֹּל כֹּל	the whole/all/everything *hak·**kōl***	ABS W/ DEF. ART.	noun
לִפְנֵיהֶם׃ לִפְנֵי	before them/in their presence *lif·nê·**hem***	--- W/ 3MP SX	prep

Scholars are divided over whether "love or hate" refers to the "love" and "hate" of God, in which case people would not know whether or not they are in covenant relationship with him. For such covenantal usage of the terms love and hate, see Mal 1:2–3: "Is not Esau Jacob's brother, declares

Yahweh, yet I loved [אהב] Jacob and I hated [שׂנא] Esau." Such a reading—which has Qoheleth stating that humans do not know whether or not they are in right relationship with God—is inconsistent with Ecclesiastes (including the previous clause!) and the rest of Scripture. Another option is to understand the "love" and "hate" as that of other humans. That is, no one knows whether the people in their lives will love or hate them. The best reading, though, is to understand the statement more generally—no one knows whether good or evil awaits them in this life. The future is obscured from humans, though not from God, whom Qoheleth repeatedly urges his audience to fear or live in right relationship with.

2a הַכֹּל כַּאֲשֶׁר לַכֹּל מִקְרֶה אֶחָד

Everything is as everything else—one fate!

הַכֹּל כֹּל	the whole/all/everything *hak·kōl*	ABS W/ DEF. ART.	noun
כַּאֲשֶׁר אֲשֶׁר	like/as *ka·'ă·šer*	--- W/ PREP כְּ	relative pron
לַכֹּל כֹּל	to the all/whole/everything *lak·kōl*	ABS W/ PREP לְ + DEF. ART.	noun
מִקְרֶה מִקְרֶה	fate/fortune/chance *miq·re*	ABS	noun
אֶחָד אֶחָד	one *'e·ḥād*	ABS	cardinal number

The Septuagint connects the last two words of the previous verse (הַכֹּל לִפְנֵיהֶם) with the first word of v. 2, which it renders with ματαιοτης, the word it most often uses to translate הֶבֶל (rendered as "Abel/Abelish" throughout this commentary). The word הַכֹּל in the Masoretic Text is only one letter different from הֶבֶל, and the letters are very similar in Hebrew (כ vs. ב). The Syriac Peshitta contains the same reading as the Septuagint. Thus, the Septuagint read the ending of 9:1 and beginning of 9:2 as הֶבֶל הַכֹּל לִפְנֵיהֶם: "Everything before them is Abel." Several modern commentaries follow this reading (e.g., Fox 2004, Alter 2010, Schoors 2013). Others disagree, arguing that the Masoretic Text is clear as it stands (e.g., Crenshaw 1987, Longman 1998, Ogden 2007). The translation here follows the Masoretic tradition.

In 2:14–15 Qoheleth lamented that the wise and fool share the same "fate" (מִקְרֶה), and in 3:19 he likewise lamented that humans and beasts share the same "fate" (מִקְרֶה). Here he again wrestles with the reality that death awaits everyone, whether righteous or wicked, ritually pure or impure, offering sacrifices or not, good or sinner, or swearing oaths or not (see clauses below). No matter how a person lives, no one can escape death's grip.

2b לַצַּדִּיק וְלָרָשָׁע

For the righteous and for the wicked,

לַצַּדִּיק צַדִּיק	to/for the righteous *laṣ·ṣad·**dîq***	MS SUBST W/ PREP לְ + DEF. ART. — adj
וְלָרָשָׁע רָשָׁע	and to/for the wicked *wə·lā·rā·**šāʿ***	MS SUBST W/ CONJ וְ + PREP לְ + DEF. ART. — adj

2c לַטּוֹב וְלַטָּהוֹר וְלַטָּמֵא

for the good, for the ritually pure, and for the ritually impure,

לַטּוֹב טוֹב	to/for the good *laṭ·**ṭôv***	MS SUBST W/ PREP לְ + DEF. ART. — adj
וְלַטָּהוֹר טָהוֹר	and to/for the clean/ritually pure *wə·laṭ·ṭā·**hôr***	MS SUBST W/ CONJ וְ + PREP לְ + DEF. ART. — adj
וְלַטָּמֵא טָמֵא	and to/for the unclean/ritually impure *wə·laṭ·ṭā·**mēʾ***	MS SUBST W/ CONJ וְ + PREP לְ + DEF. ART. — adj

2d וְלַזֹּבֵחַ וְלַאֲשֶׁר אֵינֶנּוּ זֹבֵחַ

for those who offer sacrifices and for those who don't,

וְלַזֹּבֵחַ זבח	and to/for the (ones) offering sacrifices *wə·laz·zō·**vē**·aḥ*	QAL PTCP MS W/ CONJ וְ + PREP לְ + DEF. ART. — verb

וְלַאֲשֶׁר אֲשֶׁר	and to/for (those) that *wə·la·ʾă·šer*	--- W/ CONJ וְ + PREP לְ	relative pron
אֵינֶנּוּ אַיִן	there is not to (them) *ʾê·**nen**·nû*	--- W/ 3MS SX	particle
זֹבֵחַ זבח	sacrificing/offering sacrifices *zō·**vē**·aḥ*	QAL PTCP MS	verb

2e כַּטּוֹב כַּחֹטֶא

like the good person, so the sinner,

כַּטּוֹב טוֹב	like/as the good (one) *kaṭ·**ṭôv***	MS SUBST W/ PREP כְּ + DEF. ART.	adj
כַּחֹטֶא חטא	like/as the sinner *ka·ḥō·**ṭe**ʾ*	QAL PTCP MS W/ PREP כְּ + DEF. ART.	verb

2f הַנִּשְׁבָּע כַּאֲשֶׁר שְׁבוּעָה יָרֵא׃

the one who vows, just as the one who shuns swearing a vow.

הַנִּשְׁבָּע שׁבע	the swearing/vowing (one) *han·niš·**bā**ʿ*	NIPH PTCP MS W/ DEF. ART.	verb
כַּאֲשֶׁר אֲשֶׁר	like/as *ka·ʾă·**šer***	--- W/ PREP כְּ	relative pron
שְׁבוּעָה שְׁבוּעָה	vow/oath *šə·vû·**ʿâ***	ABS	noun
יָרֵא׃ ירא	(he) feared/shunned *yā·**rē**ʾ*	QAL PF 3MS	verb

The long list of opposites drives home the author's point that the "same fate" (that is, death) awaits everyone, regardless of how they live under the sun. Note that "shuns" is the same word in Hebrew that Qoheleth uses to describe how one should live in relationship with God (ירא, "fear"). The context here, though, is not "fear" in the sense of fearing God but rather fear in the sense of being afraid to do something, thus "shunning."

3a **זֶ֣ה ׀ רָ֗ע בְּכֹ֤ל אֲשֶׁר־נַעֲשָׂה֙ תַּ֣חַת הַשֶּׁ֔מֶשׁ**

This is an evil in all that is done under the sun:

זֶ֣ה ׀ זֶה	this *ze*	---	demonstr pron
רָ֗ע רַע	evil/bad (thing) *rā*ʿ	MS PRED	adj
בְּכֹ֤ל כֹּל	in everything/all *bə·**ḵōl***	ABS W/ PREP בְּ	noun
אֲשֶׁר־ אֲשֶׁר	who/that/which *ʾă·šer-*	---	relative pron
נַעֲשָׂה֙ עשׂה	(it) is done/happens *na·ʿă·**śâ***	NIPH PF 3MS	verb
תַּ֣חַת תַּחַת	under ***ta**·ḥat*	---	prep
הַשֶּׁ֔מֶשׁ שֶׁמֶשׁ	the sun *haš·**še**·meš*	ABS W/ DEF. ART.	noun

As throughout the book of Ecclesiastes, "under the sun" is Qoheleth's way of referring to life on earth. It is not, as some would have it, contrasting a "worldly" perspective of life with a "heavenly" perspective of life.

3b **כִּֽי־מִקְרֶ֤ה אֶחָד֙ לַכֹּ֔ל**

that the same fate is for everyone,

כִּֽי־ כִּי	that *kî-*	---	conj
מִקְרֶ֤ה מִקְרֶה	fate/fortune/chance *miq·**re***	ABS	noun
אֶחָד֙ אֶחָד	one *ʾe·**ḥād***	ABS	cardinal number
לַכֹּ֔ל כֹּל	to/for the all/whole/everyone *lak·**kōl***	ABS W/ PREP לְ + DEF. ART.	noun

3c וְגַם לֵב בְּנֵי־הָאָדָם מָלֵא־רָע

and also that the heart of humans is filled with evil,

Hebrew	Gloss	Parsing	POS
וְגַם גַּם	and also/even *wə·gam*	--- W/ CONJ וְ	adv
לֵב לֵב	heart/mind of *lēv*	CST	noun
בְּנֵי־ בֵּן	sons/children of *bə·nê-*	CST	noun
הָאָדָם אָדָם	the man/human/humanity *hā·ʾā·dām*	ABS W/ DEF. ART.	noun
מָלֵא־ מלא	(it) is full of/filled with *mā·lēʾ-*	QAL PF 3MS	verb
רָע רַע	evil *rāʿ*	ABS	noun

For discussion of the human heart being filled with evil, see comments at 8:11 and the "From Text to Sermon" section for 8:10–15.

3d וְהוֹלֵלוֹת בִּלְבָבָם בְּחַיֵּיהֶם

and madness resides in their hearts during their lives—

Hebrew	Gloss	Parsing	POS
וְהוֹלֵלוֹת הוֹלֵלָה	and madness/folly *wə·hô·lē·lôt*	ABS W/ CONJ וְ	noun
בִּלְבָבָם לֵבָב	in/within their hearts/minds *bil·vā·vām*	CST W/ PREP בְּ + 3MP SX	noun
בְּחַיֵּיהֶם חַיִּים	in/during their lives *bə·ḥay·yê·hem*	CST W/ PREP בְּ + 3MP SX	noun

3e וְאַחֲרָיו אֶל־הַמֵּתִים׃

and after that? To the dead!

Hebrew	Gloss	Parsing	POS
וְאַחֲרָיו אַחֲרֵי	and after (it/him) *wə·ʾa·ḥă·rāyw*	--- W/ CONJ וְ + 3MS SX	prep

אֶל־ אֶל	to/toward *'el-*	---	prep
הַמֵּתִים׃ מות	the dead (ones) *ham·mē·**tîm***	QAL PTCP MP W/ DEF. ART.	verb

Though in v. 3a Qoheleth states that "this is an evil" on earth, he actually lists two evils. The first evil is that the same fate awaits everyone. The second is that evil and madness characterize humans, and after their evil and foolish lives, they join the dead. As Longman (1998:227) points out, "The abrupt syntax at the end of the verse [3e] is intentional and reflects the suddenness of death in the midst of life."

4a כִּֽי־מִי֙ אֲשֶׁ֣ר יְחֻבַּ֔ר אֶ֖ל כָּל־הַחַיִּ֑ים יֵ֣שׁ בִּטָּח֑וֹן

However, there is hope for whoever is joined to all the living,

כִּי־ כִּי	however/although *kî-*	---	conj
מִי֙ מִי	who? ***mî***	---	interr pron
אֲשֶׁ֣ר אֲשֶׁר	who/that/which *'ă·**šer***	---	relative pron
יְחֻבַּ֔ר חבר	(he) is joined/attached *yə·ḥub·**bar***	PUAL IMPF 3MS	verb
אֶ֖ל אֶל	to ***'el***	---	prep
כָּל־ כֹּל	all of *kol-*	CST	noun
הַחַיִּ֑ים חַיִּים	the living (ones) *ha·ḥay·**yîm***	MP SUBST W/ DEF. ART.	adj
יֵ֣שׁ יֵשׁ	there is ***yēš***	---	particle
בִּטָּח֑וֹן בִּטָּחוֹן	certainty/hope/confidence *biṭ·ṭā·**ḥôn***	ABS	noun

The translation here follows the *qere* ("what is read"), which is יְחֻבַּר ("[he] is joined"), rather than the *ketiv* ("what is written"), which is יְבֻחַר ("[he] is chosen"). The difference is the transposition of the ב and the ח.

4b כִּֽי־לְכֶ֤לֶב חַי֙ ה֣וּא ט֔וֹב מִן־הָאַרְיֵ֖ה הַמֵּֽת׃

for even a living dog is better than a dead lion.

כִּֽי־ כִּי	for/because *kî-*	---	conj
לְכֶ֤לֶב כֶּ֫לֶב	to/for/even a dog *lə·**ke**·lev*	ABS W/ PREP לְ	noun
חַי֙ חַי	living/alive/live *ḥay*	MS ATTR	adj
ה֣וּא הוּא	it *hû'*	---	personal pron
ט֔וֹב טוֹב	good *ṭôv*	MS PRED	adj
מִן־ מִן	from/than *min-*	---	prep
הָאַרְיֵ֖ה אַרְיֵה	the lion *hā·'ar·**yē***	ABS W/ DEF. ART.	noun
הַמֵּֽת׃ מות	dead (one) *ham·**mēt***	QAL PTCP MS W/ DEF. ART.	verb

The comparison between the regal lion and the despised canine highlights the worth of being alive over being dead. If both were alive, surely it is better to be a lion than a dog, but that value dissipates when the lion goes where everyone is headed: to death.

5a כִּ֧י הַחַיִּ֛ים יוֹדְעִ֖ים שֶׁיָּמֻ֑תוּ

For the living know that they will die,

כִּ֧י כִּי	for/because ***kî***	---	conj
הַחַיִּ֛ים חַיִּים	the living (ones) *ha·ḥay·**yîm***	MP SUBST W/ DEF. ART.	adj
יוֹדְעִ֖ים ידע	knowing *yô·də·**'îm***	QAL PTCP MP	verb
שֶׁיָּמֻ֑תוּ מות	that they will die *šey·yā·**mū**·tû*	QAL IMPF 3MP W/ RELATIVE PRON שֶׁ	verb

5b	וְהַמֵּתִים אֵינָם יוֹדְעִים מְאוּמָה

but the dead don't know anything,

וְהַמֵּתִים מות	and/but the dead (ones) *wə·ham·mē·**tîm***	QAL PTCP MP W/ CONJ וְ + DEF. ART.	verb
אֵינָם אַיִן	there is not to them/ they do not have *ʾê·**nām***	--- W/ 3MP SX	particle
יוֹדְעִים ידע	knowing *yô·də·**ʿîm***	QAL PTCP MP	verb
מְאוּמָה מְאוּמָה	anything *mə·**ʾû**·mâ*	---	indef pron

5c	וְאֵין־עוֹד לָהֶם שָׂכָר

and there's no longer a return for them

וְאֵין־ אַיִן	and there is not *wə·ʾên-*	--- W/ CONJ וְ	particle
עוֹד עוֹד	again/still/yet ***ʿôd***	---	adv
לָהֶם לְ	to/for them *lā·**hem***	--- W/ 3MP SX	prep
שָׂכָר שָׂכָר	wages/return *śā·**ḵār***	ABS	noun

The word translated "return" here is שָׂכָר. Though often translated as "reward" (e.g., NET, CSB, ESV), we saw above in 4:9 that this word refers to wages or a return on work. It is not the same Hebrew term that Qoheleth uses to refer to humanity's "reward" or "portion," which he will use in the following verse.

5d	כִּי נִשְׁכַּח זִכְרָם׃

because their memory is forgotten.

כִּי כִּי	for/because ***kî***	---	conj

Hebrew	Gloss / Transliteration	Parsing	Part of speech
נִשְׁכַּח שׁכח	(it) is forgotten *niš·**kaḥ***	NIPH PF 3MS	verb
זִכְרָם׃ זֵכֶר	their remembrance/memory *zik·**rām***	CST W/ 3MP SX	noun

That even their memory is forgotten means that the dead are forever banished from the realm of the living. For further discussion in Ecclesiastes on being forgotten and the problems it poses for Qoheleth, see the notes at 1:11a and 1:11d.

6a גַּם אַהֲבָתָם גַּם־שִׂנְאָתָם גַּם־קִנְאָתָם כְּבָר אָבָדָה

Also their love, their hate, and their jealousy
have already faded away,

Hebrew	Gloss / Transliteration	Parsing	Part of speech
גַּם גַּם	also/even ***gam***	---	adv
אַהֲבָתָם אַהֲבָה	their love *ʾa·hă·vā·**tām***	CST W/ 3MP SX	noun
גַּם־ גַּם	also/even *gam-*	---	adv
שִׂנְאָתָם שִׂנְאָה	their hate *śin·ʾā·**tām***	CST W/ 3MP SX	noun
גַּם־ גַּם	also/even *gam-*	---	adv
קִנְאָתָם קִנְאָה	their jealousy *qin·ʾā·**tām***	CST W/ 3MP SX	noun
כְּבָר כְּבָר	already/long ago *kə·**vār***	---	adv
אָבָדָה אבד	(it) perished/faded away/ceased *ʾā·**vā**·dâ*	QAL PF 3FS	verb

The dead lack knowledge and a return for their deeds, the memory of them fades, and the emotions they experienced and expressed likewise cease to exist.

6b	וְחֵ֥לֶק אֵין־לָהֶ֛ם ע֖וֹד לְעוֹלָ֑ם

and they no longer have a portion—forever—

וְחֵ֥לֶק חֵלֶק	and portion *wə·ḥē·leq*	ABS W/ CONJ וְ	noun
אֵין־ אַיִן	there is not *ʾên-*	---	particle
לָהֶ֛ם לְ	to/for them *lā·hem*	--- W/ 3MP SX	prep
ע֖וֹד עוֹד	again/still/yet *ʿôd*	---	adv
לְעוֹלָ֑ם עוֹלָם	for/to a long time/ forever/eternity *lə·ʿô·lām*	ABS W/ PREP לְ	noun

For discussion of humanity's "portion" or "reward" and its significance in Ecclesiastes, see the notes at 1:3a, 11d; 2:10d, 11a; "From Text to Sermon" at 2:4–11; notes at 3:22b, c; 4:4c; "From Text to Sermon" at 4:4–12; notes at 5:17c, 18c; "From Text to Sermon" at 5:13–20; notes at 7:10c, 11b; and "From Text to Sermon" at 8:10–15. The point emphasized here is that the "portion" is temporary—it must be enjoyed *while we live.*

6c	בְּכֹ֥ל אֲשֶׁר־נַעֲשָׂ֖ה תַּ֥חַת הַשָּֽׁמֶשׁ׃

in everything that is done under the sun.

בְּכֹ֥ל כֹּל	in all/everything *bə·ḵōl*	ABS W/ PREP בְּ	noun
אֲשֶׁר־ אֲשֶׁר	who/that/which *ʾă·šer-*	---	relative pron
נַעֲשָׂ֖ה עשׂה	(it) is done *na·ʿă·śâ*	NIPH PF 3MS	verb
תַּ֥חַת תַּחַת	under *ta·ḥat*	---	prep
הַשָּֽׁמֶשׁ׃ שֶׁמֶשׁ	the sun *haš·šā·meš*	ABS W/ DEF. ART.	noun

9:7–10

7a לֵךְ אֱכֹל בְּשִׂמְחָה לַחְמֶךָ

lēḵ ʾĕḵōl bəśimḥâ laḥmeḵā

Go, eat your bread in joy

7b וּשֲׁתֵה בְלֶב־טוֹב יֵינֶךָ

ûšătē vəlev-ṭôv yêneḵā

and drink your wine with a happy heart,

7c כִּי כְבָר רָצָה הָאֱלֹהִים אֶת־מַעֲשֶׂיךָ׃

kî ḵəvār rāṣâ hāʾĕlōhîm ʾet-maʿăśêḵā.

for God already delights in your deeds.

8a בְּכָל־עֵת יִהְיוּ בְגָדֶיךָ לְבָנִים

bəḵol-ʿēt yihyû vəgādêḵā ləvānîm

At all times may your clothes be white,

8b וְשֶׁמֶן עַל־רֹאשְׁךָ אַל־יֶחְסָר׃

wəšemen ʿal-rōʾšəḵā ʾal-yeḥsār.

and do not let oil be lacking upon your head.

9a רְאֵה חַיִּים עִם־אִשָּׁה אֲשֶׁר־אָהַבְתָּ

rəʾē ḥayyîm ʿim-ʾiššâ ʾăšer-ʾāhavtā

Enjoy life with the wife whom you love

9b כָּל־יְמֵי חַיֵּי הֶבְלֶךָ אֲשֶׁר נָתַן־לְךָ תַּחַת הַשָּׁמֶשׁ

kol-yəmê ḥayyê hevleḵā ʾăšer nātan-ləḵā taḥat haššemeš

all the days of your Abelish life that he gave you under the sun—

9c כֹּל יְמֵי הֶבְלֶךָ

kōl yəmê hevleḵā

all of your Abelish days.

9d כִּ֣י ה֤וּא חֶלְקְךָ֙ בַּֽחַיִּ֔ים

kî hû' ḥelqəḵā baḥayyîm

For that is your portion in life

9e וּבַעֲמָ֣לְךָ֔ אֲשֶׁר־אַתָּ֥ה עָמֵ֖ל תַּ֥חַת הַשָּֽׁמֶשׁ׃

ûva'ămāləḵā 'ăšer-'attâ 'āmēl taḥat haššāmeš.

and in your toil that you toil under the sun.

10a כֹּל֩ אֲשֶׁ֨ר תִּמְצָ֧א יָדְךָ֛ לַעֲשׂ֥וֹת

kōl 'ăšer timṣā' yādəḵā la'ăśôt

All that your hand finds to do,

10b בְּכֹחֲךָ֖ עֲשֵׂ֑ה

bəḵōḥăḵā 'ăśē

do it with your strength.

10c כִּי֩ אֵ֨ין מַעֲשֶׂ֜ה וְחֶשְׁבּ֗וֹן וְדַ֙עַת֙ וְחָכְמָ֔ה בִּשְׁא֕וֹל

kî 'ên ma'ăśe wəḥešbôn wəda'at wəḥoḵmâ biš'ôl

**For there is no working or thinking
or knowledge or wisdom in Sheol,**

10d אֲשֶׁ֥ר אַתָּ֖ה הֹלֵ֥ךְ שָֽׁמָּה׃

'ăšer 'attâ hōlēḵ šāmmâ.

where you are going.

7a לֵ֣ךְ אֱכֹ֤ל בְּשִׂמְחָה֙ לַחְמֶ֔ךָ

Go, eat your bread in joy

לֵךְ הלך	(you) go/walk *lēḵ*	QAL IMPV MS	verb
אֱכֹל אכל	(you) eat *'ĕ·ḵōl*	QAL IMPV MS	verb

בְּשִׂמְחָה֙	in joy/happiness	ABS	noun
שִׂמְחָה	*bə·śim·**ḥâ***	W/ PREP בְּ	
לַחְמֶ֔ךָ	your bread/food	CST	noun
לֶ֫חֶם	*laḥ·**me**·ḵā*	W/ 2MS SX	

7b	וּֽשֲׁתֵ֥ה בְלֶב־ט֖וֹב יֵינֶ֑ךָ

and drink your wine with a happy heart,

וּֽשֲׁתֵ֥ה	and (you) drink	PIEL IMPV MS	verb
שׁתה	*û·šă·**tē***	W/ CONJ וְ	
בְלֶב־	with a heart/mind	ABS	noun
לֵב	*və·lev-*	W/ PREP בְּ	
ט֖וֹב	good	MS ATTR	adj
טוֹב	***ṭôv***		
יֵינֶ֑ךָ	your wine	CST	noun
יַ֫יִן	*yê·**ne**·ḵā*	W/ 2MS SX	

7c	כִּ֣י כְבָ֔ר רָצָ֥ה הָאֱלֹהִ֖ים אֶֽת־מַעֲשֶֽׂיךָ׃

for God already delights in your deeds.

כִּ֣י	for/because	---	conj
כִּי	***kî***		
כְבָ֔ר	already/long ago	---	adv
כְּבָר	*ḵə·**vār***		
רָצָ֥ה	(he) was pleased with/ delighted in	QAL PF 3MS	verb
רצה	*rā·**ṣâ***		
הָאֱלֹהִ֖ים	the God	ABS	noun
אֱלֹהִים	*hā·ʾĕ·lō·**hîm***	W/ DEF. ART.	
אֶֽת־	*(direct object marker)*	---	particle
אֵת	*ʾet-*		
מַעֲשֶֽׂיךָ׃	your deeds/actions	CST	noun
מַעֲשֶׂה	*ma·ʿă·**śê**·ḵā*	W/ 2MS SX	

Given the inevitability of death and the human inability to forestall it, Qoheleth encourages his readers to take joy in the pleasures of food and drink. Wine and bread were staples of the Israelite diet, and thus they represent not luxuries out of reach of most people but rather the normal, everyday sustenance of life. We are to take joy in the most mundane of experiences—that is God's gift to humans. Further, though Qoheleth acknowledges the reality of God's judgment—and warns of it in v. 9—he also states that God "delights in" or "is pleased with" the work that we humans do. Understanding this truth should cause us to "relax and enjoy our lives" (Weeks 2022:438).

8a	בְּכָל־עֵ֕ת יִהְי֥וּ בְגָדֶ֖יךָ לְבָנִ֑ים

At all times may your clothes be white,

Hebrew	Gloss	Parsing	Part of speech
בְּכָל־ כֹּל	in/at all of *bə·ḵol-*	CST W/ PREP בְּ	noun
עֵ֕ת עֵת	time *ʿēt*	ABS	noun
יִהְי֥וּ היה	let (them) be / may (they) be *yih·yû*	QAL JUSS 3MP	verb
בְגָדֶ֖יךָ בֶּ֫גֶד	your clothes/garments *və·gā·dɛ̂·ḵā*	CST W/ 2MS SX	noun
לְבָנִ֑ים לָבָן	white *lə·vā·nîm*	MP PRED	adj

8b	וְשֶׁ֖מֶן עַל־רֹאשְׁךָ֥ אַל־יֶחְסָֽר׃

and do not let oil be lacking upon your head.

Hebrew	Gloss	Parsing	Part of speech
וְשֶׁ֖מֶן שֶׁ֫מֶן	and oil *wə·še·men*	ABS W/ CONJ וְ	noun
עַל־ עַל	on/upon *ʿal-*	---	prep
רֹאשְׁךָ֥ רֹאשׁ	your head *rō᾽·šə·ḵā*	CST W/ 2MS SX	noun
אַל־ אַל	no/not *᾽al-*	---	particle

יֶחְסָר׃ חסר	(it) will be lacking *yeḥ · sār*	QAL JUSS 3MS	verb

Both white clothing and oil upon one's head symbolize rejoicing and merriment. Qoheleth is encouraging his readers to "dress up" regularly rather than saving one's fancy clothing only for special occasions.

9a רְאֵה חַיִּים עִם־אִשָּׁה אֲשֶׁר־אָהַבְתָּ

Enjoy life with the wife whom you love

רְאֵה ראה	(you) see/experience/enjoy *rə · 'ē*	QAL IMPV MS	verb
חַיִּים חַיִּים	life *ḥay · yîm*	ABS	noun
עִם־ עִם	with *'im-*	---	prep
אִשָּׁה אִשָּׁה	woman/wife *'iš · šâ*	ABS	noun
אֲשֶׁר־ אֲשֶׁר	who/that/which *'ă · šer-*	---	relative pron
אָהַבְתָּ אהב	you loved *'ā · **hav** · tā*	QAL PF 2MS	verb

Together with food and wine, Qoheleth now encourages his readers to enjoy life with one's spouse, thus highlighting again the book's overarching concern with flourishing relationships (see further at 4:7–12). Some scholars have argued that Qoheleth envisions enjoyment with a "woman" in general rather than one's wife in particular because of the lack of a definite article ("the") on אִשָּׁה ("wife"). However, the absence of the definite article does not necessitate that reading from a grammatical standpoint (see Whitley 1979:80), and Longman aptly points out that "the command to enjoy a promiscuous lifestyle sounds like a postsexual revolution statement and not like one an Israelite wise man, no matter how confused and questioning, would make to his students" (Longman 1998:231).

9b	כָּל־יְמֵי֙ חַיֵּ֣י הֶבְלֶ֔ךָ אֲשֶׁ֤ר נָֽתַן־לְךָ֙ תַּ֣חַת הַשֶּׁ֔מֶשׁ

all the days of your Abelish life that he gave you under the sun—

כָּל־ כֹּל	all of *kol-*	CST	noun
יְמֵי֙ יוֹם	days of *yə·**mê***	CST	noun
חַיֵּ֣י חַיִּים	life of *ḥay·**yê***	CST	noun
הֶבְלֶ֔ךָ הֶבֶל	your Abel/mist/vapor/breath *hev·**le**·ḵā*	CST W/ 2MS SX	noun
אֲשֶׁ֤ר אֲשֶׁר	who/that/which *'ă·**šer***	---	relative pron
נָֽתַן־ נתן	he gave ***nā**·tan-*	QAL PF 3MS	verb
לְךָ֙ לְ	to you *lə·**ḵā***	--- W/ 2MS SX	prep
תַּ֣חַת תַּחַת	under ***ta**·ḥat*	---	prep
הַשֶּׁ֔מֶשׁ שֶׁמֶשׁ	the sun *haš·**še**·meš*	ABS W/ DEF. ART.	noun

9c	כֹּ֖ל יְמֵ֣י הֶבְלֶ֑ךָ

all of your Abelish days.

כֹּ֖ל כֹּל	all of ***kōl***	CST	noun
יְמֵ֣י יוֹם	days of *yə·**mê***	CST	noun
הֶבְלֶ֑ךָ הֶבֶל	your Abel/mist/vapor/breath *hev·**le**·ḵā*	CST W/ 2MS SX	noun

Note the close connection that Qoheleth draws between enjoyment of God's gifts in 9:7–9a with and the acknowledgment that life is still marked by Abelness in v. 9b–c. Life is not all good or all bad, but rather our lives as a whole are Abelish—marked by the same experiences of Abel in

Gen 4—and yet they are also saturated with joy in God's gifts, including even the days themselves.

9d	כִּ֣י ה֤וּא חֶלְקְךָ֙ בַּֽחַיִּ֔ים		
	For that is your portion in life		
כִּ֣י כִּי	for/because *kî*	---	conj
ה֤וּא הוּא	that *hû'*	---	demonstr pron
חֶלְקְךָ֙ חֵ֫לֶק	your reward/portion *ḥel·qə·kā*	CST W/ 2MS SX	noun
בַּֽחַיִּ֔ים חַיִּים	in life *ba·ḥay·yîm*	ABS W/ PREP בְּ + DEF. ART.	noun

9e	וּבַעֲמָ֣לְךָ֔ אֲשֶׁר־אַתָּ֥ה עָמֵ֖ל תַּ֥חַת הַשָּֽׁמֶשׁ׃		
	and in your toil that you toil under the sun.		
וּבַעֲמָ֣לְךָ֔ עָמָל	and in your toil/labor *û·va·'ă·mā·lə·kā*	CST W/ CONJ וְ + PREP בְּ + 2MS SX	noun
אֲשֶׁר־ אֲשֶׁר	who/that/which *'ă·šer-*	---	relative pron
אַתָּ֥ה אַתָּה	you *'at·tâ*	---	personal pron
עָמֵ֖ל עָמֵל	toil *'ā·mēl*	MS PRED	adj
תַּ֥חַת תַּחַת	under *ta·ḥat*	---	prep
הַשָּֽׁמֶשׁ׃ שֶׁ֫מֶשׁ	the sun *haš·šā·meš*	ABS W/ DEF. ART.	noun

Enjoyment of food, drink, a spouse, and work is humanity's "portion" or "reward," the gift of God that helps us to navigate life "under the sun," which is marked through by Abelness. For further discussion, see comments at 1:3a, 11d; 2:10d, 11a; "From Text to Sermon" at 2:4–11; notes at

3:22b, c; 4:4c; "From Text to Sermon" at 4:4–12; notes at 5:17c, 18c; "From Text to Sermon" at 5:13–20; notes at 7:10c, 11b; and "From Text to Sermon" at 8:10–15.

10a כֹּל אֲשֶׁר תִּמְצָא יָדְךָ לַעֲשׂוֹת

All that your hand finds to do,

כֹּל כֹּל	all/everything *kōl*	ABS	noun
אֲשֶׁר אֲשֶׁר	who/that/which *ʾă·šer*	---	relative pron
תִּמְצָא מצא	(you) find *tim·ṣāʾ*	QAL IMPF 2MS	verb
יָדְךָ יָד	your hand *yā·də·ḵā*	CST W/ 2MS SX	noun
לַעֲשׂוֹת עשׂה	to do/make *la·ʿă·śôt*	QAL INF CST W/ PREP לְ	verb

10b בְּכֹחֲךָ עֲשֵׂה

do it with your strength.

בְּכֹחֲךָ כֹּחַ	with your strength/ power/might *bə·ḵō·ḥă·ḵā*	CST W/ PREP בְּ + 2MS SX	noun
עֲשֵׂה עשׂה	(you) do/make *ʿă·śē*	QAL IMPV MS	verb

10c כִּי אֵין מַעֲשֶׂה וְחֶשְׁבּוֹן וְדַעַת וְחָכְמָה בִּשְׁאוֹל

For there is no working or thinking or knowledge or wisdom in Sheol,

כִּי כִּי	for/because *kî*	---	conj

אֵין אַיִן	there is not *ʾên*	---	particle
מַעֲשֶׂה מַעֲשֶׂה	working *ma·ʿă·**śe***	ABS	noun
וְחֶשְׁבּוֹן חֶשְׁבּוֹן	and thought/reckoning *wə·ḥeš·**bôn***	ABS W/ CONJ וְ	noun
וְדַעַת דַּעַת	and knowledge *wə·**da**·ʿat*	ABS W/ CONJ וְ	noun
וְחָכְמָה חָכְמָה	and wisdom *wə·ḥok·**mâ***	ABS W/ CONJ וְ	noun
בִּשְׁאוֹל שְׁאוֹל	in Sheol *biš·**ʾôl***	ABS W/ PREP בְּ	noun

10d אֲשֶׁר אַתָּה הֹלֵךְ שָׁמָּה׃

where you are going.

אֲשֶׁר אֲשֶׁר	who/that/which *ʾă·**šer***	---	relative pron
אַתָּה אַתָּה	you *ʾat·**tâ***	---	personal pron
הֹלֵךְ הלך	going/walking *ho·**lek̲***	QAL PTCP MS	verb
שָׁמָּה׃ שָׁם	to there ***šām**·mâ*	--- W/ LOCATIVE ה	adv

Qoheleth grounds his admonition to "do . . . with your strength" "all that your hand finds to do" in the knowledge that activity ceases in Sheol. Thinking, doing, planning, knowing, and wisdom will cease in Sheol, so it is all the more imperative that humans engage fully in such activities now, while we still can. Readers of the New Testament know that God will one day create the new heavens and the new earth (Rev 21:1), where such activity will resume, but the author of Ecclesiastes did not have access to this fuller revelation of God's purposes. Qoheleth's view here reflects the common understanding in the Hebrew Bible that activity ends upon death (cf. Ps 6:5: "Who can praise you in Sheol?").

From Text to Sermon

One Fate for All. A key theme in Ecclesiastes that the author develops further here is that there is one fate for everyone. He laments the singular fate for humans and beasts in ch. 3, and before that in ch. 2 he bemoans that the wise and the foolish are heading toward the same end—death. In this passage, Qoheleth returns to consider again this theme of the same fate for all (see "From Text to Sermon" at 1:1–11 for discussion of the cyclical nature of the book of Ecclesiastes). As we have seen throughout the book already, Qoheleth's discussion of difficult issues models for readers today how to struggle through those same issues. That is, his frustration with the reality that death is coming for everyone, no matter how good or evil, gives readers today the space and language to express their own frustration and confusion over the same issue. It is likely that many people will find such honesty refreshing, and listening to the words of Ecclesiastes will perhaps give the people in your congregation freedom to similarly acknowledge the aspects of life that they find unjust. Leading your people in speaking honestly to God and to one another will strengthen the horizontal, human-to-human relationships in your congregation as well as the vertical, human-to-God relationships.

Drink Your Wine with a Happy Heart. As we saw in the "From Text to Sermon" section on 8:10–15, Qoheleth does not simply leave his readers in despair. His protestations and disclosure of frustration over the injustices he sees (and that we all experience) in life are not mere bellyaching or incessant complaints over every small matter. Rather, they are one part of his process for navigating life in this broken world. A second part of his admonition (along with fearing the Lord), as we've seen throughout, is the call to enjoy life, or *carpe diem* ("seize the day"). Since we have talked about this concept in multiple places already, here we will zero in on Qoheleth's statement to "drink your wine with a happy heart" (9:7).

According to the National Survey on Drug Use and Health, in 2022, 12.2 percent of US adults and 2.9 percent of US youth (twelve to seventeen years of age) suffered from alcohol use disorder, or what is typically called alcoholism. That amounts to just over thirty million people in the United States alone. Given these statistics, it is more than likely that someone in your congregation either personally suffers from alcohol use disorder or suffers because of a loved one's struggle with alcoholism. There are a range of reasons that people drink too much alcohol, and this is not the place to adjudicate those reasons or examine in detail the psychological causes for alcoholism. However, Eccl 9:7 does offer the opportunity to speak to one aspect of alcohol use that was particularly helpful for me personally as I struggled with alcoholism. The verse says to "drink your wine with a happy heart" (9:7).

In the years that I drank heavily, it was never "with a happy heart." It was never in celebration or in community. Rather, drinking made me forget; it enabled me to shut my mind off, to go numb, to avoid the difficulties of life for a few hours. Of course, it was a doomed strategy that led to deeper isolation and much suffering. I (and I would venture many people like me) asked alcohol to do something it was never intended to do and thus made into an idol. I bowed at the altar of Bacchus instead of the altar of Christ, and it wreaked havoc on all other parts of my life, though it took me a very long time to see its devastating personal and relational effects.

Though some people should abstain completely from alcohol given the enormous temptation to worship it as a false god, Qoheleth is not a teetotaler, nor does the rest of the Bible advocate for that position. What Qoheleth does, though, is place alcohol in a particular context—one marked by joy, celebration, and relationship with God and others. Reframing alcohol use in this way will go a long way toward freeing those who drink in isolation in order to avoid life, demonstrating instead a better, fuller way of living—in community.

ECCLESIASTES 11:1–10

THE LIMITS OF HUMAN KNOWLEDGE (AND WHAT TO DO ABOUT IT)

In this short chapter, Qoheleth outlines the limits of human knowledge and offers some advice for coping with those limits. In sum, he argues that we should diversify our endeavors, be diligent to do what we can despite the unknowable future, and enjoy life as much as possible.

LARGER LITERARY CONTEXT › 11:1–10

11:1–6

1a שַׁלַּ֥ח לַחְמְךָ֖

*šal**laḥ** laḥmə**ḵā***

Send your bread

1b עַל־פְּנֵ֣י הַמָּ֑יִם

*ʿal-pə**nê** ham**mā**yim*

upon the surface of the waters,

1c כִּֽי־בְרֹ֥ב הַיָּמִ֖ים תִּמְצָאֶֽנּוּ׃

*kî-və**rōv** hayyā**mîm** timṣāʾ**ennû**.*

for in many days you will find it.

2a תֶּן־חֵ֥לֶק לְשִׁבְעָ֖ה

*ten-**ḥē**leq ləšivʿ**â***

Give a portion to seven,

2b וְגַ֣ם לִשְׁמוֹנָ֑ה

*wə**gam** lišmô**nâ***

even to eight,

2c כִּ֚י לֹ֣א תֵדַ֔ע מַה־יִּהְיֶ֥ה רָעָ֖ה עַל־הָאָֽרֶץ׃

***kî lōʾ** tē**daʿ** mah-yih**ye** rāʿ**â** ʿal-hāʾ**ā**reṣ.*

because you do not know what evil will happen upon the earth.

3a אִם־יִמָּלְא֨וּ הֶעָבִ֥ים

*ʾim-yimmāləʾ**û** heʿā**vîm ge**šem*

If the clouds are full,

3b עַל־הָאָ֣רֶץ יָרִ֔יקוּ גֶּ֖שֶׁם

*ʿal-hāʾ**ā**reṣ yā**rî**qû*

they empty rain upon the earth.

3c וְאִם־יִפּ֥וֹל עֵ֛ץ בַּדָּר֖וֹם וְאִ֣ם בַּצָּפ֑וֹן

*wəʾim-yip**pôl** ʿ**ēṣ** baddā**rôm** wəʾ**im** baṣṣā**fôn***

And if a tree falls in the south or in the north,

3d מְק֛וֹם שֶׁיִּפּ֥וֹל הָעֵ֖ץ שָׁ֥ם יְהֽוּא׃

*mə**qôm** šeyyip**pôl** hā**ʿēṣ** **šām** yə**hû**ʾ.*

the place where the tree falls, there it is.

4a שֹׁמֵ֥ר ר֖וּחַ לֹ֣א יִזְרָ֑ע

*šō**mēr** **rû**aḥ **lō**ʾ yiz**rā**ʿ*

One watching the wind will not sow,

4b וְרֹאֶ֥ה בֶעָבִ֖ים לֹ֥א יִקְצֽוֹר׃

*wərō**ʾe** veʿā**vîm** **lō**ʾ yiq**ṣôr**.*

and one who looks at the clouds will not reap.

5a כַּאֲשֶׁ֨ר אֵינְךָ֤ יוֹדֵ֙עַ֙ מַה־דֶּ֣רֶךְ הָר֔וּחַ

*kaʾă**šer** ʾênə**ḵā** yô**dē**aʿ mah-**de**reḵ hā**rû**aḥ*

Just as you do not know the path of the wind

5b כַּעֲצָמִ֖ים בְּבֶ֣טֶן הַמְּלֵאָ֑ה

*kaʿăṣā**mîm** bə**ve**ṭen hamməlē**ʾâ***

or how the bones form in the womb of the pregnant woman,

5c כָּ֗כָה לֹ֤א תֵדַע֙ אֶת־מַעֲשֵׂ֣ה הָֽאֱלֹהִ֔ים

kā**ḵâ **lō**ʾ tē**da**ʿ ʾet-maʿă**śē** hāʾĕlō**hîm

so you do not know the work of God,

5d אֲשֶׁ֥ר יַעֲשֶׂ֖ה אֶת־הַכֹּֽל׃

*ʾă**šer** yaʿă**śe** ʾet-hak**kōl**.*

who makes everything.

6a בַּבֹּ֙קֶר֙ זְרַ֣ע אֶת־זַרְעֶ֔ךָ

*ba**bō**qer zə**ra**ʿ ʾet-zarʿ**e**ḵā*

In the morning sow your seed,

6b וְלָעֶרֶב אַל־תַּנַּח יָדֶךָ

wəlāʿerev ʾal-tannaḥ yādekā

and at night do not let your hand rest,

6c כִּי אֵינְךָ יוֹדֵעַ אֵי זֶה יִכְשָׁר

kî ʾênəkā yôdēaʿ ʾê ze yikšār

for you do not know what will be advantageous,

6d הֲזֶה אוֹ־זֶה

hăze ʾô-ze

this one or that one—

6e וְאִם־שְׁנֵיהֶם כְּאֶחָד טוֹבִים׃

wəʾim-šənêhem kəʾeḥād ṭôvîm.

or if both alike will be prosperous.

1a	שַׁלַּח לַחְמְךָ		
	Send your bread		
שַׁלַּח שלח	(you) send/send off *šal·laḥ*	PIEL IMPV MS	verb
לַחְמְךָ לֶחֶם	your bread *laḥ·mə·kā*	CST W/ 2MS SX	noun

Given the overall context of the verse, "bread" may be better translated as "grain," as in the NET. See further discussion at v. 1c below.

1b	עַל־פְּנֵי הַמָּיִם		
	upon the surface of the waters,		
עַל־ עַל	on/upon *ʿal-*	---	prep

פְּנֵי פָּנֶה	face/surface of *pə·**nê***	CST	noun
הַמָּיִם מַיִם	the waters/seas *ham·**mā**·yim*	ABS W/ DEF. ART.	noun

1c כִּי־בְרֹב הַיָּמִים תִּמְצָאֶנּוּ׃

for in many days you will find it.

כִּי־ כִּי	for/because *kî-*	---	conj
בְּרֹב רֹב	in many of *və·**rōv***	CST W/ PREP בְּ	noun
הַיָּמִים יוֹם	the days *hay·yā·**mîm***	ABS W/ DEF. ART.	noun
תִּמְצָאֶנּוּ׃ מצא	you will find/obtain it *tim·ṣā·**'en**·nû*	QAL IMPF 2MS W/ 3MS SX	verb

There are two primary interpretations of the meaning of this verse. In the first instance, sending one's bread is taken to be a charitable activity in which one gives freely to those in need. In the second view, Qoheleth is seen as advocating engaging in business despite its associated risks. Thus, the "bread" "stands for any kind of commodity of trade" (Longman 1998:256) and hence the NET translation of "grain." Taken together with the following verse, it is clear that Qoheleth acknowledges the inherent risk involved in not knowing the future—a key limitation that God has placed on humans—and encourages trade or charity (depending on one's interpretation) regardless.

2a תֶּן־חֵלֶק לְשִׁבְעָה

Give a portion to seven,

תֶּן־ נתן	(you) give *ten-*	QAL IMPV MS	verb
חֵלֶק חֵלֶק	portion *ḥē·leq*	ABS	noun

לְשִׁבְעָה / שֶׁבַע	to seven / *lə·šiv·ʿâ*	ABS W/ PREP לְ	cardinal number

2b	וְגַם לִשְׁמוֹנָה
	even to eight,

וְגַם / גַּם	and also/even / *wə·gam*	--- W/ CONJ וְ	adv
לִשְׁמוֹנָה / שְׁמֹנֶה	to eight / *liš·mô·nâ*	ABS W/ PREP לְ	cardinal number

This statement takes the form of a numerical saying, well known in the Hebrew Bible (see, e.g., Job 5:19; Prov 6:16; Isa 17:6; Mic 5:5 [4]).

2c	כִּי לֹא תֵדַע מַה־יִּהְיֶה רָעָה עַל־הָאָרֶץ׃
	because you do not know what evil will happen upon the earth.

כִּי / כִּי	for/because / *kî*	---	conj
לֹא / לֹא	no/not / *lōʾ*	---	particle
תֵדַע / ידע	you know / *tē·daʿ*	QAL IMPF 2MS	verb
מַה־ / מָה	what? / *mah-*	---	interr pron
יִּהְיֶה / היה	(it) will be / *yih·ye*	QAL IMPF 3MS	verb
רָעָה / רָעָה	disaster/evil / *rā·ʿâ*	ABS	noun
עַל־ / עַל	on/upon / *ʿal-*	---	prep
הָאָרֶץ׃ / אֶרֶץ	the earth / *hā·ʾā·reṣ*	ABS W/ DEF. ART.	noun

"Evil" (רָעָה) can also mean "disaster." The translation here aims to avoid the connotation of natural disasters *only*, for the term encompasses both natural disasters, such as floods and hurricanes, and human-made disasters like war. Significantly, though, the Old Testament goes to great lengths to attribute evil/disaster to Yahweh himself, who is sovereign over all things. In Amos 3:6 Yahweh asks, "If evil/disaster happens in a city, did not Yahweh do it?" And Jonah 3:10 states, "And God saw their works, that the turned from their evil ways, and God relented concerning the evil/disaster that he said he would do to them, and he did not do it." Qoheleth's theology of God's sovereignty is consistent with the rest of the Old Testament witness; therefore, we should not understand this verse as implying that bad things just happen; rather, Qoheleth's point is that *humans* have no idea what is coming down the pike. The best course of action, then, is simply to do what we can without worrying about the things we do not know.

3a אִם־יִמָּלְאוּ הֶעָבִים

If the clouds are full,

אִם־ אִם	if/when *'im-*	---	conj
יִמָּלְאוּ מלא	(they) are full of/filled with *yim·mā·lə·'û*	NIPH IMPF 3MP	verb
הֶעָבִים עָב	the clouds *he·'ā·**vîm***	ABS W/ DEF. ART.	noun

3b עַל־הָאָרֶץ יָרִיקוּ גֶּשֶׁם

they empty rain upon the earth.

גֶּשֶׁם גֶּשֶׁם	rain ***ge***·*šem*	ABS	noun
עַל־ עַל	on/upon *'al-*	---	prep
הָאָרֶץ אֶרֶץ	the earth/land *hā·**'ā**·reṣ*	ABS W/ DEF. ART.	noun
יָרִיקוּ ריק	they empty/pour down *yā·**rî**·qû*	HIPH IMPF 3MP	verb

3c	וְאִם־יִפּ֥וֹל עֵ֛ץ בַּדָּר֖וֹם וְאִ֣ם בַּצָּפ֑וֹן

And if a tree falls in the south or in the north,

וְאִם־ אִם	and if *wə·ʾim-*	--- W/ CONJ וְ	conj
יִפּ֥וֹל נפל	(it) falls *yip·**pôl***	QAL IMPF 3MS	verb
עֵ֛ץ עֵץ	a tree ***ʿēṣ***	ABS	noun
בַּדָּר֖וֹם דָּרוֹם	in the south *bad·dā·**rôm***	ABS W/ PREP בְּ + DEF. ART.	noun
וְאִ֣ם אִם	or if *wə·**ʾim***	--- W/ CONJ וְ	conj
בַּצָּפ֑וֹן צָפוֹן	in the north *baṣ·ṣā·**fôn***	ABS W/ PREP בְּ + DEF. ART.	noun

3d	מְק֛וֹם שֶׁיִּפּ֥וֹל הָעֵ֖ץ שָׁ֥ם יְהֽוּא׃

the place where the tree falls, there it is.

מְק֛וֹם מָקוֹם	place of *mə·**qôm***	CST	noun
שֶׁיִּפּ֥וֹל נפל	that/which/where (it) will fall *šey·yip·**pôl***	QAL IMPF 3MS W/ PREP שֶׁ	verb
הָעֵ֖ץ עֵץ	the tree *hā·**ʿēṣ***	ABS W/ DEF. ART.	noun
שָׁ֥ם שָׁם	there ***šām***	---	adv
יְהֽוּא׃ הוה	it is/will be *yə·**hûʾ***	QAL IMPF 3MS	verb

There is much scholarly discussion about the form of the final verb in this verse, but its meaning remains the same no matter what one decides about its root or parsing. Those interested can read summaries of the discussion in Schoors (2013:769–71) and Fredericks (1988:222–23).

In addition to the evil/disaster mentioned in v. 2, here Qoheleth further illustrates human inability with the natural phenomena of rain and of trees falling down. When those things happen in the natural course of weather and life cycles, they remain distinctly outside of human control.

4a שֹׁמֵ֥ר ר֖וּחַ לֹ֣א יִזְרָ֑ע

One watching the wind will not sow,

שֹׁמֵ֥ר שׁמר	watching (one) of *šō·mēr*	Q (CST) PTCP MS	verb
ר֖וּחַ רוּחַ	wind *rû·aḥ*	ABS	noun
לֹ֣א לֹא	no/not *lō'*	---	particle
יִזְרָ֑ע זרע	(he) will sow *yiz·rā'*	QAL IMPF 3MS	verb

4b וְרֹאֶ֥ה בֶעָבִ֖ים לֹ֥א יִקְצֽוֹר׃

and one who looks at the clouds will not reap.

וְרֹאֶ֥ה ראה	and a seeing/looking (one) *wə·rō·'e*	QAL PTCP MS W/ CONJ וְ	verb
בֶעָבִ֖ים עָב	at the clouds *ve·'ā·vîm*	ABS W/ PREP בְּ + DEF. ART.	noun
לֹ֥א לֹא	no/not *lō'*	---	particle
יִקְצֽוֹר׃ קצר	(he) will reap *yiq·ṣôr*	QAL IMPF 3MS	verb

This verse resonates especially with readers in agricultural contexts. Humans can control neither wind nor rain, and attempting to perfectly time seeding and harvesting with the weather will result in neither planting one's crop nor reaping it at harvest time. The point, again, is that humans must not allow the unpredictability of the future to paralyze us in the present. Note the connection here with the poem in 3:1–8.

5a	כַּאֲשֶׁר אֵינְךָ יוֹדֵעַ מַה־דֶּרֶךְ הָרוּחַ

Just as you do not know the path of the wind

כַּאֲשֶׁר אֲשֶׁר	like/as *ka·ʾă·**šer***	--- W/ PREP כְּ	relative pron
אֵינְךָ אַיִן	there is not to you/ you do not *ʾ**ê**·nə·ḵā*	--- W/ 2MS SX	particle
יוֹדֵעַ ידע	know *yô·**dē**·aʿ*	QAL PTCP MS	verb
מַה־ מָה	what? *mah-*	---	interr pron
דֶּרֶךְ דֶּרֶךְ	way/road/path of ***de**·reḵ*	CST	noun
הָרוּחַ רוּחַ	the wind *hā·**rû**·aḥ*	ABS W/ DEF. ART.	noun

5b	כַּעֲצָמִים בְּבֶטֶן הַמְּלֵאָה

or how the bones form in the womb of the pregnant woman,

כַּעֲצָמִים עֶצֶם	like/as the bones *ka·ʿă·ṣā·**mîm***	ABS W/ PREP כְּ + DEF. ART.	noun
בְּבֶטֶן בֶּטֶן	in womb of *bə·**ve**·ṭen*	CST W/ PREP בְּ	noun
הַמְּלֵאָה מָלֵא	the full (one) *ham·mə·lē·**ʾâ***	FS SUBST W/ DEF. ART.	adj

The verb "form" is not in the Hebrew text. The meaning is pulled from the description in the previous clause—"the path of the wind." Thus, as we don't know the path of the wind, so we do not know the path of bones, that is, how bones are formed.

5c	כָּכָה לֹא תֵדַע אֶת־מַעֲשֵׂה הָאֱלֹהִים

so you do not know the work of God,

כָּכָה כָּכָה	thus/so/in this way *kā·kâ*	---	adv
לֹא לֹא	no/not *lōʾ*	---	particle
תֵדַע ידע	you know *tē·daʿ*	QAL IMPF 2MS	verb
אֶת־ אֵת	*(direct object marker)* *ʾet-*	---	particle
מַעֲשֵׂה מַעֲשֶׂה	work/deed/action of *ma·ʿă·śē*	ABS	noun
הָאֱלֹהִים אֱלֹהִים	the God *hā·ʾĕ·lō·hîm*	ABS W/ DEF. ART.	noun

5d	אֲשֶׁר יַעֲשֶׂה אֶת־הַכֹּל׃

who makes everything.

אֲשֶׁר אֲשֶׁר	who/that/which *ʾă·šer*	---	relative pron
יַעֲשֶׂה עשׂה	(he) does/makes *ya·ʿă·śe*	QAL IMPF 3MS	verb
אֶת־ אֵת	*(direct object marker)* *ʾet-*	---	particle
הַכֹּל׃ כֹּל	the whole/all/everything *hak·kōl*	ABS W/ DEF. ART.	noun

The root עשׂה means both "to make" and "to do." In English we are forced to choose between one of the meanings, so that God either "makes everything" or "does everything." Though it cannot be reflected in the translation, it is best to retain both meanings.

The point of this verse, as with previous verses, is to highlight the lack of human knowledge, this time knowledge of God. Furthermore, here the author explicitly compares human lack with God's abundance. We do not know everything, but certainly God does, for he "makes/does everything."

6a	בַּבֹּ֙קֶר֙ זְרַ֣ע אֶת־זַרְעֶ֔ךָ

In the morning sow your seed,

בַּבֹּ֙קֶר֙ בֹּ֫קֶר	in the morning *ba·**bō**·qer*	ABS W/ PREP בְּ + DEF. ART.	noun
זְרַ֣ע זרע	(you) sow *zə·**ra**ʻ*	QAL IMPV MS	verb
אֶת־ אֵת	*(direct object marker)* *ʼet-*	---	particle
זַרְעֶ֔ךָ זֶ֫רַע	your seed *zar·**ʻe**·ḵā*	CST W/ 2MS SX	noun

6b	וְלָעֶ֖רֶב אַל־תַּנַּ֣ח יָדֶ֑ךָ

and at night do not let your hand rest,

וְלָעֶ֖רֶב עֶ֫רֶב	and to/toward the evening/night *wə·lā·**ʻe**·rev*	ABS W/ CONJ וְ + PREP לְ + DEF. ART.	noun
אַל־ אַל	no/not *ʼal-*	---	particle
תַּנַּ֣ח נוח	(you) cause to/give rest *tan·**naḥ***	HIPH JUSS 2MS	verb
יָדֶ֑ךָ יָד	your hand *yā·**de**·ḵā*	CST W/ 2MS SX	noun

Qoheleth is not advocating working all the time, which he finds loathsome (see comments at 4:4–12 above, as well as “From Text to Sermon” there). Rather, in keeping with the context of the current passage, he is arguing that our lack of knowledge about the future should cause us to diversify our efforts, as he notes in the following clauses of this verse.

6c	כִּ֣י אֵֽינְךָ֩ יוֹדֵ֨עַ אֵ֤י זֶה֙ יִכְשָׁ֔ר

for you do not know what will be advantageous,

כִּ֣י כִּי	for/because ***kî***	---	conj

אֵינְךָ אַיִן	there is not to you *ʾê·nə·ḵā*	--- W/ 2MS SX	particle
יוֹדֵעַ ידע	knowing *yô·dēʿ*	QAL PTCP MS	verb
אֵי אַי	where? / whether/if *ʾê*	---	interr pron
זֶה זֶה	this *ze*	---	demonstr pron
יִכְשַׁר כשר	(it) will succeed/ be advantageous *yiḵ·šār*	QAL IMPF 3MS	verb

6d הֲזֶה אוֹ־זֶה

this one or that one—

הֲזֶה זֶה	the this *hă·ze*	--- W/ INTERR הֲ	demonstr pron
אוֹ־ אוֹ	or *ʾô-*	---	conj
זֶה זֶה	this *ze*	---	demonstr pron

6e וְאִם־שְׁנֵיהֶם כְּאֶחָד טוֹבִים׃

or if both alike will be prosperous.

וְאִם־ אִם	and/or if *wə·ʾim-*	--- W/ CONJ וְ	conj
שְׁנֵיהֶם שְׁנַיִם	two/both of them *šə·nê·hem*	CST W/ 3MP SX	cardinal number
כְּאֶחָד אֶחָד	as one *kə·ʾe·ḥād*	ABS W/ PREP כְּ	cardinal number
טוֹבִים׃ טוֹב	good/prosperous *ṭô·vîm*	MP PRED	adj

The ideal, of course, is for both endeavors to succeed equally well. However, humans simply do not know if one, the other, both, or neither effort will be successful. While the temptation may be to throw our hands in the air and give up, Qoheleth reinforces that we must do what we can do despite the outcome being hidden from us.

11:7–10

7a וּמָת֖וֹק הָא֑וֹר

*ûmā**tôq** hā**ʾôr***

Light is sweet,

7b וְט֥וֹב לַֽעֵינַ֖יִם לִרְא֥וֹת אֶת־הַשָּֽׁמֶשׁ׃

*wə**ṭôv** la**ʿê**nayim lir**ʾôt** ʾet-haš**šā**meš.*

and it is good for the eyes to see the sun.

8a כִּ֣י אִם־שָׁנִ֥ים הַרְבֵּ֛ה יִחְיֶ֥ה הָאָדָ֖ם

kî** ʾim-šā**nîm** har**bē** yiḥ**ye** hāʾā**dām

Indeed, if a person lives many years,

8b בְּכֻלָּ֣ם יִשְׂמָ֑ח

*bəkul**lām** yiś**māḥ***

may he rejoice in all of them.

8c וְיִזְכֹּר֙ אֶת־יְמֵ֣י הַחֹ֔שֶׁךְ

*wəyiz**kōr** ʾet-yə**mê** ha**ḥō**šek*

But may he remember the days of darkness,

8d כִּֽי־הַרְבֵּ֥ה יִהְי֖וּ

*kî-har**bē** yih**yû***

for they will be many.

8e כָּל־שֶׁבָּ֥א הָֽבֶל׃

*kol-šeb**bāʾ** **hā**vel.*

Everything that is coming is Abel.

9a שְׂמַ֧ח בָּח֣וּר בְּיַֽלְדוּתֶ֗יךָ

*śə**maḥ** bā**ḥûr** bəyaldû**tê**kā*

Rejoice, young man, in your youth;

9b וִֽיטִֽיבְךָ֤ לִבְּךָ֙ בִּימֵ֣י בְחוּרוֹתֶ֔ךָ

*wîṭîvə**ḵā** libbə**ḵā** bî**mê** vəḥûrô**te**ḵā*

may your heart be happy in your young days.

9c וְהַלֵּךְ֙ בְּדַרְכֵ֣י לִבְּךָ֔ וּבְמַרְאֵ֖י עֵינֶ֑יךָ

*wəhal**lēḵ** bədar**ḵê** libbə**ḵā** ûvəmar**ʾê** ʿê**nê**ḵā*

Walk in the paths of your heart and in the sight of your eyes,

9d וְדָ֕ע כִּ֛י עַל־כָּל־אֵ֖לֶּה יְבִיאֲךָ֥ הָאֱלֹהִ֖ים בַּמִּשְׁפָּֽט׃

*wə**dāʿ** **kî** ʿal-kol-ʾ**ē**lle yəvîʾă**ḵā** hāʾĕlō**hîm** bammiš**pāṭ**.*

but know that concerning all of these things,
God will bring you into judgment.

10a וְהָסֵ֤ר כַּ֙עַס֙ מִלִּבֶּ֔ךָ

*wəhā**sēr** **ka**ʿas millib**be**ḵā*

Banish anger from your heart

10b וְהַעֲבֵ֥ר רָעָ֖ה מִבְּשָׂרֶ֑ךָ

*wəhaʿă**vēr** rā**ʿâ** mibbəśā**re**ḵā*

and remove wickedness from your body,

10c כִּֽי־הַיַּלְד֥וּת וְהַשַּׁחֲר֖וּת הָֽבֶל׃

*kî-hayyal**dût** wəhaššaḥă**rût** **hā**vel.*

for youth and black hair are Abelish.

7a וּמָת֖וֹק הָא֑וֹר

Light is sweet,

וּמָת֖וֹק מָתוֹק	and sweet *û · mā · **tôq***	MS PRED W/ CONJ וְ	adj
הָא֑וֹר אוֹר	the light *hā · **ʾôr***	ABS W/ DEF. ART.	noun

7b **וְטוֹב לַעֵינַ֫יִם לִרְא֖וֹת אֶת־הַשָּֽׁמֶשׁ׃**

and it is good for the eyes to see the sun.

וְטוֹב טוֹב	and good *wə·ṭôv*	MS PRED W/ CONJ וְ	adj
לַעֵינַ֫יִם עַיִן	for the eyes *la·ʿê·na·yim*	ABS W/ PREP לְ + DEF. ART.	noun
לִרְאוֹת ראה	to see *lir·ʾôt*	QAL INF CST W/ PREP לְ	verb
אֶת־ אֵת	*(direct object marker)* *ʾet-*	---	particle
הַשָּֽׁמֶשׁ׃ שֶׁמֶשׁ	the sun *haš·šā·meš*	ABS W/ DEF. ART.	noun

This verse marks a transition from the previous section, where Qoheleth advocated taking action despite uncertainty and the human inability to know the future. Here Qoheleth turns to reflect (again) on the value of being alive, urging readers to embrace a joyful life as fully as possible, though with the knowledge that many travails await us. Despite all of that, it is indeed "good for the eyes to see the sun."

8a **כִּ֣י אִם־שָׁנִ֤ים הַרְבֵּה֙ יִחְיֶ֣ה הָאָדָ֔ם**

Indeed, if a person lives many years,

כִּי אִם־ כִּי אִם־	indeed/surely if *kî ʾim-*	---	conj
שָׁנִים שָׁנָה	years *šā·nîm*	ABS	noun
הַרְבֵּה רבה	to be many/much *har·bē*	HIPH INF ABS	verb
יִחְיֶה חיה	(it) will be *yiḥ·ye*	QAL IMPF 3MS	verb
הָאָדָם אָדָם	the man/human/humanity *hā·ʾā·dām*	ABS W/ DEF. ART.	noun

8b **בְּכֻלָּ֣ם יִשְׂמָ֑ח**

may he rejoice in all of them.

בְּכֻלָּ֣ם כֹּל	in all of them *bə·kul·**lām***	CST W/ PREP בְּ + 3MP SX	noun
יִשְׂמָ֑ח שׂמח	let him/may he rejoice *yiś·**māḥ***	QAL JUSS 3MS	verb

8c **וְיִזְכֹּר֙ אֶת־יְמֵ֣י הַחֹ֔שֶׁךְ**

But may he remember the days of darkness,

וְיִזְכֹּר֙ זכר	and/but let him/ may he remember *wə·yiz·**kōr***	QAL JUSS 3MS W/ CONJ וְ	verb
אֶת־ אֵת	*(direct object marker)* *ʾet-*	---	particle
יְמֵ֣י יוֹם	days of *yə·**mê***	CST	noun
הַחֹ֔שֶׁךְ חֹ֫שֶׁךְ	the darkness *ha·**ḥō**·šek̲*	ABS W/ DEF. ART.	noun

8d **כִּֽי־הַרְבֵּ֥ה יִהְי֖וּ**

for they will be many.

כִּֽי־ כִּי	for/because *kî-*	---	conj
הַרְבֵּ֥ה רבה	to be many/much *har·**bē***	HIPH INF ABS	verb
יִהְי֖וּ היה	they will be *yih·**yû***	QAL IMPF 3MP	verb

8e	כָּל־שֶׁבָּ֖א הָֽבֶל׃

Everything that is coming is Abel.

כָּל־ כֹּל	all/every *kol-*	ABS	noun
שֶׁבָּ֖א בוא	that/which comes/is coming *šeb·bā'*	QAL PTCP MS W/ PREP שֶׁ	verb
הָֽבֶל׃ הֶ֫בֶל	Abel/mist/vapor/breath *hā·vel*	ABS	noun

This verse illustrates well the tension seen throughout the entire book. Humans can and should rejoice as much as possible, yet we must also remember that there will be many dark days, for all of life is marked by Abel.

9a	שְׂמַ֧ח בָּח֣וּר בְּיַלְדוּתֶ֗יךָ

Rejoice, young man, in your youth;

שְׂמַ֧ח שׂמח	(you) rejoice/take joy *śə·maḥ*	QAL IMPV MS	verb
בָּח֣וּר בָּחוּר	youth/young man *bā·ḥûr*	ABS	noun
בְּיַלְדוּתֶ֗יךָ יַלְדוּת	in your youth/young days *bə·yal·dû·tê·kā*	CST W/ PREP בְּ + 2MS SX	noun

Though Qoheleth uses a term specifically for a "young man" (בָּחוּר), we should not take that to mean his instruction applies to males only. Rather, young people in general should take joy, or rejoice, in their younger days. However, we should not read into this statement notions of "sowing one's oats" or living recklessly.

9b	וִֽיטִֽיבְךָ֤ לִבְּךָ֙ בִּימֵ֣י בְחוּרוֹתֶ֔ךָ

may your heart be happy in your young days.

וִֽיטִֽיבְךָ֤ יטב	be good/pleasing / make merry/happy *wî·ṭî·və·kā*	HIPH JUSS 3MS W/ CONJ וְ + 2MS SX	verb

לִבְּךָ לֵב	your heart/mind *lib·bə·**ḵā***	CST W/ 2MS SX	noun
בִּימֵי יוֹם	in days of *bî·**mê***	CST W/ PREP בְּ	noun
בְחוּרוֹתֶךָ בְּחוּרִים	your youth/young days *və·ḥû·rô·**te**·ḵā*	CST W/ 2MS SX	noun

The word for "youth" here (בְּחוּרִים) differs from the word used in v. 9a (יַלְדוּת), but the meaning is the same, and this line repeats the sentiment in the previous line (synonymous parallelism).

9c וְהַלֵּךְ בְּדַרְכֵי לִבְּךָ וּבְמַרְאֵי עֵינֶיךָ

Walk in the paths of your heart and in the sight of your eyes,

וְהַלֵּךְ הלך	and (you) walk/go about *wə·hal·**lēḵ***	PIEL IMPV MS W/ CONJ וְ	verb
בְּדַרְכֵי דֶּרֶךְ	in paths/ways of *bə·dar·**ḵê***	CST W/ PREP בְּ	noun
לִבְּךָ לֵב	your heart/mind *lib·bə·**ḵā***	CST W/ 2MS SX	noun
וּבְמַרְאֵי מַרְאֶה	and in sight/vision of *û·və·mar·**ʾê***	CST W/ CONJ וְ + PREP בְּ	noun
עֵינֶיךָ עַיִן	your eyes *ʿê·**nɛ̂**·ḵā*	CST W/ 2MS SX	noun

Qoheleth is essentially encouraging young people to do the things they want to do. This is not altogether different from modern parents encouraging their children to pursue interests and hobbies that appeal to them, that will bring them joy. As the next clause makes clear, this is not a call to foolish, wanton living. As any parent will attest, "Find something you love and do that" does not mean, "Indulge your basest desires with no regard for consequences."

9d	וְדָ֗ע כִּ֛י עַל־כָּל־אֵ֥לֶּה יְבִיאֲךָ֥ הָאֱלֹהִ֖ים בַּמִּשְׁפָּֽט׃

but know that concerning all of these things,
God will bring you into judgment.

Hebrew	Gloss	Parsing	Part of speech
וְדָ֗ע ידע	but (you) know/ acknowledge/recognize *wə·dāʿ*	QAL IMPV MS W/ CONJ וְ	verb
כִּ֛י כִּי	that *kî*	---	conj
עַל־ עַל	on/upon/concerning *ʿal-*	---	prep
כָּל־ כֹּל	all of *kol-*	CST	noun
אֵ֥לֶּה אֵלֶּה	these (things) *ʾēl·le*	---	demonstr pron
יְבִיאֲךָ֥ בוא	(he) will bring you / cause you to enter *yə·vî·ʾă·ḵā*	HIPH IMPF 3MS W/ 2MS SX	verb
הָאֱלֹהִ֖ים אֱלֹהִים	the God *hā·ʾĕ·lō·hîm*	ABS W/ DEF. ART	noun
בַּמִּשְׁפָּֽט׃ מִשְׁפָּט	in/into judgment/justice *bam·miš·pāṭ*	ABS W/ PREP בְּ + DEF. ART.	noun

Lest we think that Qoheleth is urging his readers to live recklessly and pursue desires that are wicked, unwise, or otherwise inappropriate, he tempers his advice with the warning that God will indeed judge what we do. Thus, in keeping with the book's overall theological message, Qoheleth urges readers to pursue and embrace joy—but within the boundaries of a relationship with God (that is, "fear of God").

מִשְׁפָּט refers both to "judgment" and "justice" in Hebrew. The word does not carry the negative connotations that we often associate with "judgment" in modern culture. Rather, it refers simply to God's just measurement of what is good and right (or evil and wrong). God is not "judgy," but he is just and righteous, and therefore our thoughts and actions should acknowledge his justice/judgment and we should adjust our lives accordingly.

10a	וְהָסֵר כַּ֫עַס מִלִּבֶּךָ

Banish anger from your heart

וְהָסֵר סור	and (you) cause to turn aside/remove/ward off *wə·hā·**sēr***	HIPH IMPV MS W/ CONJ וְ	verb
כַּ֫עַס כַּ֫עַס	vexation/anger/grief ***ka**·ʿas*	ABS	noun
מִלִּבֶּךָ לֵב	from your heart/mind *mil·lib·**be**·ḵā*	CST W/ PREP מִן + 2MS SX	noun

The range of meaning of כַּעַס ("anger") is broad, but it always has a somewhat negative connotation (e.g., worry, grief, vexation). The lack of an exactly corresponding term in English should be addressed in preaching or teaching on this passage, lest we unnecessarily limit that which Qoheleth urges his young readers to banish from their hearts. Essentially, he is arguing that in addition to pursuing joy, young people should also reject the sorts of emotions that overtake or otherwise dampen a happy heart.

10b	וְהַ֣עֲבֵ֣ר רָעָ֖ה מִבְּשָׂרֶ֑ךָ

and remove wickedness from your body,

וְהַעֲבֵר עבר	and (you) cause to pass by/send/remove/take away *wə·ha·ʿă·**vēr***	HIPH IMPV MS W/ CONJ וְ	verb
רָעָה רָעָה	evil/wickedness *rā·**ʿâ***	ABS	noun
מִבְּשָׂרֶךָ בָּשָׂר	from your body/flesh *mib·bə·śā·**re**·ḵā*	CST W/ PREP מִן + 2MS SX	noun

As in v. 9, Qoheleth here combines the admonition to reject negative emotions (כַּעַס, "anger, grief," v. 10a) with a call to pursue the Lord, to "remove wickedness from your body." Again, we should not read Qoheleth's advice hedonistically, for his calls to joy are embedded within the context of living in relationship with the Creator.

10c	כִּֽי־הַיַּלְד֥וּת וְהַשַּׁחֲר֖וּת הָֽבֶל׃

for youth and black hair are Abelish.

כִּֽי־ כִּי	for/because *kî-*	---	conj
הַיַּלְד֥וּת יַלְדוּת	the youth/young days *hay·yal·**dût***	ABS W/ DEF. ART.	noun
וְהַשַּׁחֲר֖וּת שַׁחֲרוּת	and the blackness *wə·haš·ša·ḥă·**rût***	ABS W/ CONJ וְ + DEF. ART.	noun
הָֽבֶל׃ הֶבֶל	Abel/mist/vapor/breath ***hā**·vel*	ABS	noun

This clause provides the reason for banishing anger/grief/vexation and rejecting evil: like Abel, youth is fleeting.

Scholars and translations are divided over how to understand the word שַׁחֲרוּת ("black hair"), which appears only here in the Hebrew Bible. It could be related to the word שַׁחַר, which means "dawn," as in the time of day when the sun rises (e.g., Gen 19:15; Jonah 4:7). On the other hand, the word could derive from the verb שחר, which means "to be black." The latter interpretation is preferred here on comparison with the use of "grey" or "grey hair" to indicate old age in the Hebrew Bible (e.g., Lev 19:32; Prov 16:31; 20:29).

From Text to Sermon

You Can (and Should) Do What You Can (and Should) Do. The theme of 11:1–6 is that humans do not know very much. Two possible responses to our finiteness often present themselves. In the first instance, we can imagine that we actually do know a lot and proceed arrogantly on that assumption. This is the way of the rich fool in Jesus's parable in Luke 12. Supposing that his future was certain, the man built larger barns than he already had in preparation for a life of ease, "but God said to him, 'Fool! This night your soul is required of you, and the things you have prepared, whose will they be?'" (Luke 12:20 ESV). The book of James offers similar advice to the person who thinks the future is certain: "Now listen, you who say, 'Today or tomorrow we will go to this or that city, spend a year there, carry on business and make money.' Why, you do not even know what will happen tomorrow. What is your life? You are a mist that appears for a little while and then vanishes" (Jas 4:13–14 ESV). The second response to the unknowability of the future is to do nothing at all. This is the way of the fool.

Qoheleth urges us to avoid both of these responses and instead proceed in a third way—namely, what we can and should do with the full knowledge that we ultimately do not know what will happen. Like James urged his readers, "You ought to say, 'If it is the Lord's will, we will live and do this or that.'" This third, better way of being in the world acknowledges and operates within both divine sovereignty and human responsibility.

The Mysterious Work of God. As part of his larger discussion of human finiteness, in v. 5 Qoheleth uses the imagery of the path of the wind and a baby being formed in a mother's womb to illustrate that humans "do not know the work of God, who makes everything." Like the unknowable future, the mystery of God forces us to acknowledge that we are human and God is God. However, the great temptation that Adam and Eve faced—and that all of us face at some point (usually at many points!)—is to put ourselves in the place of God. Like our first ancestors, we think that God is untrustworthy or somehow withholding good from us, and so we reject the fundamental truth that humans are human and God is God, choosing to worship ourselves rather than our Creator.

In John 3, Jesus uses similar imagery to help Nicodemus see that he is human and lacks the knowledge of God's mysterious work in people. Meeting under cover of night, Jesus tells the Pharisee that "unless someone is born again, he cannot see the kingdom of God" (John 3:3 ESV). Nicodemus, understandably confused, protests that such a thing is utterly impossible: "Can he enter his mother's womb a second time and be born?" (3:4 ESV). Here Jesus likely draws from Ecclesiastes to help the "teacher of Israel" understand (3:10 ESV). "Do not be amazed that I told you that you must be born again," Jesus responds. "The wind blows where it pleases, and you hear its sound, but you don't know where it comes from or where it is going. So it is with everyone born of the Spirit." That is, "Just as you do not know the path of the wind or how the bones form in the womb of the pregnant woman, so you do not know the work of God, who makes [and, it turns out, remakes] everything" (Eccl 11:5).

More than simply forcing Nicodemus to acknowledge his finiteness, though, Jesus's analogy points Nicodemus to the truth of God's immense love for his creation. This love is most manifest in the death and resurrection of Christ, which restores the broken relationship between humans and God, thus undoing the disastrous effects of Adam and Eve's—and our—self-worship.

ECCLESIASTES 12:9–14

THE END OF THE MATTER

This passage brings us to the conclusion of our journey through the book of Ecclesiastes, through which we learned the importance of (1) speaking honestly and plainly about the sin-marred, Abelish world in which we live; (2) embracing as fully as God allows the gifts that he gives us; and (3) living in relationship with God, or fearing him. The book's closing returns to this final part of Qoheleth's program for flourishing in an upside-down world, arguing that fearing God and obeying his commands is in fact what it means to be human.

LARGER LITERARY CONTEXT › 12:9–14

12:9–10

9a וְיֹתֵ֗ר שֶׁהָיָ֥ה קֹהֶ֖לֶת חָכָ֑ם

*wəyō**tēr** šehā**yâ** qō**he**let ḥā**kām***

And more than Qoheleth being wise,

9b עֹ֗וד לִמַּד־דַּ֙עַת֙ אֶת־הָעָ֔ם

*ʿ**ôd** limmad-**da**ʿat ʾet-hāʿ**ām***

he also taught the people knowledge,

9c וְאִזֵּ֣ן וְחִקֵּ֔ר תִּקֵּ֖ן מְשָׁלִ֥ים הַרְבֵּֽה׃

*wəʾiz**zēn** wəḥiq**qēr** tiq**qēn** məšā**lîm** har**bē**.*

and he weighed, searched out, and made clear many proverbs.

10a בִּקֵּ֣שׁ קֹהֶ֔לֶת לִמְצֹ֖א דִּבְרֵי־חֵ֑פֶץ

*biq**qēš** qō**he**let lim**ṣō**ʾ divrê-**ḥē**feṣ*

Qoheleth sought to find delightful words

10b וְכָת֥וּב יֹ֖שֶׁר דִּבְרֵ֥י אֱמֶֽת׃

*wəkā**tûv** **yō**šer div**rê** ʾĕ**met**.*

and frankly wrote truthful words.

9a וְיֹתֵ֗ר שֶׁהָיָ֥ה קֹהֶ֖לֶת חָכָ֑ם

And more than Qoheleth being wise,

וְיֹתֵ֗ר יוֹתֵר	and more/surplus/excess *wə·yō·**tēr***	ABS W/ CONJ וְ	noun
שֶׁהָיָ֥ה היה	that (he) was *še·hā·**yâ***	QAL PF 3MS W/ PREP שֶׁ	verb
קֹהֶ֖לֶת קֹהֶלֶת	Qoheleth *qō·**he**·let*	ABS	noun

חָכָם חָכָם	wise *ḥā·kām*	MS PRED	adj

9b עוֹד לִמַּד־דַּעַת אֶת־הָעָם

he also taught the people knowledge,

עוֹד עוֹד	again/yet/still *'ôd*	---	adv
לִמַּד־ למד	he taught/trained *lim·mad-*	PIEL PF 3MS	verb
דַּעַת דַּעַת	knowledge *da·'at*	ABS	noun
אֶת־ אֵת	*(direct object marker)* *'et-*	---	particle
הָעָם עַם	the people *hā·'ām*	ABS W/ DEF. ART.	noun

9c וְאִזֵּן וְחִקֵּר תִּקֵּן מְשָׁלִים הַרְבֵּה׃

and he weighed, searched out, and made clear many proverbs.

וְאִזֵּן אזן	and he weighed *wə·'iz·zēn*	PIEL PF 3MS W/ CONJ וְ	verb
וְחִקֵּר חקר	and (he) searched out/ investigated/explored *wə·ḥiq·qēr*	PIEL PF 3MS W/ CONJ וְ	verb
תִּקֵּן תקן	(he) made straight/clear *tiq·qēn*	PIEL PF 3MS	verb
מְשָׁלִים מָשָׁל	proverbs/sayings/parables *mə·šā·lîm*	ABS	noun
הַרְבֵּה׃ רבה	to be many/much *har·bē*	HIPH INF ABS	verb

10a	בִּקֵּשׁ קֹהֶלֶת לִמְצֹא דִּבְרֵי־חֵפֶץ		
	Qoheleth sought to find delightful words		
בִּקֵּשׁ בקשׁ	(he) sought/asked/requested *biq·**qēš***	PIEL PF 3MS	verb
קֹהֶלֶת קֹהֶלֶת	Qoheleth/gatherer/assembler *qō·**he**·let*	ABS	noun
לִמְצֹא מצא	to find/discover/come across *lim·**ṣō'***	QAL INF CST W/ PREP לְ	verb
דִּבְרֵי־ דָּבָר	words/matters/things of *div·rê-*	CST	noun
חֵפֶץ חֵפֶץ	delight/desire/pleasure ***ḥē**·feṣ*	ABS	noun

10b	וְכָתוּב יֹשֶׁר דִּבְרֵי אֱמֶת׃		
	and frankly wrote truthful words.		
וְכָתוּב כתב	and writing *wə·kā·**tûv***	QAL PASS PTCP MS W/ CONJ וְ	verb
יֹשֶׁר יֹשֶׁר	upright/straight/correct ***yō**·šer*	ABS	noun
דִּבְרֵי דָּבָר	words/matters/things of *div·**rê***	CST	noun
אֱמֶת׃ אֱמֶת	truth *'ĕ·**met***	ABS	noun

Ecclesiastes 12:9–14 comprises the epilogue of the book of Ecclesiastes. The history of interpretation is divided over whether these final five verses are the words of Qoheleth himself, summarizing his work from a third-person perspective, or whether they come from a second person who compiled the "words of Qoheleth, son of David, king in Jerusalem" (1:1). We cannot answer that question here, and it ultimately does not make much difference in interpretation unless one views the bulk of the book as unorthodox (as many scholars do). As interpreted in this volume, Ecclesiastes is far from unorthodox and instead represents the honest struggle of a realist sage in Israel. Thus, whether this is the third-person perspective of Qoheleth or a second narrator, the message and theology of the book remain the same.

12:11–12

11a דִּבְרֵ֨י חֲכָמִ֜ים כַּדָּ֣רְבֹנ֗וֹת

*div**rê** ḥăḵā**mîm** kaddorvō**nôt***

The words of the wise are like goads,

11b וּכְמַשְׂמְר֖וֹת נְטוּעִ֑ים בַּעֲלֵ֣י אֲסֻפּ֑וֹת

*ûḵəmaśmə**rôt** nəṭû**ʿîm** baʿă**lê** ʾăsup**pôt***

and like embedded nails are masters of collections.

11c נִתְּנ֖וּ מֵרֹעֶ֥ה אֶחָֽד׃

*nittə**nû** mērō**ʿe** ʾe**ḥād**.*

They were given by one shepherd.

12a וְיֹתֵ֣ר מֵהֵ֔מָּה בְּנִ֖י הִזָּהֵ֑ר

*wəyō**tēr** mē**hēm**mâ bə**nî** hizzā**hēr***

And beyond these, my son, be warned:

12b עֲשׂ֨וֹת סְפָרִ֤ים הַרְבֵּה֙ אֵ֣ין קֵ֔ץ

*ʿă**śôt** səfā**rîm** har**bē** ʾ**ên** **qēṣ***

there is no end to the making of many books,

12c וְלַ֥הַג הַרְבֵּ֖ה יְגִעַ֥ת בָּשָֽׂר׃

*wə**la**hag har**bē** yəgi**ʿat** bā**śār**.*

and much study is weariness to the body.

11a דִּבְרֵ֨י חֲכָמִ֜ים כַּדָּ֣רְבֹנ֗וֹת

The words of the wise are like goads,

דִּבְרֵ֨י דָּבָר	words of *div·rê*	CST	noun

חֲכָמִים חָכָם	wise (ones) *ḥă·ḵā·**mîm***	MP SUBST	adj
כַּדָּרְבֹנוֹת דָּרְבָנָה	like the goads *kad·dor·vō·**nôt***	ABS W/ PREP כְּ + DEF. ART.	noun

11b **וּכְמַשְׂמְרוֹת נְטוּעִים בַּעֲלֵי אֲסֻפּוֹת**

and like embedded nails are masters of collections.

וּכְמַשְׂמְרוֹת מַסְמֵר	and like nails/spikes *û·ḵə·maś·mə·**rôt***	ABS W/ CONJ וְ + PREP כְּ	noun
נְטוּעִים נטע	planted/embedded *nə·ṭû·**ʿîm***	QAL PASS PTCP MP	verb
בַּעֲלֵי בַּעַל	masters of *ba·ʿă·**lê***	CST	noun
אֲסֻפּוֹת אֲסֻפָּה	collections *ʾă·sup·**pôt***	ABS	noun

The meaning of בַּעֲלֵי ("masters of") is clear, but אֲסֻפּוֹת ("collections") appears only here in the Hebrew Bible and has presented interpretive difficulties. Based on its root (אסף, "to add") and later usage, it seems to mean "collection" or something similar. Nevertheless, as Longman points out, translations tend to interpret the phrase in a way that emphasizes the parallelism with "words of the wise" in the previous clause—"collected sayings" (ESV) or "collections" (NASB)—thus leaving untranslated the word בַּעֲלֵי ("masters of"). However, "recent studies of parallelism . . . have successfully challenged the idea that parallelism is based on true synonymity, noting that the second colon always sharpens or progresses the thought of the first colon" (Longman 1998:276). Thus, whereas the first colon refers in general to the words of the wise, the second refers more specifically to those who have mastered collections, what we might call scholars of a particular body of literature.

11c נִתְּנוּ מֵרֹעֶה אֶחָד׃

They were given by one shepherd.

נִתְּנוּ	they were given/granted	NIPH PF 3CP	verb
נתן	*nit·tə·**nû***		
מֵרֹעֶה	from/by shepherd	QAL PTCP MS	verb
רעה	*mē·**rō**·'e*	W/ PREP מִן	
אֶחָד׃	one	ABS	cardinal number
אֶחָד	*'e·**ḥād***		

12a וְיֹתֵר מֵהֵמָּה בְּנִי הִזָּהֵר

And beyond these, my son, be warned:

וְיֹתֵר	and more/beyond	ABS	noun
יוֹתֵר	*wə·yō·**tēr***	W/ CONJ וְ	
מֵהֵמָּה	from these	---	personal
הֵמָּה	*mē·**hēm**·mâ*	W/ PREP מִן	pron
בְּנִי	my son	CST	noun
בֵּן	*bə·**nî***	W/ 1CS SX	
הִזָּהֵר	(you) be warned/careful	NIPH IMPV MS	verb
זהר	*hiz·zā·**hēr***		

"These" refers to the preceding "words of the wise" and "masters of collections." That is, the reader should beware of books beyond the accepted tradition. Note that the intended reader of the book becomes clear here: "my son." We will be familiar with a father addressing his son from reading the book of Proverbs (e.g., Prov 1:8, 10, 15).

12b עֲשׂוֹת סְפָרִים הַרְבֵּה אֵין קֵץ

there is no end to the making of many books,

עֲשׂוֹת	to do/make	QAL INF CST	verb
עשׂה	*'ă·**śôt***		
סְפָרִים	documents/books/scrolls	ABS	noun
סֵפֶר	*sə·fā·**rîm***		

הַרְבֵּה רבה	to be many/much *har·bē*	HIPH INF ABS	verb
אֵין אַיִן	there is not *ʾên*	---	particle
קֵץ קֵץ	end/limit *qēṣ*	ABS	noun

12c וְלַהַג הַרְבֵּה יְגִעַת בָּשָׂר׃

and much study is weariness to the body.

וְלַהַג לַהַג	and study *wə·la·hag*	ABS W/ CONJ וְ	noun
הַרְבֵּה רבה	to be many/much *har·bē*	HIPH INF ABS	verb
יְגִעַת יְגִעָה	weariness/wearying of *yə·gi·ʿat*	CST	noun
בָּשָׂר׃ בָּשָׂר	body/flesh *bā·śār*	ABS	noun

To this every preacher can say, “Amen.”

12:13–14

13a סוֹף דָּבָר
sôf dāvār
The concluding word,

13b הַכֹּל נִשְׁמָע
*hak**kōl** niš**mā**ʿ*
the entirety has been heard.

13c אֶת־הָאֱלֹהִים יְרָא
*ʾet-hāʾĕlō**hîm** yərāʾ*
Fear God

13d וְאֶת־מִצְוֺתָיו שְׁמוֹר
*wəʾet-miṣwô**tāyw** šə**môr***
and keep his commandments

13e כִּי־זֶה כָּל־הָאָדָם׃
*kî-**ze** kol-hāʾā**dām**.*
because this is the whole of humanity.

14a כִּי אֶת־כָּל־מַעֲשֶׂה הָאֱלֹהִים יָבִא בְמִשְׁפָּט
kî** ʾet-kol-maʿă**śe** hāʾĕlō**hîm** yā**vī**ʾ vəmiš**pāṭ
For God will judge every deed,

14b עַל כָּל־נֶעְלָם
*ʿ**al** kol-neʿ**lām***
including every hidden thing,

14c אִם־טוֹב וְאִם־רָע׃
*ʾim-**ṭôv** wəʾim-**rāʿ**.*
whether good or evil.

13a	סוֹף דָּבָר		
	The concluding word,		
סוֹף סוף	end/conclusion/totality *sôf*	CST	noun
דָּבָר דָּבָר	word/matter/thing *dā·vār*	ABS	noun

13b	הַכֹּל נִשְׁמָע		
	the entirety has been heard.		
הַכֹּל כֹּל	the whole/all/everything *hak·kōl*	ABS W/ DEF. ART.	noun
נִשְׁמָע שׁמע	(it) was/has been heard/ listened to *niš·mā‘*	NIPH PF 3MS	verb

These two clauses introduce the book's summative, concluding word, which should guide our interpretation of the entire treatise.

13c	אֶת־הָאֱלֹהִים יְרָא		
	Fear God		
אֶת־ אֵת	*(direct object marker)* *'et-*	---	particle
הָאֱלֹהִים אֱלֹהִים	the God *hā·'ĕ·lō·hîm*	ABS W/ DEF. ART.	noun
יְרָא ירא	(you) fear/have reverence for *yə·rā'*	QAL IMPV MS	verb

"Fear" is a particularly important word for the book of Ecclesiastes and the Hebrew Bible as a whole, as it is shorthand for biblical faith, describing a human's posture toward and relationship with God. For fuller discussion of this concept, see "From Text to Sermon" below.

13d	וְאֶת־מִצְוֺתָיו שְׁמוֹר

and keep his commandments

וְאֶת־ / אֵת	*(direct object marker)* / *wə · 'et-*	--- W/ CONJ וְ	particle
מִצְוֺתָיו / מִצְוָה	his commands/ commandments / *miṣ · wô · **tāyw***	CST W/ 3MS SX	noun
שְׁמוֹר / שׁמר	(you) keep/observe/ give heed to / *šə · **môr***	QAL IMPV MS	verb

Typical Hebrew sentence structure is verb-subject-direct object. In this clause and the previous, the author fronts the direct objects ("God" in v. 13c and "commandments" in v. 13d), placing them before the verb (with embedded subject) for emphasis.

13e	כִּי־זֶה כָּל־הָאָדָם׃

because this is the whole of humanity.

כִּי־ / כִּי	for/because / *kî-*	---	conj
זֶה / זֶה	this / *ze*	---	demonstr pron
כָּל־ / כֹּל	whole/all/everything of / *kol-*	CST	noun
הָאָדָם׃ / אָדָם	the man/human/humanity / *hā · 'ā · **dām***	ABS W/ DEF. ART.	noun

Some English translations supply a word in this clause, such as "duty" ("this is the whole *duty* of humanity," NIV, ESV, KJV), or otherwise expand the statement for clarification, such as the NASB's "this applies to every person" and the CSB's "this is for all humanity." However, the Hebrew text makes sense as it stands, and in fact it communicates a significant theological statement that could be missed if we modify the clause. Rather than being the "duty" or responsibility of every human, or even something that "applies to every person" (though of course those notions are implied), the author is making a statement about what it means to be a human being. The whole, all, everything of being a human in a world marked by Abelness is fearing God and keeping his commands, or put another way, living in right relationship with him. See "From Text to Sermon" below for further discussion.

14a	כִּי אֶת־כָּל־מַעֲשֶׂה הָאֱלֹהִים יָבִא בְמִשְׁפָּט		
	For God will judge every deed,		
כִּי כִּי	for/because *kî*	---	conj
אֶת־ אֵת	*(direct object marker)* *'et-*	---	particle
כָּל־ כֹּל	all/every/whole *kol-*	CST	noun
מַעֲשֶׂה מַעֲשֶׂה	deed/action *ma·'ă·śe*	ABS	noun
הָאֱלֹהִים אֱלֹהִים	the God *hā·'ĕ·lō·hîm*	ABS W/ DEF. ART.	noun
יָבִא בוא	(he) will bring/bring about/ cause to come *yā·vī'*	HIPH IMPF 3MS	verb
בְמִשְׁפָּט מִשְׁפָּט	in/into judgment/justice *və·miš·pāṭ*	ABS W/ PREP בְּ	noun

The verse woodenly reads, "For every deed God will bring into judgment," which is rendered more idiomatically here. Ecclesiastes ends on a final word of warning concerning how we humans live: God is just and will therefore judge what we do. This warning provides the "stick" for living a faithful life, whereas the vision of life that Ecclesiastes presents—in which humans enjoy the gifts of God and the benefits of living in right relationship with him—is the "carrot."

14b	עַל כָּל־נֶעְלָם		
	including every hidden thing,		
עַל עַל	in addition to/together with *'al*	---	prep

כָּל־ כֹּל	all/every/whole *kol-*	CST	noun
נֶעְלָ֑ם עלם	hidden/concealed thing *ne'·lām*	NIPH PTCP MS	verb

The God who is sovereign is also omniscient, so Ecclesiastes reminds readers that "every hidden thing" will eventually be brought into judgment. This stands in one sense as a warning to live faithfully, but in another sense it is a reason for hope, for we can be certain that God will bring justice for everything.

14c אִם־ט֖וֹב וְאִם־רָֽע׃

whether good or evil.

אִם־ אִם	if/whether *'im-*	---	conj
ט֖וֹב טוֹב	good *ṭôv*	MS PRED	adj
וְאִם־ אִם	and if/whether *wə·'im-*	--- W/ CONJ וְ	conj
רָֽע׃ רַע	evil *rā'*	MS PRED	adj

In the Masoretic tradition, it is customary to repeat the second-to-last verse after reading the final verse of Isaiah, the Book of the Twelve (the Minor Prophets), Lamentations, and Ecclesiastes "so that the book does not end with a threat" (Fox 2004:85; see also Longman 1998:281; Weeks 2022:697). Here that would mean repeating Eccl 12:13 to close the reading of the book.

From Text to Sermon

Frank Words of Truth and Firmly Planted Nails. I grew up in the Deep South, which is (rightly) known for its hospitality and politeness (among other, not-as-flattering characteristics). Because of the cultural pressure to be nice—at least to a person's face—being frank was never highly valued. In fact, speaking hard truths plainly is a good way to make enemies down there. Throughout the book of Ecclesiastes, though, we have seen the teacher tell the truth openly and honestly, and here in the last few verses, he is lauded as a person who "frankly wrote truthful words" (12:10b).

As a young seminarian struggling with drug and alcohol abuse, self-imposed social isolation, and an overwhelming sense that nothing in life mattered, I started reading Ecclesiastes because I thought, "If there's a guy who wrote a whole book of the Bible saying that everything is 'meaningless,' then maybe there's some hope for me." I soon learned that Qoheleth *did not* say that everything is meaningless, but I also learned I was right about his frankness, about his clear statement of what is what in the world. The author of Ecclesiastes does not hold back from describing life the way that he saw it—and the way that so many of us experience it. There is injustice, frustration, and agony. Things don't go the way they should. The righteous are scorned, the wicked praised, and death is coming for all of us, no matter what we do. Such truthful words awakened my heart again, gave me hope for a different sort of life, and they made me turn again to the God who inspired those words. As we saw in 3:16–22, Qoheleth models disclosure, or telling the truth about our experiences, which is a primary way of healing after trauma. The church needs this book, and the people in our congregations need to see frank truth-telling modeled—both in Scripture and in one another.

Verse 11 of chapter 12 reminds us, though, that frank words of truth are not always so encouraging, at least not in the moment. They are like "goads" and "embedded nails," both of which a shepherd uses to poke and prod reluctant animals. These are not the rod and staff of Ps 23, as Longman (1998:280) points out, tools that conjure warm images of the shepherd protecting his sheep from predators who would do them harm. Rather, these tools inflict pain on the animals themselves and thus recall the common biblical theme that discipline is good, even though it is painful, keeping us on the way of wisdom when we would stray to the way of folly if left to ourselves. Indeed, "the Lord disciplines the one he loves and punishes every son he receives" (Heb 12:6 CSB, quoting Prov 3:12).

Fearing God. The last two verses of Ecclesiastes give us the hermeneutical lens through which we are to read the rest of the book, and indeed through which we should examine the entirety of human life. At least two avenues for fruitful discussion present themselves.

First, we would do well to consider what exactly it means to "fear God." The word "fear" has a wide range of meaning, and its primary usage in modern culture is not typically religious. Therefore, it may be good to spend time talking with your congregation about the differences between the various types of fear that we experience today, such as being afraid of the dark, fear of heights, the fear produced by a scary movie or book, and the fear induced by living with an abusive spouse or parent. Particularly in the last example, there exists the danger that people who have experienced abuse will associate fearing God with fearing an abusive husband or father. It will be important to demonstrate that fearing God is something altogether different, and indeed it refers to living in right relationship with God. Such fear is not cowering fear, but it is the appropriate response to the knowledge that God is God and we are not, that he is altogether above and beyond us, wiser and more powerful than humans can ever imagine. And yet we must hold his transcendence in tension with his desire to be near his people. That is, the Lord likewise loves us more deeply than we could ever imagine—to the point of sending his own Son to die a sinner's death so that he might make right what was made wrong in the garden so long ago and so that humans might once again live in right relationship with him. Thus, the fear of God must be understood in the context of a relationship with God—a relationship that God alone made possible.

Second, and following from the meaning of "fear," the last part of v. 13 offers another avenue for meaningful reflection on living in relationship with God. The translation of v. 13 above woodenly reflects the Hebrew: "because this is the whole of humanity." English translations often supply a word or two to clarify (in their opinion) the author's message: "that is the whole duty of everyone" (NRSV); "this is everyone's duty" (NLT); "this is the duty of all mankind" (NIV); "this is the whole duty of man" (ESV). However, the term "duty" is altogether absent in the Hebrew text. The author is not telling readers that our *duty* is to live in relationship with God; rather he is stating that "the whole of humanity" is living in relationship with him. Put another way, what it means to be human, really and fully human, is to fear God, or to live in right relationship with him. Fearing God is not our *duty*; it is our *being*.

WORKS CITED

Alter, Robert. 2010. *The Wisdom Books: Job, Proverbs, and Ecclesiastes*. New York: Norton.

Anderson, William H. U. 1998. "The Curse of Work in Qoheleth: An Exposé of Genesis 3:17–19 in Ecclesiastes." *Evangelical Quarterly* 70:99–113.

Bartholomew, Craig G. 2009. *Ecclesiastes*. Baker Commentary on the Old Testament Wisdom and Psalms. Grand Rapids: Baker Academic.

Blenkinsopp, Joseph. 2003. *Isaiah 56–66*. Anchor Bible 19. New York: Doubleday.

———. 2011. *Creation, Un-Creation, Re-Creation: A Discursive Commentary on Genesis 1–11*. London: T&T Clark.

Bollhagen, James. 2011. *Ecclesiastes*. Concordia Commentary. St. Louis: Concordia.

Brown, William P. 2011. *Ecclesiastes*. Interpretation: A Bible Commentary for Teaching and Preaching. Louisville: Westminster John Knox.

Crenshaw, James. 1987. *Ecclesiastes*. Old Testament Library. Philadelphia: Westminster.

Curtis, Edward M. 2013. *Ecclesiastes and Song of Songs*. Teach the Text Commentary Series. Grand Rapids: Baker Books.

DCH = Clines, David J. A. 1993–2016. *The Dictionary of Classical Hebrew*. 8 vols. Sheffield: Sheffield Academic.

Ellis, Robert. 2010. "Amos Economics." *Review and Expositor* 107:463–79.

Ellul, Jacques. 1990. *Reason for Being: A Meditation on Ecclesiastes*. Grand Rapids: Eerdmans.

Fishbane, Michael. 1985. *Biblical Interpretation in Ancient Israel*. Oxford: Clarendon.

Fox, Michael V. 1977. "Frame Narrative and Composition in the Book of Qohelet." *Hebrew Union College Annual* 48:83–106.

———. 2004. *Ecclesiastes*. JPS Bible Commentary. Philadelphia: Jewish Publication Society.

Fredericks, Daniel C. 1988. *Qoheleth's Language: Re-Evaluating Its Nature and Date*. Lewiston, NY: Edwin Mellen.

———. 1993. *Coping with Transience*. Sheffield: JSOT Press.

Fredericks, Daniel C., and Daniel J. Estes. 2010. *Ecclesiastes and Song of Songs*. Apollos Old Testament Commentary. Downers Grove: IVP Academic.

Galling, Kurt. 1932. "Koheleth-Studien." *Zeitschrift für die alttestamentliche Wissenschaft* 50: 276–99.

Gordis, Robert. 1945. *The Wisdom of Ecclesiastes*. New York: Behrman.

Herman, Judith. 1997. *Trauma and Recovery: The Aftermath of Violence—From Domestic Abuse to Political Terror*. New York: Basic Books.

Krüger, Thomas. 2001. *Qoheleth*. Minneapolis: Fortress.

Longman III, Tremper. 1998. *Ecclesiastes*. New International Commentary on the Old Testament. Grand Rapids, Eerdmans.

Meek, Russell L. 2015. "'I Was King over Israel in Jerusalem': Inerrancy and Authorial Ambiguity in Ecclesiastes." *Journal for the Evangelical Study of the Old Testament* 4:63–85.

———. 2022. *Ecclesiastes and the Search for Meaning in an Upside-Down World*. Peabody, MA: Hendrickson.

Miller, Douglas B. 2002. *Symbol and Rhetoric in Ecclesiastes: The Place of* Hebel *in Qohelet's Work*. Academia Biblica 2. Atlanta: SBL Press.

Morabito, Melissa S., Linda M. Williams, and April Pattavina. 2019. "Decision Making in Sexual Assault Cases: Replication Research on Sexual Violence Case Attrition in the U.S." Final Technical Report #252689. *National Criminal Justice Reference Service*. https://www.ncjrs.gov/pdffiles1/nij/grants/252689.pdf.

Ogden, Graham S. 2007. *Qoheleth*. Readings: A New Biblical Commentary. Sheffield: Sheffield Phoenix.

Peterson, Andrew. 2009. *North! Or Be Eaten*. Book 2 of The Wingfeather Saga. Colorado Springs: Waterbrook.

Samet, Nili. 2015. "The Gilgamesh Epic and the Book of Qoheleth: A New Look." *Biblica* 96.3:375–90.

Schoors, Antoon. 2013. *Ecclesiastes*. Historical Commentary on the Old Testament. Leuven: Peeters.

Seow, C. L. 1997. *Ecclesiastes: A New Translation with Introduction and Commentary*. Anchor Bible 18C. New Haven: Yale University Press.

Shaffer, A. 1967. "The Mesopotamian Background of Qoh 4:9–12." *Eretz Israel* 8:246–50. (Hebrew)

———. 1969. "New Information on the Origin of the 'Threefold Cord.'" *Eretz Israel* 9:159–60. (Hebrew)

Verheij, Arian. 1991. "Paradise Retried: On Qohelet 2:4–6." *Journal for the Study of the Old Testament* 50 (1991):113–15.

Waltke, Bruce K. 2004. *Proverbs 1–15*. New International Commentary on the Old Testament. Grand Rapids: Eerdmans, 2004.

Weeks, Stuart. 2022. *Ecclesiastes 5:7–12:14: A Critical and Exegetical Commentary*. International Critical Commentaries. London: T&T Clark.

Whitley, C. F. 1979. *Koheleth: His Language and Thought*. Beihefte zur Zeitschrift für die alttestamentliche Wissenschaft 148. Berlin: de Gruyter.

INDEX OF BIBLICAL REFERENCES

NOTE: The primary purpose of a Scripture index in a book like this, where biblical passages are being treated directly, is not to present the reader with every biblical reference found in the book, but to offer ones that lie outside the range of each of the passages treated. Hence, this index presents references to such outside passages, plus verses from the passages treated in this book *but only when these are cross-referenced in a discussion of another verse found in these passages.*

Old Testament

ABOUT THE AUTHOR

Russell L. Meek (PhD, Midwestern Baptist Theological Seminary) is associate professor of Old Testament and Hebrew at William Tennent School of Theology. His most recent books include *Ecclesiastes and the Search for Meaning in an Upside-Down World* (Hendrickson, 2022) and the co-authored *Book-by-Book Guide to Biblical Hebrew Vocabulary* (Hendrickson, 2019). You can find him in the virtual world at russmeek.com, but he prefers the real world with his wife and their three sons in north Idaho, where you'll find them gardening, cooking, and exploring the wild.